W9-BNL-775

THE PARKER SISTERS

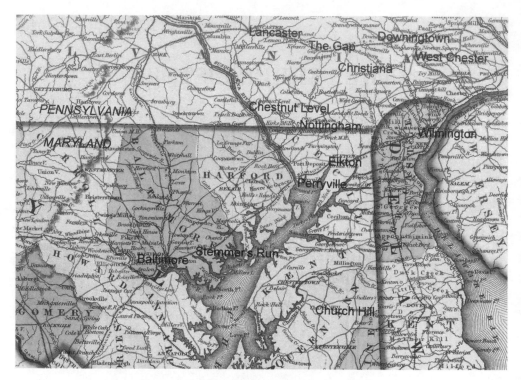

The Maryland/Pennsylvania border area, 1855.
(Original map by J. H. Colton & Co., 1855.)

THE PARKER SISTERS

A BORDER KIDNAPPING

Lucy Maddox

TEMPLE UNIVERSITY PRESS
Philadelphia · Rome · Tokyo

BUNCOMBE COUNTY PUBLIC LIBRARIES

TEMPLE UNIVERSITY PRESS
Philadelphia, Pennsylvania 19122
www.temple.edu/tempress

Copyright © 2016 by Temple University—Of The Commonwealth System
   of Higher Education
All rights reserved
Published 2016

Text design by Levi Dillon

Library of Congress Cataloging-in-Publication Data

Maddox, Lucy.
  The Parker sisters : a border kidnapping / Lucy Maddox.
     pages cm
  Includes bibliographical references and index.
   ISBN 978-1-4399-1318-5 (cloth : alkaline paper) — ISBN 978-1-4399-1320-8
(e-book)   1. Parker, Elizabeth, approximately 1841–   2. Parker, Rachel, 1834–1918.
3. Free African Americans—Pennsylvania—Chester County—Biography.   4. African
American girls—Pennsylvania—Chester County—Biography.   5. Kidnapping—
Pennsylvania—Chester County—History—19th century.   6. Borderlands—Social
aspects—Pennsylvania—History—19th century.   7. United States. Fugitive slave
law (1850).   8. Slave trade—Maryland—Baltimore—History—19th century.
9. Slave trade—Louisiana—New Orleans—History—19th century.   I. Title.
  F157.C4M33 2016
  306.3'620922—dc23
  [B]

                                                                    2015013664

♾ The paper used in this publication meets the requirements of the American
National Standard for Information Sciences—Permanence of Paper for Printed
Library Materials, ANSI Z39.48-1992

Printed in the United States of America

9 8 7 6 5 4 3 2 1

For Jim

CONTENTS

1. Introduction   *1*

2. The Line   *23*

3. The Parkers' World   *45*

4. Border Justice   *69*

5. Elizabeth's Story   *93*

6. Baltimore   *117*

7. Legal Justice   *145*

8. Freedom   *165*

9. Afterward   *189*

Acknowledgments   *199*

Appendix   *201*

Notes   *211*

Bibliography   *233*

Index   *241*

THE PARKER SISTERS

1

INTRODUCTION

O N A MID-DECEMBER EVENING in 1851 in rural Chester County, Pennsylvania, Elizabeth Parker walked out of Matthew Donnelly's kitchen and into the farmyard. Donnelly, the man for whom she was working, had sent her out to find the slop bucket. Elizabeth went, even though she thought it was an odd request. Donnelly had just come in from spending fifteen minutes out in the yard; why hadn't he brought in the bucket himself? Elizabeth found the bucket, but she never made it back into the house; she was grabbed by two men, bound and gagged, and hurried off to a Baltimore slave pen. Two months later, Elizabeth, who was not yet a teenager, was in New Orleans; two weeks after that, she had been sold and put to work as a slave. Shortly after Elizabeth's abduction, her seventeen-year-old sister Rachel was taken from the home of another Chester County farmer and rushed to the same Baltimore slave pen. This time, the abductor—the same man in both cases—was pursued to Baltimore and arrested before Rachel could be sent away and sold. The pursuit, however, cost the life of Rachel's employer, Joseph Miller, who was more than likely murdered but whose death was never officially resolved. The abductor of Elizabeth and Rachel, Thomas McCreary, was indicted but never convicted. He went free, while the two girls, who had committed no crime, both spent months in jail.[1]

The stories of the kidnappings of the Parker girls are remarkable. The stories that surround the kidnappings are also remarkable—stories of the exasperated white citizens of Chester County who determined to bring the two black girls home and of the legal and political machinations that let a known kidnapper and possible murderer go free. These are stories that belong to a particular place and time, the midcentury border between North and South, between slavery and freedom. The landscape of the border became increasingly tense, especially for its black inhabitants, as the debates about slavery and the rights of states became more contentious. By the time of the passage of the Fugitive Slave Act (or Fugitive Slave Law) of 1850, the border country had become a dangerous place to be for most black people. Both fugitive slaves and free blacks were targets for the slave catchers, since both could be taken across the state line and sold. Living in a free state like Pennsylvania in the 1850s did not guarantee freedom for anyone who was black.

The people who watched the Parker episode unfold could find it hard to describe or account for without comparing it to the most sensational fiction. The Philadelphia Female Anti-Slavery Society called the story of the Parker sisters "so tragic, so deeply pathetic, that, were they the theme of a romance, they would thrill the soul of every reader." A local Chester County newspaper referred more specifically to Elizabeth Parker's case as "extraordinary," "a story of Romance," one that "would almost afford a subject for another 'Uncle Tom's Cabin.'" Harriet Beecher Stowe did in fact put the Parker story into one of her books, although not into her famous novel. In *The Key to Uncle Tom's Cabin*, the book in which she collected a mass of historical evidence to support the picture of slavery she had constructed in the novel, she gave a brief account of the Parker abductions to illustrate her point about the reality and extent of the kidnapping of free blacks. The Parkers' story became known, Stowe pointed out, but others did not: "Around the [slave] trader are continually passing and repassing men and women who would be worth to him thousands of dollars in the way of trade,—who belong to a class whose rights nobody respects, and who, if reduced to slavery, could not easily make their word good against him. The probability is that hundreds of free men and women and children are all the time being precipitated into slavery in this way."[2]

In 2012, the Chester County township of East Nottingham erected a commemorative sign as a reminder of the events comprising what came to be called the "Parker case": the kidnappings, the death of Joseph Miller, and the extraordinary communal effort that ultimately led to a successful rescue of the two girls. The marker reads:

> Emboldened by the 1850 Fugitive Slave Law, Maryland slave catchers kidnapped Rachel and Elizabeth Parker from the Nottingham area in 1851. Rachel's employer Joseph Miller was murdered in a failed attempt to rescue her from Baltimore. Public outrage led Pennsylvania officials to seek the sisters' release in a Maryland civil court case that secured their freedom in 1853. The forcible enslavement of two young free black women galvanized anti-slavery sentiment.

As the township's marker suggests, this is a story about how a disastrous law affected the small farming communities of Chester County in ways that had significant, widening consequences for the state and the nation as well. But it is also a story about families, especially the Parker family, whose lives and fates were deeply embedded in the daily rounds of their community and, at the same time, in the madness and violence consuming all of antebellum America. The marker is one effort to do justice to the people involved in the "Parker case" and to recognize their place in a crucial and dangerous moment in U.S. history.

Chester County lies on the southeastern border of Pennsylvania, adjoining the northern boundaries of both Maryland and Delaware. In the late eighteenth century, those state boundary lines became part of the longer and more famous line drawn by Charles Mason and Jeremiah Dixon; Chester County therefore found itself on the border between the free states north of the line and the slave states south of it. That border was enormously significant, and slavery made all the difference in defining its meaning, to whites as well as blacks. As an early historian of the region put it, the "Mason and Dixon line was the imaginary demarcation between two wholly antagonistic social and political orders." Pennsylvania had been effectively free since it instituted gradual abolition in 1780 through the country's first emancipation law. The law had stipulated that while no more slaves could be brought into the state, anyone who had been born into slavery before 1780 would remain in bondage for life; children born to slave mothers after 1780 would serve until the age of twenty-eight, when they would be freed. The immediate impact of the change was limited, since the slave population of Pennsylvania had always been comparatively small (which made gradual abolition relatively easy to accomplish). At the time the abolition law was passed, there were 470 slaves in Chester County; in 1800, that number had decreased to 58, and by 1840, the federal census could count only 64 slaves in the entire state.[3]

In neighboring Maryland, by contrast, even though the slave population had begun declining around 1830 and even though many Marylanders were declaring the institution of slavery moribund, more than eighty-seven thousand slaves remained in the state in 1860. Many of these were in the northern counties, where the state line might be only a few miles, or even a mile, away. The knowledge that stepping across a county line could mean the whole difference between being completely subject to a master and being at least relatively free to choose one's own movements must have been constantly on the minds of the slaves of border states like Maryland. Of course, that knowledge was also very present in the minds of slaveholders in those states and in the minds of the "borderers," slave catchers who roamed the area looking for runaways or, often, for anyone they could plausibly claim to be a runaway and who seemed vulnerable—such as the young Parker sisters.

Not surprisingly, many Maryland slaves took advantage of the proximity of the Pennsylvania line to flee across it, in spite of the dangers of getting there. Runaway slaves began coming north into Chester and neighboring counties early. Enough had come by the 1820s that an organized but clandestine network of local people had formed to assist the fugitives—a network of the kind that would later be called the Underground Railroad. Most of these fugitives had not traveled far. In the records of runaways who were captured in Chester County and returned to claimants between

1820 and 1839, 96 out of 119 came from Maryland, and of those, 20 were from Cecil County, just below the Pennsylvania line.

The stream of runaways who left Maryland for Pennsylvania prompted years of friction between the two states. The Parker kidnappings tapped into a sectional history that had become increasingly acrimonious. Maryland did not like that Pennsylvania sheltered its runaway slaves and suspected that Pennsylvanians were enticing them away. Pennsylvania did not like that Maryland had slaves in the first place or that Marylanders felt free to come into Pennsylvania and seize suspected runaways, sometimes by violence. Quakers in Pennsylvania, already troubled by the number of kidnappings, had organized a Society for the Protection of Free Negroes Held in Bondage as early as 1775, with the stated purpose of protecting free blacks from abduction and redeeming those who had already been taken. By the nineteenth century, the two state legislatures were putting a lot of time and energy into efforts to make life difficult for each other. The legislature of Maryland produced a series of resolutions after 1816 addressing what it called in an 1823 report "the growing evils occasioned the citizens of [Maryland], by the encouragement runaway slaves receive from some of the citizens of Pennsylvania." The Pennsylvania legislature responded by instituting new state laws that made it even harder for Maryland slaveholders to retrieve runaways who had crossed the border. The interstate conflict over the legal status of fugitives and those who harbored them would continue until 1850, when the Fugitive Slave Law took the issue out of the states' hands and put the rendition of fugitives under federal control.[4]

While the two state legislatures squabbled and resolutions went back and forth, the fugitives kept coming. Determining the number of runaway slaves who crossed into Pennsylvania from the South is impossible, as one researcher after another has had to acknowledge. Documentation and reporting were seldom unbiased; in places less friendly to the return of fugitive slaves, the press was likely to report only successful escapes or rescues. In other places, the arrest of a runaway was unlikely to make it into the news (or into the records) unless the arrest had turned violent. The evidence that can be pieced together, however, suggests that the numbers were very large, that they only increased as the country moved toward civil war, and that the consternation of slaveholders across the South was wide and deep. The flight of slaves out of Maryland led the governor of South Carolina to declare in 1850 that, on the question of its future as a slave state, "Maryland is hopeless." Some Pennsylvanians were disturbed by the influx of fugitives into their state, some outraged enough to try to stop it. G. A. Doyle of Carlisle circulated a prospectus, in 1846, for a newspaper with the express aim of helping slaveholders, especially those from Maryland and Virginia, to find their fugitives who had fled to Pennsylvania. Doyle proposed locating men strategically along the Pennsylvania border to supply him with information about runaways and those who helped them. (Apparently, Doyle's plans never came to fruition.)[5]

Many of the runaways who made it to Pennsylvania were directed to safe houses, the places that were becoming known as stations on the Underground Railroad, most of them owned by Quakers. In one of these houses in Chester County, Nathan Evans, the son of an active Quaker agent, kept a diary in which he recorded for a time the number of refugees who arrived at the Evans home seeking aid and were helped to make their way north. For the four months of 1842 in which Nathan kept records, a total of ninety people found their way to the Evans home or were brought there. They came in groups, some as small as two and others as large as sixteen. All ninety were kept until they could be safely sent on to the next agent or station. Scattered evidence from other Underground Railroad agents suggests that the Evans numbers were not unusual; people fleeing slavery came through southeastern Pennsylvania in a steady stream until the beginning of the Civil War. An early historian of Chester County attested that there was so much traffic on the southern route of the Underground Railroad through the county that "it became necessary to have several branches, and these branch routes interlaced the more northern lines in several places."[6]

The number of escapees from Maryland roused slaveholders around the state to take action. A "Mutual Protection Society for the Eastern Shore of Maryland" was proposed as early as 1825 with the intention of cracking down on free blacks, who were thought to encourage slaves to abscond. At a slaveholders' meeting in Annapolis in 1842, attendees requested that the state legislature post guards at railroad stations and steamboat docks to catch fugitives and offer rewards for the identification of anyone encouraging or helping a slave to run away. Their legislative package did not pass, but two years later the legislature did put into place a system of bounties that included $100 for anyone who successfully captured a runaway slave in a free state. In 1846, the citizens of Queen Anne's County held a meeting "for the purpose of asking further action in reference to the frequent loss of their slaves by absconding, and of adopting such measures as might be deemed advisable for the better security of such property in future." In that same year, slaveholders in neighboring Kent County organized their own "Mutual Protection Society." A similar organization was formed in Frederick County in 1849 and another in Baltimore County in 1850.[7]

Any newspaper, of whatever political persuasion, could find exciting copy in the number of escaping slaves. An antislavery paper in Ohio reported in September that the flight of slaves from Maryland was causing "great commotion" among slaveholders. The paper noted with satisfaction the "absconding of whole gangs and families of slaves, who are seldom ever caught." Three months later, the same paper again reported on the excitement in Maryland, this time referring to the "panic" among slaveholders, "especially on the state's Eastern Shore." The *Village Record* in Chester County reported early in 1850 that "every day but swells the number of absconding slaves from Maryland." About the same time, a Delaware pro-slavery newspaper, the *Blue Hen's Chicken*, also reported on the increasing number of runaways from Maryland and Delaware, though with alarm rather than complacency. Noting that slave property was "insecure" in both states, the paper concluded, "[Soon] we shall not have a slave worth keeping. The young and hearty who are able to work, run away, leaving behind the old and children, too young to be of much service." A newspaper in Maryland's Cecil County, the *Elkton Democrat*, directed blame for some of the state's trouble squarely at next-door Chester County. Reporting on the recent flight of eight slaves from Cecil, the *Democrat* announced that the owners were offering a reward of $1,000. The money was being put up, however, not for the apprehension of the slaves, but for the arrest of "the individual who enticed them away, who is believed to be a well-known abolitionist of Chester County, Pennsylvania." The money apparently went unclaimed.[8]

One runaway who fled slavery in Maryland and made it safely to Chester County was a young man from Kent County named Isaac Mason. In a memoir written late in his life, Mason recounted making the decision to run away in 1846, when he learned that the man who claimed him as his property intended to sell him south. Mason fled, making his way through Delaware and into Chester County. Like many others who were fleeing from Maryland and states farther south, Mason stopped running when he got to Pennsylvania, believing that he had reached a place of safety. He recalled that, in crossing from Delaware to Pennsylvania, he felt that he had "stepped from bondage into liberty, from darkness into light." (Some fugitives relaxed after crossing the line into Pennsylvania because they thought they had made it to Canada.)[9]

Mason had in fact found safety, at least for a while, and, like many other fugitives, he seems to have had little trouble finding work among the farmers of Chester County. He was hired by at least four different employers over three years, the last a farmer named Joshua Pusey who hired him in 1849. Mason felt secure enough in his contract with Pusey to plan to marry and set up his own household. Before the wedding could take place, however, one of Mason's neighbors and friends, a fellow runaway named Tom Mitchell, was kidnapped by three men who dragged Mitchell from his house at night and drove away with him, leaving his frantic wife and children behind. One of those men who took Tom Mitchell was the same Thomas McCreary who would abduct the Parker sisters two years later. After Mitchell's kidnapping, Mason decided to postpone his marriage, get out of Chester County, and head for Canada: "That kind of work thoroughly frightened me, and I resolved that I would break the Pusey bargain and leave that region immediately. Mitchell's captors were drovers, and they knew him as a slave and of his whereabouts, and they made good use of their knowledge; they got fifty dollars for him."[10]

Isaac Mason's experience as a runaway was typical in several ways. In the first place, like most of the other fugitives who passed through Chester County, he came across the Pennsylvania border from Maryland. Second, Mason stopped in Chester County and planned to stay there because it seemed welcoming; he, Tom Mitchell, and many others found assistance, work, other fugitives, and a sense of relative safety—as short-lived as it turned out to be for both Mason and Mitchell. Finally, Mason's primary reason for leaving both Maryland and Pennsylvania was a common one: he feared being sold south, a prospect that was realistic and understandably terrifying. In the plantation areas of the Deep South, slaves from the Eastern Shore of Maryland were considered especially valuable. Sidney George Fisher, the owner of Cecil County's Mount Harmon plantation, who was himself strongly opposed to slavery, noted in his diary in 1846 that a neighbor had just "sent some of the negroes off to Baltimore on their way to his estate in Georgia. The negroes here dread nothing on earth so much as this and they are in great commotion about it. . . . They regard the South with perfect horror and to be sent there, is considered as the worst punishment inflicted on them, & is reserved for one offence alone by the custom of the neighborhood, an attempt to run away." Historians of slavery have not failed to note the irony in Fisher's seemingly detached observation: slaves often ran away because they feared being sent south, and to be sent south was a frequent punishment for running away.[11]

Although Mason and others found refuge among the rural populations of the southern counties of Pennsylvania, very few in that population would describe themselves as being antislavery, much less as being sympathetic to abolitionism. Southern Pennsylvania was, in fact, more sympathetic to the fugitive in practice than in theory. In 1847, Isaac S. Flint wrote to the *Pennsylvania Freeman* about his problems in trying to bring the antislavery message to the small towns of Chester County. Flint found the town of Oxford to be "the most pro-slavery corner of Chester County," where the hostility to the antislavery cause was "ignorant and bitter." Flint noted that it was difficult to find meeting spaces anywhere around Oxford for antislavery gatherings. Another antislavery activist, Charles Burleigh, consistently encountered opposition to his lectures in Chester County. A member of the Pennsylvania Yearly Meeting of Progressive Friends, Burleigh was an ardent supporter of the Meeting's principles, campaigning with equal passion for temperance and vegetarianism and against the death penalty and slavery. He lectured frequently in the towns and villages of the state, especially on the antislavery message. At a meeting in West Chester in 1837, Burleigh's speech was interrupted twice: the first time when cayenne pepper was thrown on the stove, producing fits of coughing and wheezing throughout the hall, and again when the audience was pelted with eggs.[12]

Burleigh continued to be met by eggs as well as by less material forms of resistance in the years he traveled the county. He learned to expect limited support and to value whatever support he did find. After a meeting in 1846 at the Little Elk Meeting House in Nottingham, Burleigh wrote that "abolitionists are not very numerous there, and pro-slavery is rather bolder to show its brassy front than in many communities." Yet Burleigh found an encouraging sympathy for the slave and especially for the fugitive even among those who had little sympathy for the antislavery movement and its representatives. He especially appreciated the honesty of the farmers and working men of the county: "It was gratifying to hear those unlearned men pouring out their strong indignation against tyranny—and generous sympathy for the needy. There were no orators there, but plain, blunt men, who talked right on what they felt was true. They were men too much in earnest to polish their speech, and round off their sentences." It was these Nottingham men, or their compatriots, who would a few years later offer the remarkably courageous resistance that kept the Parker sisters out of slavery.[13]

Burleigh did not have such ready sympathy for the elite of the community, especially the ministers. Nor, apparently, did some of them feel warmly toward him and his intrusions onto their turf. On a visit to Oxford in 1847, Burleigh found his abolitionist message resisted by the local Presbyterian minister, John Miller Dickey, who was at that time deeply involved in the colonization movement, an organized effort to encourage blacks in the United States to relocate to Africa. Probably at Dickey's instigation, Burleigh was arrested for selling antislavery literature, not because of its content but because he was violating the Sabbath by selling it on a Sunday. While the local constable was taking care of the details of the arrest, Burleigh addressed the crowd that had gathered, defending his actions and his cause. Dickey responded, speaking, according to Burleigh, "partly in defense of his church from the imputation of being pro-slavery, and partly in a personal attack upon myself as a disorganizer; an enemy of the Government, the Church, and the Sabbath; a rejecter of the Old Testament and as much of the New as does not suit my notions, etc." The constable finished his paperwork, the back-and-forth speeches ended, and Burleigh spent six days in jail in West Chester, a stay that he declared to be quite restful and comfortable. On a return visit to Oxford a few years later, when he spoke against the Fugitive Slave Law (which he called the National Kidnapping Law), Burleigh was once again greeted by an egg-throwing audience. This time, however, he was satisfied that Dickey, whom he called "the clerical ruffian," had no part in the demonstration, since he was out of town that evening. (Dickey may never have lost his disgust with abolitionists, but he did rouse himself to action when the Parkers were kidnapped and Joseph Miller was killed. Along with other prominent citizens of the county, he would be instrumental in securing the return of the two sisters to Chester County.)[14]

One place near Oxford that was open to antislavery gatherings, and eventually suffered for it, was Hosanna Meeting House, a small black church that hosted speakers like Burleigh, Flint, and Frederick Douglass. According to local legend, Harriet Tubman used the church as a pick-up or exchange station for runaways crossing into Lancaster County. Free blacks from nearby communities and from as far away as Philadelphia would come to Hosanna on Saturday evenings, when the church meetings were held. Fugitives could mix with the congregation and then conceal themselves in one of the visitors' wagons, to be transported to the next friendly reception. The antislavery activity at Hosanna ceased, however, after the passage of the Fugitive Slave Law. A new minister who arrived shortly after the passage of the law disapproved of harboring fugitives, an activity that had become illegal and punishable under the new law. His stand split the congregation, and the minister and his supporters were accused by the rest of the members of being complicit with the kidnappers and slave catchers. The church was forced to close.[15]

The influx of fugitive slaves raised fears among many in Chester County about the possibilities for violent conflicts between the fugitives and the people who came into the state looking for them. These fears were exacerbated by the Christiana "riot" of 1851 in neighboring Lancaster County. There, a Maryland slaveholder, Edward Gorsuch, was

Hosanna Meeting House.
(Photo by the author.)

killed in a confrontation with a group of African Americans, many of them fugitives themselves, who were protecting the men Gorsuch had come to capture. A West Chester newspaper suggested, nervously, that the flood of fugitives into Chester County could produce another Christiana if nothing were done to stop it: "Runaway slaves are generally voted not only a nuisance, but a danger to the peace and good order of a community wherein they may locate. That such an immigration engendering scenes like the late Christiana murder, will be tolerated for any length of time, in Pennsylvania, can hardly be expected."[16]

Fear of violence was only one reason for resisting the influx of runaways. Many in Chester County also had political and economic reasons for being concerned. John Swayne, a county farmer, wrote to state senator William Jackson in 1843 that the county was becoming a dumping ground for the wrong kind of people, who were crowding out the right kind:

It is obvious that an increasing prejudice is abroad against those of a dark skin. . . . Their numbers are rapidly increasing by the ingress of perhaps the worst class the slave states produce—the idle or infirm who are sent away, the vicious and insubordinate who run away. Thus the interests of masters and slaves concur in throwing into this state perhaps this naborhood [*sic*] in particular those who as working men are driving away working citizens, for whom they are a very inferior substitute.[17]

Swayne might have had reason to be concerned about population *trends* in his part of the world, but the actual population *numbers* were quite small. There were only 5,223 African Americans living in all of Chester County in 1850, out of a total population of over 61,000. Swayne's township of East Marlborough had only 121 black residents in 1850. Of these, 39, or about one-third, were born outside Pennsylvania and were thus part of the "ingress" of undesirables from slave states that disturbed Swayne: 17 were born in Delaware, 20 in Maryland, and 1 each in Virginia and the District of Columbia. The numbers were higher for the neighboring township of New Garden. There, of a total black population of 284, 104 were born outside the state: 70 in Delaware, 30 in Maryland, 2 in Virginia, and 2 in New Jersey. In these two adjacent townships, then, out of a total black population of just over 400, nearly 150 were born outside Pennsylvania, and all but 6 of those came from the slave states of Delaware and Maryland. It is reasonable to assume that many of those born outside the state, if not most, were fugitives.[18]

John Swayne worried that unreliable immigrants were taking jobs away from more dependable local workers. To others in the county, especially among its Quaker and free black populations, the same trends that bothered Swayne were taken as encouraging signs of success. In spite of a general distrust of abolitionists and concern about runaways coming into the state, the large number of free blacks, former slaves, Quakers, and others with antislavery sentiments made Chester and the other border counties of Pennsylvania—a state founded by Quakers—more receptive than most to fugitives from slavery. In 1850, there were 37 Quaker meetings in Chester County alone, with large numbers in the adjoining counties as well. In all of Pennsylvania there were 142 meetings (as opposed to a total of 26 in Maryland). By the 1770s, the Yearly Meeting of Philadelphia had voted to disown any slaveholding members, and the Quakers remained the religious group most closely identified with antislavery sentiment in Pennsylvania, especially after the network of stations on the Underground Railroad was established. Many Quaker homes became stations, or safe houses, and many Quaker men and women became agents who supplied funds, hid runaways, or otherwise aided fugitives in their flight to the North. Of the 132 agents who were known to have been active on the Underground Railroad in Chester County, at least 82 were Quakers. An additional 31 known agents in the county were African American. Less is known about this latter group, but at least some of them were former slaves themselves, such as Benjamin Freeman, who moved to West Chester and settled there after being manumitted in Queen Anne's County, Maryland.[19]

It was individual Quakers who were politically active. The Society of Friends, in general, did not condone any kind of conflict or law breaking, including violation of the laws regarding slavery. As one historian has put it, "Moral opposition to slavery was a core Quaker tenet, although political action was not." Another has characterized the majority of Quakers as viewing slaveholding "as a sin to be banned from the Society, not as a condition from which Afro-Americans must be delivered." The Baltimore Yearly Meeting of Friends had made its position clear in 1842, stating that its membership would "avoid involving ourselves with the associations that have sprung up around us, for the avowed purpose of promoting the abolition of slavery in our country by political or other means of a coercive nature. . . . The Society of Friends, in thus taking up a testimony against slavery, publicly and openly, did not desire to invade the privileges of their neighbors, nor in any way improperly to interfere with them. With us it is purely a religious concern." Even though Quakers made up a very large percentage of known Underground Railroad agents in the area, those activist Friends were a small minority of the total population of Quakers. An 1881 history of Chester County noted that "nearly all" of those who "assisted the fugitive to freedom were members of the Society of Friends, although the majority of that society, while averse to slavery, took no part in the labors, and, with few exceptions, refused the use of their meeting houses for anti-slavery lectures." When the London Grove meeting quietly ignored a request from the Chester County Anti-Slavery Society to use its house, a member of the Society wrote to the *Pennsylvania Freeman*, the newspaper of the Pennsylvania Abolition Society, complaining that the London Grove Friends were "lamentably ignorant in relation to the great questions which are now rocking with agitation the civilized world, and it is the duty of abolitionists to endeavor to enlighten them." (London Grove evidently remained unmoved.)[20]

Disagreement about the response to slavery split the Society in Pennsylvania, as it split other religious organizations, including tiny Hosanna Meeting House. Quakers attending the Marlborough Conference in Chester County in 1845 raised the possibility of separating from the Pennsylvania Yearly Meeting on the grounds that it was not progressive enough; by 1853, the dissatisfied members had organized as the Pennsylvania Yearly Meeting of Progressive Friends, which would continue to meet for more than eighty years at Longwood, near Kennett Square. The Pennsylvania Anti-Slavery Society, an organization whose founders were primarily Quakers, also became increasingly irritated by the Friends' timidity when it came to endorsing the abolitionist cause. In a statement signed in 1851 by J. Miller McKim and James Mott (a prominent Quaker), the Anti-Slavery Society accused the state's Quakers of having lost their fervor and become soft on slavery. "The hostility of the Friends to slavery," the statement declared, "is a thing of the past."[21]

The Philadelphia Yearly Meeting defended itself against the criticism, declaring that "our Society has steadfastly maintained a testimony against all wars and fightings, tumults, violence and shedding of blood, and against forcible resistance to oppression." The statement continued with an endorsement of black passivity that brought to the boiling point much abolitionist blood, including that of some Quakers. "[We] have counselled [slaves] to endeavor to serve with patience and fidelity while in bondage, and to commit their cause into the hands of a merciful and omnipotent Father in heaven." Clearly, many Quakers did not take nearly as strong or as public a stance as the Anti-Slavery Society would have liked; they even disagreed among themselves about what that stance should be. At the same time, their doctrinal opposition to slavery, the documented aid given to fugitives by some of their number, and their generally tolerant ways continued to draw both runaways and free blacks to communities with large Quaker populations. Their presence contributed significantly to creating in Pennsylvania's southern counties what one scholar has called an "anti-slavery borderland" that was "an early version of the Civil War emancipation borderland."[22]

Isaac Mason thus had good reasons to stop running when he reached Chester County and to contemplate a settled life there. But he had equally good reasons to change course abruptly—to leave the county and go north as quickly and as quietly as possible—when his neighbor Tom Mitchell was kidnapped. If the proximity of Chester County to the northern counties of Maryland, especially Kent and Cecil Counties, made it easy for slaves in that region of Maryland to cross the line between slavery and freedom without traveling very far, the slave catchers and kidnappers could cross with equal ease—in both directions. A captured fugitive or a kidnapped free black person taken in Pennsylvania could be spirited across the state line and into slave territory quickly. As Elizabeth Parker would discover, if the abduction was carefully planned, it might even go unnoticed until after the kidnappers and their victim were well away.

Elizabeth and her sister Rachel would also discover that free blacks kidnapped in Pennsylvania were likely to find themselves quickly handed over to a slave trader, often in Baltimore, and sent south to be sold. By the 1840s, Baltimore had become the busiest slave-exporting port in the upper South. For the kidnapper, Baltimore thus offered not only a conveniently located slave market but also a choice of experienced traders who were always looking for good, quick deals. Many of the people who were shipped out of Baltimore were destined for the slave markets of New Orleans. Two of the largest exporters, Hope Slatter and Austin Woolfolk, each sent more than twenty-five hundred people to New Orleans over the course of their careers. Joseph S. Donovan shipped more than twenty-one hundred, and the Campbell brothers, to whom Thomas McCreary brought both Elizabeth and Rachel Parker, sent a total of nearly thirteen hundred people, including Elizabeth Parker, between 1844 and 1856. Elizabeth was among many free persons who were shipped off from Baltimore to slavery in the Deep South. Occasionally a slave trader would refuse to take someone who was known to be kidnapped and arrange to send the person home, especially if the law or the Quakers were sniffing around. The evidence suggests, however, that many, like Elizabeth, were simply merged in the crowd and found themselves exchanging a slave pen in Baltimore for one in New Orleans.[23]

Some slave catchers who came into Pennsylvania from the South were looking for particular runaways for whom they had warrants. Others came in search of anyone, fugitive or free, whom they might successfully claim to be a slave and thus sell for profit, probably to a slave trader. The kidnappings in the state began early. A group of seventy-three African Americans in Philadelphia sent a petition to Congress in 1800 protesting the kidnapping of free blacks in their city. R. C. Smedley notes that there were reports of "some cases of kidnapping and shooting of fugitives who attempted to escape" in the small town of Columbia as early as 1804. Since the town had been founded in 1787 by a strongly antislavery Quaker, Samuel Wright, who specifically encouraged both emancipated and fugitive slaves to harbor there, it became a particular target of the slave catchers and kidnappers. Columbia was only one of many small communities with primarily African American populations that came to dot the southern Pennsylvania border, including some in Chester County: all of these villages attracted the attention of kidnappers. The Pennsylvania Abolition Society declared in 1822 that the taking of black people had become such a lucrative business that the kidnappers were "emboldened to keep up a regular chain of communication and barter from Philadelphia to the Eastern shore of the Chesapeake." The number of kidnapped people sold into slavery was great enough to lead at least one scholar to describe the trade as "the other underground railroad"— the one going from north to south.[24]

By the 1840s, the kidnapping problem had worsened. The *Cincinnati Gazette* noted in May 1843 that kidnapping "is increasing all along the border of the free states. Several instances have occurred lately in which wives and children, born free and known to be so, have been torn from their homes, and forced into slavery. We suppose this is a sort of retaliation for the free states allowing abolitionists to steal slaves." The reports of kidnappings continued through the 1840s, although only a few of those instances were prosecuted or otherwise became public. Among the few documented cases in the five years between 1844 and 1849, Pennsylvania had its share: in 1844, two Maryland men were arrested and tried for kidnapping a black man from West Chester; in 1846 Thomas Finnegan was convicted of kidnapping a free black family from Adams County; two men were arrested in 1847 for kidnapping Mary Whiting from Chambersburg and selling her to a Baltimore slave dealer; in 1848, a woman and her several children were kidnapped from Pine Grove Forge in Lancaster County, three men tried to kidnap a girl from Downingtown, and a seventeen-year-old boy was kidnapped from Chester County and never seen again. In 1849, one white man and one black man kidnapped a free black boy from Chester County and took him to Baltimore to sell him, and in the same year, Thomas McCreary and two others kidnapped Tom Mitchell in Chester County.[25]

Not surprisingly, the raids into southeastern Pennsylvania to arrest or steal people produced resistance, some of it armed, much of it violent. However, the troubles caused by slave hunters before midcentury were not disturbing enough to prevent Chester County from enticing visitors and potential new residents by presenting itself as a bucolic and peaceful paradise. This boosterish account of the town of Oxford was sent to the *Baltimore Sun* in May 1847 by a correspondent signing himself "Rudolph":

Gentlemen—Have you ever been here in this county? If you have not, you certainly have missed visiting one of the freshest and best looking, most highly cultivated, and most healthy parts of creation. This town is beautifully situated, being high and dry, and having a paradise of country all around it. . . . Indeed it is one of the freshest looking and most beautiful and picturesque villes I have ever visited. It contains about 300 hospitable, industrious, prudent, temperate, good looking, progressive, intelligent people; three good sized stores, with excellent assortments of goods and

No. 1 owners; a handsome Presbyterian church; an excellent temperance hotel; and the "Oxford Female Seminary"—an institution of the very first class—the principals of which are the Revs. John M. and Saml. Dickey.... This is, according to the recent law and election, a temperance town.[26]

Five years after Rudolph's rhapsodic description, the aura of physical and moral healthiness that he found so desirable in the neighborhood of Oxford was diminished, at least temporarily, by the abduction of the Parker sisters and the murder of one of the county's white citizens. Because of the kidnappings, the Dickeys, especially John, would become embroiled in a distressing and frustrating legal battle; Oxford and its rural environs would attract unwelcome attention from the national press; and the people of Oxford and neighboring communities, especially the black people, would live with increasing anxiety.

A major reason for the changes between 1847 and 1852—and, arguably, a major reason behind the kidnapping of the Parker sisters—was the passage of the Fugitive Slave Act in September 1850. The act effectively took the fugitive slave issue away from the states and put it into the hands of the federal government. Among its provisions was the requirement that the citizens of any state must, by law, cooperate in the identification and arrest of fugitives. By making the taking of fugitives easier and the protection of them more difficult, the new law outraged opponents of slavery across the country. It was this law, especially its stipulation that every citizen was legally bound to assist in the remanding of fugitive slaves, that pushed Harriet Beecher Stowe to publish *Uncle Tom's Cabin*. Anyone who could even consider supporting the new law, she wrote, could not possibly understand the realities of slavery; her novel would therefore put it before them in *"a living dramatic reality."* Eber Pettit, an Underground Railroad agent in New York, spoke for many when he declared that "slavery in the United States after the Fugitive Slave Act assumed its most hideous aspect.... [The Act] was undoubtedly the most barbarous law enacted by any civilized nation in the nineteenth century." Since the new regulations also made kidnapping easier, they changed, practically overnight, the landscape for all African Americans,

The town of Oxford, Pennsylvania, 1866.

*(Photo by Alexander McCormick; courtesy of
the Chester County Historical Society.)*

both free and fugitive, especially along the borders between free and slave states. As one Pennsylvania writer put it, the act "made every white man of the North a blood-hound and negro-hunter for the white men of the South."[27]

In southeastern Pennsylvania, the act narrowed or closed down possibilities for many African Americans, producing widespread fear, costing some their freedom and some their lives, at the same time that it opened up irresistibly lucrative possibilities for people like Thomas McCreary. McCreary had been an active slave catcher and occasional kidnapper before the passage of the Fugitive Slave Act, but, according to much local opinion at the time, he got bolder after 1850. His abduction of Elizabeth and Rachel Parker in 1851, within two weeks of each other, was by all accounts a very bold act.

In an area grown increasingly used to the disappearance of black people, the kidnappings of the Parker sisters were different. They stirred up what the newspapers liked to refer to as "high excitement" along the border and generated editorial comment far beyond it. William Still, in his history of the Underground Railroad, wrote of the kidnappings that "it may be said, without contradiction, that Chester county, at least, was never more aroused by any one single outrage that had taken place within her borders, than by these occurrences." The *Massachusetts Spy* expressed its astonishment at the brashness of Thomas McCreary's action: "We do not believe that the annals of crime, outrage, and wrong, legalized or otherwise, ever furnished a more startling picture of slavery in this country, than does the case of Rachel Parker, and the other collateral circumstances attending it." What made this case so shocking, in a time when kidnapping had lost some of its ability to shock, was the mysterious death of Joseph Miller. It was from Miller's house that Rachel Parker was abducted; it was Miller who organized the search party that pursued McCreary and Rachel to Baltimore; it was Miller who filed kidnapping charges against McCreary. A few hours after filing, Miller went missing from the train taking him home from Baltimore. A few hours after that, his body was found hanging from a tree near the tracks at a place called Stemmer's Run, not far from Baltimore. No one knew how he had gotten to that tree, or why, but everyone had an opinion. Miller's death was immediately read by some as a brazen, cruel murder; by others as an unexpected but explicable suicide; and by still others as a legitimate move in the war, as yet undeclared but still deadly, between slave and free states.[28]

The excitement over the Parker case lasted through two trials, five burials of Joseph Miller with four exhumations in between, a battle between two governors, many accusations that the security of the entire Union was being threatened, much fist shaking across state lines, the involvement of dozens if not hundreds of people, the expense of large sums of money, and the passage of a full year in which Rachel and Elizabeth Parker were kept enslaved or in jail.

2

THE LINE

WHILE THE PASSAGE of the new Fugitive Slave Act had seemed years overdue to some, it was nearly unthinkable to others, especially in the North, where news of the passage produced immediate outrage and anger. As William Still described the reaction, "The deepest feelings of loathing, contempt and opposition were manifested by the opponents of Slavery on every hand. Anti-slavery papers, lecturers, preachers, etc. arrayed themselves boldly against it on the ground of its inhumanity and violation of the laws of God." Among the most eloquent denouncers of the legislation was Boston's Theodore Parker, who declared the law both politically corrupt and morally shameful:

> It subverts the purposes of the Constitution, it destroys Justice, disturbs domestic Tranquility, hinders the common Defense and the general Welfare, and annihilates the Blessings of Liberty. . . . It contradicts the very substance of the Christian Religion—the two great commandments of Love to God, and Love to man, whereon "hang all the Law and the Prophets." It makes natural humanity a crime; it subjects all the Christian virtues to fine and imprisonment.

Other opponents of the law, more succinct than the fiery Parker, simply called it evil or, as Samuel May put it, an "enactment of Hell!" William Newman, an escaped slave from Virginia who became a Baptist minister in Ohio, declared that in passing the law, the U.S. Congress had made it clear that the "real and true mission" of the federal government was to preserve slavery. Newman announced that his personal resistance to the new law would be as violent as it needed to be: "Even fugitive slaves pity the nation that makes colored men slaves and white men kidnappers. . . . I am frank to declare that it is my fixed and changeless purpose to kill any so-called man who attempts to enslave me or mine, if possible, though it be Millard Fillmore himself."[1]

The 1850 law was the culmination of a series of attempts by Congress to help slaveholders retain or retrieve their human property. The first fugitive slave law had been instituted in 1793. In spite of periodic attempts to change it and make it more enforceable, the original legislation was still in effect nearly sixty years later, when the new, stronger law was finally passed. Under the old law, a slaveholder had the legal right to retrieve a runaway from any state, slave or free, as long as he obtained a certificate from a judge or magistrate attesting to his ownership of the slave. The old law also imposed a penalty of $500 on anyone who interfered with or tried to prevent the arrest of a fugitive. Because that law had the side effect of encouraging the kidnapping of free blacks, especially in the border states, Pennsylvania passed its own law in 1826, designed to curtail the kidnappings that were on the increase. Pennsylvania's law declared that a fugitive could be apprehended only by a constable with a warrant; it would be considered kidnapping for a slaveholder to take it upon himself to apprehend a fugitive. The Pennsylvania law stood until 1842, when in *Prigg v. Pennsylvania*, the U.S. Supreme Court declared it unconstitutional, ruling further that only the federal government could legislate on the subject of fugitive slaves.

For Pennsylvanians, the consequence of the striking down of their state law with its protections was that, as the *Philadelphia Inquirer* pointed out, "a large class of persons were left without any protection from abduction; since, if the negro stealer could only escape with his victim to a slave State, he would be able to dispose of him beyond recall."

The Prigg decision left a loophole, however, by ruling that while Pennsylvania was required to allow slaveholders to enter the state in search of fugitives and have them arrested there, Pennsylvania was not required to provide any assistance to those slaveholders. Taking advantage of this opening, the Pennsylvania legislature in 1847 joined Massachusetts, Vermont, Connecticut, New Hampshire, and Rhode Island in passing its own personal liberty law. Exploiting the Prigg loophole as far as possible, Pennsylvania *prohibited* any officer of the state from assisting in the apprehension of a fugitive and denied judges and other magistrates in the state any authority in fugitive slave cases. The law also attempted to discourage slaveholders from entering the state in search of fugitives by making it illegal for runaways to be held in Pennsylvania jails and declaring that anyone who tried to use force on them would be guilty of a misdemeanor. In essence, the law declared that the state of Pennsylvania would no longer have anything to do with the pursuit or arrest of runaway slaves.[2]

The public argument following the passage of the personal liberty laws made it clear that what one person (or newspaper or party or state) saw as a fugitive slave problem and therefore a matter of property rights, another saw as a kidnapping problem and therefore a moral issue. Some of the loudest and most impassioned voices in that argument came out of Pennsylvania and Maryland, since it was by crossing their shared border that Maryland slaves were becoming protected fugitives in Pennsylvania and thus making a muddle of (among other things) the concept of states' rights. Many in Maryland accused Pennsylvania of having created a threat to the stability of the entire union by trying to circumvent federal law regarding fugitive slaves. J. R. Dorsey, for example, in his *Documentary History of Slavery in the United States, by a Native of Maryland* (1851), declared that "no state in the Union has violated the solemn compact on the subject of fugitive slaves more violently than Pennsylvania." Pennsylvania's personal liberty act, Dorsey wrote, was "one of the most odious and unconstitutional measures that has been enacted in any of the non-slaveholding States." Others in Maryland warned that Pennsylvania's law threatened at least to weaken and perhaps to destroy the system of slavery in Maryland by treating slaveholders who were in search of their property as trespassers and threatening them with prosecution. From Maryland's perspective, Pennsylvania was being a bad neighbor and a bad citizen of the Union.[3]

The *Pennsylvania Freeman* responded to attacks like these by arguing that, in fact, the opposite was true: Pennsylvania was deliberately trying to be a fair-minded neighbor and law-abiding citizen. According to the *Freeman*, the whole reason for the passage of the 1847 personal liberty law was that Pennsylvania had been *too* concerned to be a good neighbor in the past and thus *too* accommodating to Maryland's slavery interests. The 1826 law had done nothing to interfere with what slaveholders construed as their legal rights and had even allowed them to put alleged runaways in Pennsylvania jails to await trial, which the *Freeman* saw as evidence of "a most neighborly and accommodating spirit upon our part." Maryland had no quarrel with the arrangement, the *Freeman* argued, until one of her citizens was convicted of kidnapping by a Pennsylvania court. Then Maryland's spirit of goodwill quickly evaporated: the state hired lawyers to bring the Pennsylvania law to the Supreme Court, where they were successful in having it declared unconstitutional. Since the federal government had thus abandoned its responsibility for protecting free blacks in Pennsylvania, the state had been forced to create its own law "for the protection of our free, colored citizens from the bands of kidnappers that infest our Southern border, whose operations were often aided by constables and magistrates in our State. Numbers of our free colored citizens of Pennsylvania, men, women and children, were *captured and carried into slavery*, and such outrages became *so frequent and so flagrant* as to demand an effective remedy." That argument, not surprisingly, carried little or no weight in Maryland.[4]

With the passage of the 1850 Fugitive Slave Act, the lines that had been drawn in the localized arguments about Pennsylvania's 1847 law remained essentially in place. Now, however, they were drawn across a much larger map. The Act originated as a bargaining chip, a part of the compromise agreement finally settled on by pro- and antislavery factions in Congress to prepare for the admission of new states to the Union. The compromise package, introduced by Henry Clay, allowed for the admission of California as a free state and the abolition of the slave trade (but not of the ownership of slaves) in the District of Columbia. These measures were balanced first by the stipulation that the new states of New Mexico and Utah should be allowed to determine for themselves whether they were slave or free, and second by what turned out to be the real clincher in the deal—the institution of stronger fugitive slave provisions. In lobbying for the fugitive slave part of the compromise, Daniel Webster, whose strong support for the bill helped to get it passed, declared in language that was a coded but recognizable reference to abolitionists that any northerners should be able to support it as long as they were not "carried away by some fanatical idea or some false impression."[5]

The provisions of the new Fugitive Slave Act were designed to protect the property of slaveholders. Since states like Pennsylvania had been refusing to cooperate with slaveholders from other states, the law took all authority in the matter of runaway slaves away from the states and vested it entirely in the federal government. It provided for commissioners, one or more per county, to be appointed by the circuit courts, and gave them extraordinary authority to adjudicate claims for fugitive slaves. Anyone apprehending a purported runaway could bring that person to one of these or to a judge, who would make a determination in the case. In place of a salary for commissioners, the law allowed them two levels of payment: $5 for each fugitive they released and $10 for each one they returned to a claimant. Commissioners were also authorized to arrest anyone caught harboring a fugitive or interfering with the arrest of one; such offenders were subject to a $1,000 fine and up to six months in prison. Two provisions of the act especially outraged the opponents of slavery. First, accused runaways were not allowed to speak on their own behalf, and second, the commissioners and judges were instructed to make their determinations in each case in a "summary manner." In a hearing to determine whether someone was slave or free, therefore, the matter was, by law, to be settled as quickly as possible and with no explanation or comment from the person whose case was being heard.

In the eyes of many in the North and especially in the border states, what was being called a compromise was actually an egregious and shameful capitulation to southern interests. As one abolitionist asked,

"When will Northern doughfaces learn that a compromise in this country means a complete victory to the slave power?" The antislavery interests recognized immediately that the new law, by denying due process to those accused of being fugitive slaves and mandating that their cases be dealt with quickly, gave new encouragement to kidnappers while at the same time discouraging anyone from coming to the aid of either fugitives or kidnap victims. (The *New York Evening Post* bluntly called the new law "an act for the encouragement of kidnapping.") The law also encouraged corruption on the part of the newly appointed commissioners, who could earn twice as much by ruling in favor of someone's claim to a fugitive than by ruling against it. Stanley Campbell has estimated that over the life of the law, commissioners remanded into slavery more than 80 percent of the accused who were brought before them and released only 6 percent. The rest escaped or were rescued.[6]

The implications of the new law were enormous for Pennsylvania, already a magnet for runaway slaves and thus for slave catchers and kidnappers. Within weeks of the passage of the Act, a gathering of African Americans in Philadelphia passed a series of resolutions in response to the legislation, stating plainly their refusal to comply with its mandates: "We shall never refuse aid and shelter and succor to any brother or sister who has escaped from the prison-house of Southern bondage, but shall do all we can to prevent their being dragged back to a slavery inconceivably worse than death." Frustrated antislavery activists predicted an increase in both legal and illegal apprehensions of black residents and major setbacks in their attempts to protect them. William Still, writing some years later about the immediate effects of the Act, asserted that "it is hardly too much to say, that Pennsylvania was considered wholly unsafe to nine-tenths of her colored population." A newspaper in Washington County, Pennsylvania, renounced the act as "iniquitous, "repugnant," even "bloody," and declared that while it could not endorse open resistance to any law, neither could it support this misguided new one: "A law so loose in its character, so defective in its details, so open to frauds and so liable to become the means of doing great injustice and mischief, we cannot sanction.... We can see no redeeming feature in this Fugitive Slave Law—nothing we can praise, nothing that we can approve." Miller

McKim, a founding member of the Pennsylvania Anti-Slavery Society, wrote to a friend not long after the passage of the law about

> the anguish and confusion that have been produced in this part of the country by this infamous statute. It has turned Southeastern Pennsylvania into another Guinea Coast, and caused a large portion of the inhabitants to feel as insecure from the brutal violence and diabolical acts of the kidnapper, as are the unhappy creatures who people the shores of Africa. Ruffians from the other side of the Slave-line, aided by professional kidnappers on our own soil, a class of men whose "occupation," until lately, had been "gone," are continually prowling through the community, and every now and then seizing and carrying away their prey.[7]

In his 1911 history of African Americans in Pennsylvania, Edward Turner argued that fears aroused by the Fugitive Slave Act resulted in increased resistance from local blacks and the appearance of more organized forms of resistance. As a consequence, according to Turner, slave catching became more difficult and dangerous, and the kidnappings actually slowed down. The evidence from most newspapers and from the accounts of those who kept an eye on such things, however, indicates that while violent resistance might have increased after 1850, it did so in response to an *increased* number of kidnappings, attempted and successful, in Pennsylvania and elsewhere. The Pennsylvania Anti-Slavery Society reported that 1851 had been an especially dark year for fugitives, freedmen, and opponents of slavery in the state:

> The Fugitive Slave Law was then in its fullest force. The escaped bondman, frightened from his refuge, was flying before his pursuers, in search of a more secure resting place; a panic pervaded our entire colored population. . . . One year ago our record showed a catalogue of twenty-six cases of alleged slaves delivered up from this State under the Fugitive law, besides numerous cases of kidnapping and attempts to kidnap, and other instances of outrage and violence perpetrated under cover of that infamous enactment.

The proslavery press was inclined to offer more inflammatory and, often, less reliable versions of the results of the law. In October 1852, the *Kent* [County] *News* in Maryland reported that a party from Maryland had gone north intending to arrest Frederick Douglass as a fugitive slave—apparently unaware that he had purchased his own freedom years before. The same story predicted a massive raid on Pennsylvania by righteous slaveholders: "There are also known to be several thousand fugitive slaves in Columbia, Lancaster, Harrisburg, and Pittsburgh, the owners of several hundred of whom have already taken steps for their recovery, and there will soon be a great storm in that direction."[8]

While the paper's "great storm" prediction was exaggerated and deliberately apocalyptic, the reality was troubling enough. Pauli Murray, whose great-grandparents settled in the small free black community of Hinsonville, Pennsylvania, just eight miles from the Maryland line, notes that the "exposed little Negro settlements" along the state border became constant targets of raiders after the passage of the Fugitive Slave Law. "Slaveowners and their agents now charged into free states at will with their cumbersome legal papers, accompanied by a United States marshal and a *posse comitatus*, and demanded the return of Negroes who had established themselves in a community and lived there for many years as free persons. Under cover of the law, bands of marauders with faked warrants also came over the line." The slave hunters from Maryland were a distressing presence, especially in the small towns and rural communities. R. C. Smedley described them as "coarse" and "swaggering" men who "inspired a feeling of detestation wherever they appeared, [and] none favored their nefarious enterprises except the very lowest and meanest of the population. Among such they were accustomed, not unfrequently, to find spies and informers."[9]

William Parker, a runaway from Maryland who had arrived in southeastern Pennsylvania in 1839 and would achieve notoriety for his role in what came to be known as the Christiana "riot," attested to the extent of the problem:

> Kidnapping was so common . . . that we were kept in constant fear. We would hear of slaveholders or kidnappers every two or

three weeks, sometimes a party of white men would break in a house and take a man away, no one knew where, and, again, a whole family would be carried off. There was no power to protect them or prevent it. So completely roused were my feelings, that I vowed to let no slaveholder take back a fugitive, if I could but get my eye on him.

Parker put his vow into action; he and a few like-minded others formed a kind of vigilante group, pursuing kidnappers and willingly matching violence with violence. At one point Parker's group chased some kidnappers who had stolen a young girl from the home of Moses Whitson, a Chester County Quaker. Parker and his men overtook them before they got out of the county, freed the girl, and beat up the unidentified kidnappers, two of whom, Parker said, later died.[10]

Parker's account confirms that kidnappers had black as well as white informants in Chester County and that their skin color provided no protection from his vengeance. His group severely beat at least two black men who were informing on fugitives, burned the house of another, and ran another out of the county. Parker later explained his actions: "The frequent attacks from slaveholders and their tools, the peculiarity of our position, many being escaped slaves, and the secrecy attending these kidnapping exploits, all combined to make an appeal to the Lynch Code in our case excusable. Ourselves, our wives, our little ones, were insecure, and all we had was liable to seizure." As Pauli Murray describes slave hunting in the county, "Treachery was part of this lawless business. . . . White and colored informers in Chester County who worked with slave catchers and kidnappers in Maryland cared little whether their victim was a fugitive, a freedman or a free-born person." At least one fugitive, a man named Henry Harris, was betrayed by a black man who posed as a fortune teller, promising that if Harris would give him the name of his owner and the name Harris had used as a slave, he would put a spell on the owner that would protect Harris. The fortune teller relayed the information to the owner, and Harris was captured and sold to Mississippi.[11]

It was probably William Parker who inspired a passage in James H. W. Howard's 1886 novel *Bond and Free* about the escape of a slave couple from Virginia to Canada. Much of the action of the novel is set in a fictional town in southeastern Pennsylvania, near the Susquehanna River. Howard pauses in his narrative to pay tribute to men like Parker and to suggest that the extent of their efforts on behalf of fugitives can never be fully known: "So many fugitives had been attacked, imprisoned, kidnapped, and returned South from the town of H— that a few noble-hearted negro men banded together and vowed to protect, at the cost of their lives, their brethren in their efforts to obtain freedom. The bloody work done by these organizations, in defense of freedom, will never be known until judgment-day. Many a kidnapper and betrayer was beaten and driven out of the neighborhood by this little band of heroes."[12]

Among those who earned a reputation along the border was Thomas McCreary of Cecil County, Maryland, the man who would kidnap Rachel and Elizabeth Parker from Chester County in December 1851. McCreary had begun his career as a slave catcher and kidnapper well before he took the Parker sisters. The Pennsylvania Anti-Slavery Society had tried to get him sent to jail in 1849 for helping to kidnap a child in Downingtown, Pennsylvania. By that point, he was known to the antislavery press as an active slave catcher and had already earned from them the title of "the infamous McCreary." A Pennsylvania grand jury indicted him in the Downingtown kidnapping case, but he managed to get free on a technicality. That episode was typical of McCreary's entire history with the law, the courts, and the press. He kept up his reputation as an efficient slave catcher and a ruthless kidnapper while he also, by one means or another, kept himself out of jail and usually out of court.[13]

McCreary's defenders labeled him a "borderer," a description as appropriate to his reputation as to the map of his activities. His territory was the Pennsylvania/Maryland border portion of the Mason-Dixon Line, and his public identity was defined in large part by that line. He was known among the antislavery activists in Pennsylvania as a criminal, a thug, a notorious man-stealer. Within Cecil County, on the other hand, McCreary was known not as a kidnapper but as the person who "looks after runaway negroes" or, more prosaically, as the local "nigger trader." Before his 1849 indictment in the Downingtown kidnapping, McCreary had been a mail carrier, picking up the mail the train dropped off in his home town of Elkton and delivering it, by carriage, as far as the village of Chestnut Level in Lancaster County, Pennsylvania. He was removed from that job in 1849, perhaps because of his indictment in the Downingtown kidnapping, but he was subsequently allowed to keep the contract for the route and hire someone else to do the actual mail carrying.[14]

On occasion, legally or not, McCreary made the rounds with the mail himself. His route took him through southern Chester County, probably through the towns of Nottingham and Oxford and close to the farm where Rachel Parker lived with the family of Joseph Miller. This was already familiar turf for him; he had family in that part of the county, including a brother, Jesse, who lived near Joseph Miller, and at least two farmer nephews. He knew how things worked in the area, and he knew who the newcomers were among the African American population. Using his frequent trips across the state line as a means of scouting out the territory for vulnerable targets, McCreary became known in southeastern Pennsylvania not only as a kidnapper but also as an irresponsible agent for the mails. A disgruntled resident on his route who was tired of late or missing mail observed that "McCreary the contractor is known for kidnapping" and that his slave chasing was interfering with his duty to oversee timely deliveries. The complainant was less disturbed by the kidnapping distraction than by the resulting irregularity of the mail: "If Mr. McCreary does not pay more attention to the mail route than he has been doing . . . he will undoubtedly be reported to the Department."[15]

McCreary had made the news four times in 1849, more than two years before he became embroiled in the Parker case. In that single year, he was involved or suspected of involvement in at least three Pennsylvania kidnapping incidents, each of which aroused significant outrage in the state and beyond. The first of these was the Downingtown incident, which took place in late March or early April, when a fifteen-year-old boy, Henry Lee Brown, was lured away from the town. Having been promised a job as a coachman, Brown was instead hustled off to Walter Campbell's slave pen in Baltimore—the same pen to which both of the Parker sisters would be taken. Somehow Campbell learned that the boy was in fact free and sent him back to Pennsylvania. Two men, one white and one black, were arrested on charges of kidnapping Brown and tried in Chester County. Both were sentenced to prison and fined $500. Those convictions closed out the story as far as the newspapers were concerned, the *Pennsylvania Freeman* expressing the hope that the stiff sentences would "prove a terrible warning to others."[16]

The Pennsylvania Society for Promoting the Abolition of Slavery, however, was convinced there was more to it. The Society was sure enough of Tom McCreary's involvement in the abduction to charge him with kidnapping and win an indictment from a Pennsylvania grand jury. In the account of its activities for 1849, the Society reported that its members had worked with "a number of citizens of Chester County" to get McCreary into court. "The matter was laid before the Grand Jury, and a true bill found. Gov. Johnston, of this state, promptly issued his requisition, but the possession of McCreary was not obtained in consequence of the neglect of an officer employed for the purpose." This was not the last time that a governor of Pennsylvania would try in vain to bring McCreary to trial in his state. Nor was it the last time that McCreary would escape prosecution under very suspicious circumstances. If there is a story behind the instance of official "neglect" that the Abolition Society mentions in the Downingtown case—and certainly there is *some* story—it has not been told, and the neglectful officer has not been identified. Whatever the explanation might be, McCreary went scot-free, as he always would.[17]

The second and best-publicized of McCreary's 1849 exploits was the abduction from Chester County of Tom Mitchell—the man whose disappearance had frightened Isaac Mason into leaving the county. Mitchell had run away from slavery in Maryland and had been living in Pennsylvania as a free man long enough that even his wife did not know he was a former slave. In mid-August 1849—only a few months after his indictment for the kidnapping of Henry Lee Brown—McCreary and two or three accomplices broke into Mitchell's house in the small town of Unionville at midnight, threatened his wife with a gun, and spirited the half-dressed Mitchell off by train to Baltimore, where he was deposited in the pen of slave trader Jonathan Wilson. McCreary had bought

Mitchell "on the fly" from his former owner in Maryland, a Mrs. Hayes. That is, McCreary paid Mrs. Hayes an unspecified sum of money on the condition that, if he found Mitchell, he could claim ownership of the fugitive. Since Jonathan Wilson did extensive business with New Orleans and kept a second pen there, McCreary probably intended for Mitchell to be shipped to New Orleans and sold there as soon as possible.[18]

Mitchell had been working for a Quaker named George Martin for the last four years. When Martin learned of the abduction, he did what Rachel Parker's employer would do two years later: he took a train to Baltimore and headed straight for the slave pens. Accompanied by another Quaker from Chester County, Samuel Pennock, Martin went to Wilson's pen, found Mitchell there, identified him, and stated that Mitchell had lived with him for some time as a free man. Much to Martin's surprise, he was arrested on the spot, on the grounds that, if Mitchell had been working for him, then Martin owed Mitchell's former owner $1,000 to compensate him for the lost labor of his slave. Martin was released after his lawyers pointed out that debtors were liable only in the state where the debt was incurred, and Martin therefore could not legally be prosecuted in Maryland.[19]

As for Tom Mitchell, some of the press, especially the antislavery papers, announced that he had been sold south and might never be heard from again. Isaac Mason was much closer to the mark when he wrote that "the Quakers, moved with sympathy for the wife and children, and knowing the worth of the captive, raised five hundred dollars and went south, purchased his freedom and brought him back." In fact, the rescuers did not have to go very far south: Mitchell never left Baltimore. He was held at Jonathan Wilson's pen while sympathizers back home in Chester County, led by George Martin and a farmer named Enoch Swayne, raised the $600 needed to purchase him. The bill of sale, signed by the slave trader Wilson, specified that the reason for his sale was "to return to Pennsylvania for the purpose of granting his freedom."[20]

In tracing McCreary and Mitchell to Baltimore, George Martin and Samuel Pennock were following what amounted to a Chester County tradition of pursuing kidnappers, one that resulted in the return of an unknown number of captives but would also result in the death of Joseph Miller two years later. When Enoch Swayne and his fellow citizens raised the money to purchase Tom Mitchell, they were following an equally remarkable county tradition, this time one that would later benefit Elizabeth Parker. Some kidnap victims in the county, like Mitchell, were purchased from the slave dealers to whom they had been sold. In other cases, fugitives were hidden away until the pursuing owners gave up on finding them and agreed to take a small purchase price and go home. In many cases, the purchase money was raised by subscription. One such case occurred as early as 1830, when fourteen white men in Chester County and an unspecified "number of colored persons" subscribed $105—a very low price—to purchase the freedom of Henry Cooper, a runaway from Maryland. While three of the group subscribed $10, most put up $5; the "colored persons" together chipped in $9.50. As part of this particular arrangement, Cooper agreed to pay back his benefactors as he was able. He and Tom Mitchell were only two of the many former slaves who gained their freedom through the organized philanthropy of county citizens.[21]

A week after Mitchell's return, Chester County residents organized an "indignation meeting" to protest his kidnapping, running announcements in the local papers:

> The people of Chester County and vicinity, without distinction of party, will meet en mass [*sic*], at the house from which Thomas Mitchell was recently dragged from his family by Maryland kidnappers, to express their indignation at such deeds of daring outrage; and to adopt such measures as will most effectually prevent the future occurrence of such inhuman atrocities. The company will proceed from the house to a neighboring grove, where they will be addressed by several eminent speakers from Philadelphia and elsewhere, who have volunteered their services. That every man, woman and child, of the surrounding country may be present, is the wish of
>
> THE PEOPLE.

Now legally free, Mitchell remained in Chester County and worked for the Swayne family for the next twenty years.[22]

The press reactions to the Mitchell episode divided, not at all surprisingly, along the Mason-Dixon Line. The *Albany* (NY) *Evening Journal* took from it a message about the desperate measures of slaveholders who were seeing their way of life threatened: "Northern men, who have human feeling in their bosoms, should beware how they place themselves in the power of these Southern slaveholders, for their desperation, seeing the hand writing on the wall, drives them to every expedient and extremity." The Cecil County *Whig* also saw the incident as a warning to friends of the slave, specifically those in Pennsylvania, but where the New York paper found desperation among slaveholders, the Maryland paper found renewed and strengthened resolve. Maryland had things to teach the arrogant Pennsylvanians, according to the *Whig*, and Tom McCreary was the man for the job: "So long as slaves are enticed away and protected in their escape by [Pennsylvania's] laws, they will be stolen back. And though we have no sympathy with McCreary in this business of his, Pennsylvanians will find, that notwithstanding their threats, he will go into their midst and take negroes from under their very noses, until they learn to respect the laws of Maryland and of the United States." McCreary might not have been universally perceived as a favorite son in Maryland, but he was a son, and the view from inside Maryland was that he was only giving the meddling Pennsylvania abolitionists what they needed and deserved.[23]

McCreary was back in the news in a kidnapping case in September 1849, although this time his participation was only rumored. A woman named Ann Brown was apprehended in Wilmington, Delaware, with the captors claiming that she was a fugitive slave. Among those who came to Brown's aid was Thomas Garrett, the remarkably effective Quaker agent of the Underground Railroad in Wilmington who had already, by his account, aided hundreds of fugitives. The kidnappers tried to sell Brown to Garrett for $100 when they saw that their attempt to claim her as a slave was not likely to succeed in court. Garrett indignantly refused to have anything to do with giving money to kidnappers, so they simply scurried back into Maryland, and Brown was released. *Frederick Douglass's Paper*, reporting on the case, commented, "We understand that the infamous McCreary, the head kidnapper in the abduction of Thomas Mitchell, was actively engaged in this case." The rumors were never proved, and McCreary and the kidnappers stayed out of court and out of jail.[24]

McCreary aroused the indignation of the Pennsylvania antislavery activists once more at the end of 1849, his fourth appearance in the news that year, although this time he seems to have acted within the limits of Maryland law. In fact, it seems fair to say that in this case, it was the law, rather than McCreary's actions, that was the real source of outrage. At the time, free blacks who were not already Maryland residents were prohibited by law from entering the state. Breaking this law could result in a substantial fine; if the transgressor could not pay the fine, he or she could be imprisoned and sold into slavery. For some unexplained reason, a sixteen-year-old Pennsylvania boy named John Jackson found his way into Elkton, Maryland (McCreary's home), and was immediately arrested and fined. Since the boy had no way of paying such a large fine, he was freed by antislavery sympathizers in Philadelphia who raised the money for him. Remarkably, and again inexplicably, John Jackson returned to Elkton and was once again arrested. This time, no rescuers appeared, and the boy was sold as a slave—to Thomas McCreary. While there is no evidence to link McCreary to Jackson's two appearances in Elkton, his record certainly raises suspicions, and it is not surprising that he was there to place the winning bid when the boy was auctioned.[25]

Men like McCreary were sometimes called slave catchers and sometimes called kidnappers. Which term one used depended largely on how one felt about the ethics, morality, and politics of the whole business of the rendition of fugitive slaves. In Maryland, the distinction was important: in the press and in other forms of public address, it was de rigueur to defend the pursuit of fugitive slaves as the legal exercise of property rights and to condemn kidnapping as criminal. When McCreary was arrested for kidnapping Rachel Parker, his hometown newspaper, the *Cecil Whig*, appropriately headlined its report "The Slave Arrest, or the Kidnapping—as the Case May Be." The *Whig* came down solidly on the "arrest" side. In Pennsylvania, on the other hand, the two terms were often used interchangeably, for both legal and philosophical reasons. A Maryland slave who escaped to Pennsylvania became, under Pennsylvania law, a free person; it was therefore easy to interpret the capture of that person as an act of kidnapping. The more important reasons for the collapsing of the two terms were probably less precise and more deeply embedded in the ideological differences separating proslavery and antislavery groups. Making a distinction between illegal kidnapping and the legal capture of fugitives, as historian Lois Horton has pointed out, seemed to give credibility to the whole system of slavery. For abolitionists and others opposed to slavery, who began with the premise that every person is a free person, it made sense to criminalize both, to see the capture of both fugitives and free blacks as a form of kidnapping. In antislavery discourse, therefore, *kidnap* became the usable term, the one that sufficed to cover all instances of the capture of black people. In Ellwood Griest's 1873 novel *John and Mary; or, The Fugitive Slaves*, which is set in Lancaster County and based on an actual attempt by Marylanders to arrest a family of fugitive slaves, the Pennsylvania characters speak unreflectingly of the pursuers as kidnappers.[26]

Thomas McCreary was well known under both rubrics—slave catcher and kidnapper—and to both camps: those who chased fugitive slaves and those who chased slave catchers. In the summer of 1851, a few months before the Parker kidnappings, McCreary was involved in an affair that gives some idea of his reputation and standing among the two groups. The affair, which began in Delaware and moved to Maryland, was reported by Thomas Garrett in a letter to the *Pennsylvania Freeman*. The newspaper's opinion was unambiguous: "It is a base affair, and unspeakably base are the men that have been employed in it." McCreary was a rather minor player in this episode, but, significantly, it was to him that the major players turned when they needed help. If there was a fugitive slave problem in or around Cecil County, Tom McCreary was the go-to guy.[27]

Garrett's story began with the removal of two people from jail: Elizabeth Williams in West Chester, Pennsylvania, and John Kinnard in New Castle, Delaware. Both were taken by a Delaware man, George

McCrone, who claimed that they were fugitive slaves who belonged to him. In West Chester, McCrone took advantage of the provisions of the still-new Fugitive Slave Act: he removed Williams from jail, brought her before a commissioner, and had her quickly—"in a summary manner," as the law prescribed—declared his property. He also, apparently, took advantage of some malleable officials, since the hearing before the commissioner took place at four o'clock in the morning and McCrone was off to Delaware with Williams before the rest of West Chester was stirring. The peculiar scheduling did not go unnoticed for long. Even the West Chester *Village Record*, generally inclined to tread lightly on the subject of fugitives, felt nervous about the appearance of unseemly collusion in the matter: "Every one felt that the Inspectors of the prison had done wrong if they had any agency in an arrangement for delivering Williams up to a state of bondage—or even to trial—at such an unseasonable hour. . . . We trust the Directors of the prison will exonerate themselves from any collusion in this matter. They are all gentlemen of high and honorable feelings, and we are sure that they mean no wrong."[28]

In New Castle, McCrone again took advantage, this time of Delaware's vagrancy laws, which allowed sheriffs to arrest unemployed free blacks and then sell their labor to the highest bidder. In his account of the case, Garrett commented that the vagrancy laws attracted unscrupulous buyers like McCrone, who were, in his opinion, essentially kidnappers. The people whose labor they purchased often disappeared after a short time, and Garrett was convinced they were sold into slavery: "On inquiry for them the answer is, Oh! They have run away. This business has been carried on for the last ten years to an alarming extent, and no doubt will continue to be, till the law is striken [*sic*] from the statute books of the state." McCrone put Williams and Kinnard in the charge of another Delaware man, Arnold Naudain, and sent the party off to Elkton to catch the train for Baltimore, where Williams and Kinnard were to be deposited in a slave pen and sold.[29]

The party did not arrive in Elkton, however, until after the last train had left. Finding himself saddled with the two captives, Naudain took them to a secure hiding place: the attic room in the house of Tom McCreary, located conveniently near the train station. McCreary agreed to hold Williams and Kinnard in his attic (where he would also hold Elizabeth Parker a few months later) until the following night, when the next train to Baltimore would arrive. And then things began to go wrong. Here is Thomas Garrett's version of the events:

> About 10 o'clock next morning the cry of murder! Murder! was heard from the house of McCreary. When the inhabitants rushed to ascertain the cause, they found Kinnard partly out of the window hallooing lustily; McCreary holding him by the shoulders to prevent him from jumping out, and Naudain assisting. They had hand-cuffs which they were endeavoring to put on him to secure him. . . . The Sheriff, by the advice of the citizens, put the two colored people in jail for safe keeping, till there was time to make more inquiry respecting them.

It is not clear what the results of the further inquiries were or what finally became of Williams and Kinnard, but Garrett was certain that McCrone had transacted similar kinds of business before, purchasing free blacks who had been jailed for minor offenses or for being unemployed, or simply claiming that free blacks were actually his slaves and then selling them in Baltimore. He was also sure that Naudain would not suffer for his part in the business: "Arnold S. Naudain has the character of a religious and respectable man, and I presume will hardly lose caste with his neighbors for this high handed act." McCreary seems not to have been implicated in the removal of the two people from jail, but he was certainly known to Naudain and his companions, and known to have a handy attic room in Elkton that he was willing to make available to them.[30]

Given McCreary's success in evading prosecution by the law, a group of outraged Pennsylvanians decided to take matters into their own hands. A few months after the episode in Elkton, and only a few days before McCreary abducted Rachel Parker, the group attempted to arrest him at the end of his mail route in Lancaster County. McCreary had recently been making frequent mail runs himself, even though he was aware that the Pennsylvania authorities were on the lookout for him. The timing of the trips suggests strongly that the relentless McCreary was scouting the Parkers, making plans, possibly lining up accomplices. A "posse" of unidentified Pennsylvanians ambushed McCreary on the last of these runs, while he was staying at an inn near Lancaster. According to the brief news reports, McCreary defended himself against the surprise attack first with a Bowie knife—his signature weapon—and then with a revolver, shooting through the bottom of a chair that one of the posse had raised in self-defense. The confrontation ended in anticlimax with no arrest, the posse withdrawing, and McCreary hurrying back to Maryland.[31]

This version of the event differs somewhat from the one provided by McCreary himself, which was eventually included in his obituary:

> He was several times waylaid and fired upon by parties in ambush, and had a desperate encounter at Chestnut Level with seven men, who undertook to arrest him in a bar-room of the hotel at that place. . . . With his revolver and bowie-knife he caused his assailants to beat a hasty retreat, having cut the whiskers of the leader of the band by a ball fired through the bottom of a Windsor chair which the man held up between McCreary and himself, as he advanced upon him to make the arrest. After the encounter McCreary thought it prudent to make a hasty retreat, which he did, lest the party might return reinforced.[32]

In this version, McCreary is in masterful control of both the situation and the story. Brandishing a knife and a gun, apparently ready for trouble, he singlehandedly vanquishes a group of seven "assailants" in a bar-room—a perfect setting for the rough-and-ready McCreary to show up a bunch of temperance-minded abolitionists. He gets away, as he always does, this time by choosing to make a "prudent" retreat; he definitely is not routed. (And that detail of the shot-off whiskers is a nice touch.)

McCreary's hometown newspaper, the *Cecil Whig*, defended his actions on the grounds that in firing at the Pennsylvanians he was only doing his duty as a government employee: "protect[ing] the U.S. Mail, which he has contracted safely to carry." About a week later, McCreary was arrested and put on trial for kidnapping Rachel Parker. This time, the *Whig* had a more challenging task in defending him. Given the mounting evidence that Rachel was in fact free and not a runaway slave, the newspaper at first speculated that McCreary had made an honest mistake but then settled on a more politically satisfying explanation for his arrest of a free person: the abolitionists made him do it. Maybe McCreary should have been more careful about whom he abducted, according to the *Whig*, but morally he was in the clear. The paper cast McCreary's career in an almost mythically romantic light, calling him a "borderer" who had been "created by the times" and defining him as one who "goes in the night and by daring and speed carries the slave to his owner;—perchance, sometimes mistaking the description, he carries off a free negro. Whose fault is it?" The *Whig* answered its own rhetorical question, this time specifically identifying the abolitionists of Pennsylvania as the ones who "create such men as McCreary." Those abolitionists, according to the *Whig*, were "the veriest curse ever yet inflicted on the negro race; and for stating this consequence, we are charged with encouraging the lawless and daring actions of McCreary. If so, so be it." A week later, the *Whig* reiterated its defense of McCreary and its warning to Pennsylvania in even stronger terms: "When the time comes that the owner of a fugitive slave can go safely under the law and arrest him, McCreary's mission will be ended; till then, we presume his 'sorties' may be nightly expected." If the choice was between siding with a known kidnapper and siding with the abolitionists, the *Whig* was fully prepared to line up behind the kidnapper. There was no contest.[33]

3

THE PARKERS' WORLD

THE PARKER SISTERS were victims of the Fugitive Slave Act. As African American children born in the rural Pennsylvania of the mid-nineteenth century, however, Rachel and Elizabeth had in many ways been victims since birth; their victimization did not begin with the passage of that act. They were inheritors of a system that had replaced slavery in Pennsylvania, as in other states, without significantly altering the economic order that slavery had helped to make possible or the social order that had sustained it. The Parkers had a nominal freedom that slaves did not have but little more in the way of possibilities for mobility, economic security, or participation in the larger civic life of their community, much less that of the nation. They and their peers were still subject to larger forces and movements that circumscribed their lives, limited their freedom, and submerged their individual selves in material realities that can be difficult to retrieve now except as patterns, trends, and statistics. What those realities were for Elizabeth Parker is suggested by her response to being "rescued" from enslavement. When she was offered a choice between the actual slave life she got to know briefly in New Orleans and the life of approximated slavery she had known in rural Pennsylvania, Elizabeth first chose the real thing: she wanted to stay in the city; she did not want to go home. She was not free in New Orleans, but life there must have *felt* freer to her than life as a young black girl in a small Pennsylvania township.

Many African Americans passed through East and West Nottingham and the other border townships of Pennsylvania in the years before the war. However, the resident population of free blacks in the two Nottinghams at midcentury remained small. It was especially small in West Nottingham, where Rachel and Elizabeth were born. Out of a total population of 728 people counted in the 1850 census, only 33 were black; 4 of these, including Rachel Parker, were children living in white households. Black children were scarce enough in the township that everyone knew when one was born. James Brown, who had been eleven years old at the time of Rachel's birth in 1834, went to see the newborn because he had been told that African American babies were born white and, never having seen one before, he wanted to find out for himself. William McCreary, a nephew of Thomas's who lived only a few miles from the Millers' farm, reported that there were not many "colored persons" in his neighborhood: "They are not very plenty about there." He could name only three black families other than the Parkers. The scarcity of black families can be explained in part by the fact that by the time slavery ended in the state, as Gary Nash and Jean Soderlund have pointed out, the easily available land in eastern Pennsylvania was largely already taken. It was also the case that living in the southern townships was simply dangerous; the few blacks who did find a way to settle along the border were recognizably at risk from kidnappers. James Mullen, a West Nottingham farmer who lived half a mile from the Parkers when the girls were born, said that he used to ask Rachel "if she was not afraid the kidnappers would get her," since "several colored persons had previously been taken off."[1]

The sisters were the daughters of Rebecca and Edward Parker, known locally as Beck (or Little Beck) and Ned; Rachel was born in 1834 and Elizabeth sometime around 1841. They had at least one brother, James, and possibly other siblings as well, although the evidence is vague and sometimes conflicting. When witnesses were asked in court about the make-up of the Parker family, they gave varying accounts. Mary Wilkinson, from whose father the Parkers once rented a house, testified that

Beck had five children; she recalled seeing all five. Rebecca Morrison testified that Beck actually had seven children, not five. Morrison identified the two youngest of these as Harriet and Henry; they were, Morrison said, the children of a man named "Glasgow," with whom Rebecca had lived after her marriage to Ned Parker broke up. Robert Hughes also recalled that Rebecca "took up with a colored man named Glascoe" after Ned left, but he remembered seeing only three children—Rachel, James, and Elizabeth. One witness recalled a fourth child, Washington, who died sometime before 1850; another remembered Washington as well as a child named Joseph; and yet another recalled a child named Robert. If Beck did have children named Washington, Joseph, or Robert, there are no other traces of them in the records.

Other courtroom witnesses offered their memories of Beck, sketching in her movements since her childhood. The statements about Beck's origins give a picture that is far from complete but nonetheless revealing, not only about her but also about the general circumstances of free blacks in the area. Beck was born in Lancaster County, where she and her mother, who was also named Rebecca, lived with a Quaker family named Milner. There is no record of who Beck's father was or whether she had siblings. Nathan Milner gave Beck's birth date as 1813; he remembered that, when he first knew them, mother and daughter went by the name Chandler.[2] He described Beck as being "under the care" of his grandmother; his phrasing suggests that Rebecca probably was not able to care for her daughter herself. Rebecca and Beck had not been with the Milners very long when, in 1818, Rebecca was sent to the Lancaster County almshouse—another indication that she must have been ill or infirm. She evidently died there, and young Beck began, or perhaps continued, her movement from one white household to another. John Taylor testified that after Rebecca was sent away, he packed Beck into an oxcart and moved her from the Milners' to William Brown's house, also in Lancaster County, where she was put to work. Beck stayed on at Brown's for ten years. Because of this connection, she was sometimes known as "Billy Brown's Beck."[3]

If Nathan Milner was right about Beck's age, she was about five years old when she was first separated from her mother and began working for

William Brown. Even allowing some leeway in the estimation of dates, it is still clear that Beck was very young when her mother was sent away and she was put to work in the household of strangers. If Milner's memory was accurate and Beck was only five years old when she began working, her experience would not have been unusual or inconsistent with that of other children of the dependent poor, black and white, in her area. Putting the children of the poor out to work was not considered exploitative, nor was hiring them. Rather, locating black children in white homes where they would work for their keep had for a long time been considered a charitable undertaking. Even those who were doctrinally opposed to slavery, such as the Quakers, were not hesitant to take in black children on terms that were, in reality, very close to those of the master-slave relationship. In 1779, the Quaker members of Concord Monthly Meeting (in Pennsylvania) actively encouraged black parents to apprentice their children to white masters, for the good of the whole family.[4]

Between 1802 and 1825—years that included the stay of Beck's mother in the Lancaster County almshouse—the trustees of the poor in adjacent Chester County bound out 237 children to work, or about ten per year. Approximately 20 percent of these children were black, and their average age when they left the almshouse was just over six and a half. Therefore, a working black child of five, living in a white family, was not an anomaly. Unlike Beck, many of the other working children in antebellum Pennsylvania were not orphans. The Managers of the Temporary Home for Colored Children in Philadelphia announced their intention in 1850 to take "destitute colored children" who had at least one parent and were therefore ineligible for the orphans' shelter "and to place them out as soon as suitable places can be obtained for them." In November 1857, the Philadelphia House of Refuge, which took in children whose situations or histories would later mark them as "juvenile delinquents," sent its agent out to surrounding rural counties looking for farmers who might want to take on apprentice boys. Because of financial problems in the city, the agent said, the Refuge expected to be "inundated with poor boys and girls" over the coming winter.[5]

In her study of almshouses in Philadelphia's outlying areas, including Chester and Lancaster Counties, Monique Bourque concludes that the poor in rural areas were not as nameless and faceless as we might assume; many of them were familiar not only to one another and to the administrators of the almshouses but also to the larger communities through which they moved. Beck was clearly well known in several communities, both as a child and as an adult. She lived out her life in Lancaster and Chester Counties, but within that relatively small geographical space she did a lot of moving about, from place to place and from household to household. She remained with William Brown until 1828, when she was about fifteen. Brown moved west then, and Beck went to live with another Lancaster County farmer, John Kirk, where she stayed for five or six years. When Kirk also moved away, Beck worked for a while for a Dr. Webster. For at least part of this time, she was apparently using the name Rebecca McKew.[6]

In November 1833, after fifteen years of living with at least four white families, Beck claimed her own home: then about twenty years old, she married Edward Parker, who was almost twice her age, in East Nottingham in Chester County. Ned (as he was called) came from the adjacent township of West Nottingham, where he had been raised by his grandfather. People who knew him did not forget him; he was so knock-kneed, they said, that he almost seemed deformed. The justice of the peace who married Beck and Ned remembered exactly when the ceremony took place because it was the "night the stars fell"—a reference to what we now recognize as the Leonid meteor shower, which occurred on November 13, 1833. (A later chronicler of the Parkers' story mentions the falling stars but declares them "a phenomenon we know nothing about." One wonders what the married couple thought about the mysterious stars that fell on their wedding night.)[7]

Beck and Ned lived together in at least two different places in Chester County. Beck did laundry for nearby farms and boarding houses, sometimes living onsite for as much as a week while she did the washing. After Rachel was born in 1834, Beck began bringing the baby with her when she came to wash. At least two other children, Jim and Elizabeth, were born before Beck was thirty. In 1843 or 1844, about ten years after their wedding, the Parkers' marriage ended. Ned left Beck, taking Jim with him and leaving the two girls with their mother. The reason for

Ned's leaving, according to local memory, seems to have been another woman. He showed up in the township of East Marlborough about that time with a woman he called, for some reason, Eliza Parker; she declared her name to be Kitty Hun. She left Ned twice, the first time in the spring of 1844 because he would not marry her. Ned apparently relented and did marry Eliza/Kitty, but she seems to have left him again anyway, this time for good. Ned may or may not have remarried, but he did not come back to Beck and the girls. By 1845, he was living with a white farmer named William Chalfant. He had bound out young Jim, who was still less than ten years old, as an apprentice to Chalfant.[8]

At some point after Ned's departure, Beck began living with George Glasco. Glasco appears to have been at best a ne'er-do-well, and possibly dangerous. In 1843, he was convicted of assault with intent to kill for pulling a gun on a man and threatening to "blow him through," then pelting him with stones. He served six months in solitary confinement at the Chester County jail for that conviction. In 1844, he spent time in the county poorhouse. It seems most likely that Beck lived with him for a while between his departure from the poorhouse and 1848. In that year, he was back in court, charged with fornication and bastardy. The woman involved was not Beck, so she had probably separated from Glasco by then. In the Chester County death records for 1850, there is an entry for a child named Henry Glascow, age five, as well as an entry for a Henry Glascous, age five. The death of Harriett A. Glascous, also age five, is recorded in that year as well. Henry Glascow died in April of dropsy. Harriett Glascous died in November of diarrhea. The frustrating gaps, variant spellings, and likely errors in the records make positive identification of these children truly difficult. But certain possibilities do suggest themselves. Since one county resident who knew Beck testified that she had two children by George Glasco named Henry and Harriet, it is at least possible that Beck had twins by George Glasco who died six months apart in 1850, when they were five years old. If so, both Rachel and Elizabeth were away and working before these siblings were born. It is also possible that Beck took in Glasco's two children and cared for them for a while.[9]

What emerges from these incomplete records, recollections, and testimonies is the picture of a family whose shape keeps shifting and blurring. Partly this is due to the paucity of records that would allow us to track them better. But it is also due to the fact that, almost from the beginning, the Parkers spent more time in other people's families than in their own, living in an economic dependency that has been described as a twilight zone between slavery and freedom. The story of the child Beck—whose mother had been sent to a poorhouse where she would soon die—being brought in an oxcart to work in a white household where she would become "Brown's Beck" is enormously compelling. It is also predictive. From that moment on Beck moved from one white family to another, changing her name, having three or perhaps five or maybe even seven children, at least three of whom (Rachel, Jim, and Elizabeth) also began working for a series of white families when they were very young—probably as young as Beck herself when she climbed into John Taylor's oxcart.[10]

Of Beck's children that we know about, it was Elizabeth who gave her the most trouble. She began as a live-in worker when she was possibly as young as four and certainly no more than six. Beck might have sent her out so early because she could not support all of her children, but it could also have been because she found this child especially difficult; Elizabeth's older sister Rachel did not go out to work until she was about ten years old. A Chester County resident who knew the family observed that "Elizabeth was never a favorite of her mother's." Beck and Elizabeth fought. They had a serious argument late in 1851, when Elizabeth was ten or eleven, that had more long-term consequences than either could have imagined at the time.[11]

Beck, at that point, was working for John Anderson, a Lancaster County farmer, who was paying her fifty cents a week and providing her with room and board. Rachel and Elizabeth, both now virtually on their own, used to visit her there; Anderson's daughter recalled that Elizabeth came four or five times. On the last of Elizabeth's visits to the Anderson farm, in late November 1851, Beck became angry with her daughter for some reported transgression or misbehavior; she gave Elizabeth a "whaling," according to John Anderson, and told her never to come back. Apparently Elizabeth never did return to her mother—until she was brought home from Baltimore after her kidnapping experience. Anderson was persuaded that none of the trouble, including the court-room trials, would have happened if Beck had not beaten Elizabeth: "The whipping Elizabeth got," he insisted, "is the sole cause of all these proceedings." There was some truth to Anderson's claim. He said that Elizabeth "wandered off at that time," and it was about the time of the whaling that William McCreary reported seeing Elizabeth walking on the road past his house, "when she told me she was in search of a place." By that point, she had already worked for, and left, five families, and she and Beck were now estranged. She was soon taken in by Matthew Donnelly, from whose house she was kidnapped a month later.[12]

Rachel was a more tractable child than Elizabeth; a local contributor to the West Chester *Village Record* commented in the aftermath of the kidnappings, "Elizabeth is younger by some three or four years than Rachel, and though a smart, active girl, does not bear so good a character as her sister." Rachel's comparatively easy temperament may explain why she remained at home longer than Elizabeth did. Her first employer was a farmer named James Y. Smith; she lived with his family for a year before going to the Miller farm, where she remained for nearly seven years. She probably would have stayed longer had Thomas McCreary not come along and changed everything.[13]

This family history was not particularly unusual for that time and that place. Beck and her children were inheritors of a pattern that had begun at least as far back as the emancipation of slaves in Pennsylvania. With a growing free black population that needed work and a farm economy without slave labor to support it, farmers began turning to apprenticeships and, more commonly, to the practice of hiring live-in black workers who were less expensive than either slaves or white workers. In 1820, nearly half (44 percent) of African Americans in Chester and adjoining Delaware Counties, of both sexes and all ages, lived with a white head of household. By 1850, that percentage had decreased, but the practice of using live-in labor, especially on farms, remained. Joan Jensen has estimated that in Chester County's Kennett Township, at least a third of farm families had live-in female help in 1850; many of those workers were black, and a significant number of them were children.[14]

Because the black families who lived in the border counties were either thinly scattered about or clustered in a few all-black settlements, the neighbors of Beck's family were largely white. She and her children were therefore accustomed to moving among white people: they not only worked for them but also went to church with them, visited their homes, bought food at the same stores, and passed them on the roads. Beck's children played with the children of white neighbors, and Rachel even went to school with white children for a while. On Beck's wedding day, she came, more than once, to the house of a white neighbor, Hannah Melrath, to borrow something for the occasion. Rachel Kimbel, a white woman, was present at Rachel's birth; she dressed the newborn and christened her with her own name. Rachel and James often went fishing with Thomas McCreary's nephew John. Rachel knew John E. Brown, a white man, well enough to tease him: when Brown came to Joseph Miller's farm to borrow a horse for his wedding, "Rachel laughed at [him] about getting married."[15]

The great majority of people in the southern part of Chester County, white and black, lived on farms. The size of the farms varied widely, as did the number of people employed on each one. According to the 1850 census, there were nearly three and a half times as many farmers in East and West Nottingham as there were workers in all other occupations combined. Five hundred and forty-five people identified themselves as farmers, followed by thirty-nine carpenters, twenty-seven blacksmiths, twenty-four shoemakers, nineteen wheelwrights, fourteen merchants, thirteen papermakers, and eleven millers. No other profession or occupation had more than ten self-identified practitioners. These figures do not include hired farm workers, who listed themselves simply as "laborer," or farm wives. In addition, the work done in many of the other occupations—carpenter, wheelwright, blacksmith, miller—would have been a necessary adjunct to farming.[16]

These farming communities could be tightly knit and homogeneous. When Thomas McCreary was tried for kidnapping, twelve of these

Farm workers in Chester County, Pennsylvania, 1896.
(Photo by Clara Nelson; courtesy of the Chester County Historical Society.)

rural Pennsylvanians, all white men, came to Baltimore to testify on Rachel's behalf. Ten of them were from either East or West Nottingham and the remaining two were from Lancaster County, close to the West Nottingham line. Ten of the twelve were farmers. Only two identified themselves as Quakers; four were Presbyterians, two were Methodists, and three claimed no church membership. Most of these witnesses were asked by McCreary's lawyer if they belonged to any antislavery society or any organization "for preventing the arrest and recovery of slaves." All said no—and said it firmly. Some acknowledged belonging to temperance societies, but everyone, including the Quakers, denied belonging to anything resembling an abolitionist group. Lewis Melrath swore that he had "taken part in no meetings of the kind, concerning runaway negroes. I don't go in for that." Twenty-five-year-old William Morris answered the defense's question about antislavery organizations by announcing, presumably with amusement, "I belong to no society, except the society said to be the 'Broad-footed Society.'" Asked to explain what that was, Morris replied, "It is a name generally applied in our neighborhood to those who belong to no society."[17]

Morris's answer to the defense lawyer encodes some attitudes that are inherent, if generally unspoken, in the entire Parker kidnapping story. His response draws a line between two groups who were present in the courtroom that day: William Morris and the other rural Pennsylvanians on one side, and the Baltimore lawyers for Thomas McCreary on the other. None of the Pennsylvanians would have had to ask what the Broad-footed Society was, since they all belonged to the same "neighborhood," where some things were just "generally" known. Furthermore, the very presence of all those Pennsylvania farmers in the Baltimore courtroom was a sign that the Parker girls were taken to be as much a part of that neighborhood as Joseph Miller was. William Morris and his friends, by testifying on behalf of Rachel and Elizabeth Parker, were only taking care of their own.

Morris's statement also goes a long way toward neutralizing the defense's effort to make a connection between the prosecution of kidnapping and organized abolitionism—for which the hatred in Maryland and other slave states ran deep. McCreary's lawyers would have known very well what a Baltimore jury would think about the testimony of people who were even suspected of being abolitionists; one of their tactics, therefore, was to raise the specter of abolitionism with every witness they questioned. Anti-abolitionist sentiment in Maryland was not new. In 1836, Governor James Thomas had given over a significant portion of his annual address to denouncing "incendiary abolitionists," whom he described as "misguided and wickedly disposed citizens" who were trying to "inflict a mortal wound upon the Union by arraying one portion against another." Increasingly, however, anti-abolitionist feeling in Maryland focused specifically on Pennsylvania. In a pamphlet published in Baltimore in 1843, John L. Carey denounced both abolitionists and Pennsylvanians in the same breath, accusing both of being hypocritically self-righteous and self-congratulatory on the subject of slavery. Pennsylvania, he wrote, had gotten rid of its slaves not for moral reasons but only because the state's economy no longer required them. Would Pennsylvania retain the moral high ground if Maryland suddenly freed hundreds of slaves who headed in its direction? The abolitionists, according to Carey, had only done damage: through their arrogant meddling they had made the South even more defiant, held back the progress of the colonization effort, and everywhere disrupted the "preciously simple and confident" relationship between master and slave. Abolitionists were Pharisees, professors of a sentimental morality: "With these we of Maryland have nothing to do. They are lashing themselves into an insane fury about a thing which does not concern them, which they do not understand, which they can not touch without wounding us—for it is a domestic affair and relates to our hearths and household relations."[18]

"Abolitionist" had become such a loaded and inflammatory term by midcentury that few people were willing to apply it to themselves or accept it calmly when it was attached to them by others. John Dixon Long, a Methodist minister who left Maryland for Philadelphia because he did not want his children to grow up in a slave state, wrote that the word "abolitionist" had done more to silence antislavery sentiment in the South than any other word in the language, since it could endanger one's life to be defined by the word: "Once let a *negro-catcher*, or a *grogshop politician*, point you out, and say as you walk the streets 'There goes an abolitionist!' You are at the mercy of the mob, unless your wealth and political influence shield you." Even the Quakers, by and large, discouraged their members from joining any societies that were avowedly abolitionist and generally refused to allow their meeting houses to be used for abolitionist gatherings. In some states, including Pennsylvania, openly abolitionist Quakers in the 1840s could be, and often were, disowned by their meetings.[19]

The Pennsylvania witnesses, therefore, not only were denying any sympathy with abolition; they also were sending the message that, as far as they were concerned, the Parkers were local people, and the only organization to which one needed to belong in order to step up to their defense was the neighborhood. This is certainly not to say that race did not matter to the witnesses or that in defending the Parkers they were suggesting that the Parkers were their equals in any sense. These were men who often spoke of "niggers" as well as "darkeys" in the courtroom (when asked about Rachel's size, James Smith described her as being "about as big as the common little niggers about there"), and who seemed to take it as a given that black children would be taken out of their own families and put to work in white households for little or no pay. Racial equality had no place in their world, but neither did the kidnapping of "their" black people, who lived among them, worked for them, knew their customs and histories and probably a lot of their secrets—people who belonged to their neighborhood. Rachel and Elizabeth were part of that group.[20]

The responses of the rural Pennsylvanians who came to the aid of Rachel and Elizabeth are consistent with Ellwood Griest's 1873 fictional portrayal of a farming community along the Octoraro River, on the border of Lancaster and Chester Counties. Griest, a Quaker, was born in West Nottingham, worked as a blacksmith in Christiana before the Civil War, and edited the Lancaster *Inquirer* after the war. His novel, *John and Mary; or, The Fugitive Slaves*, describes an episode in which a fugitive slave couple with a young child is helped by whites who would ordinarily have kept their distance from all black people. The story, according to Griest, was drawn from actual events in his own experience. Griest describes the farming community around the Octoraro as acting less out of political or ideological convictions than out of personal and practical impulses. His farm families, he says, lived in a part of the country that was not generally antislavery, much less abolitionist. In fact, "there was a bitter prejudice against the negro, and a general conviction that he was better off in slavery than in freedom, if he had a 'good master.'" On the other hand, his farmers did believe that slaves were often wronged and mistreated, and they were quick to sympathize with suffering. They were also, Griest says, influenced by the Quakers in their midst: "The opposition of Friends, passive though it generally was, to the system of slavery, had much to do with preventing the growth of a proslavery movement." As a result, "the presence of the weary and stricken fugitive always brought out a sentiment favorable to his protection, and but few could be found hardy enough to openly advocate the return of one to bondage." The protagonist of the novel, Billy Brown, harbored a "strong and inveterate prejudice against the colored race" but was at the same time a "pre-eminently just man, and would not knowingly permit a wrong to be done to any one when in his power to prevent it." Griest's apolitical, unreflectingly racist but compassionate people could well have been the ones—or first cousins of the ones—filling that Baltimore courtroom at McCreary's trial.[21]

If the farmers understood that kidnapping was unjust and immoral, they also understood that it was economically harmful, since it depleted the number of available black workers. As one local historian put it, "Farmers and mechanics were disturbed in their domestic service by the frequency with which attacks were made upon their many and useful colored employees and by the apprehensions to which they were all constantly exposed." Many of those "useful colored employees" were children from families like the Parkers. By 1844, three of Beck's children (maybe her only three), all age ten or younger, were living with white families. Seven years later, these three were still living with white families, although all three had changed employers at least once. In East and West Nottingham, where Elizabeth and Rachel were living, the 1850 census counted a total black population of 220. Of these, twenty-six, including the two Parker girls, were living with white families. (Elizabeth was living with the Hutcheson family at that point, in a household that also included two other African Americans: sixteen-year-old Hannah Johnson and thirty-eight-year-old George Glasco, the man with whom Rebecca Parker had lived for a while.)[22]

While almost all of the heads of households with live-in black help were farmers, a few were listed as practicing a trade. One of the three people in East Nottingham who listed his occupation as "moulder" was Matthew Donnelly, the man with whom Elizabeth was living when she was kidnapped. Donnelly's household at the time was a relatively small one, consisting of Donnelly; his wife, Sarah; their seven-year-old son, FitzHenry; Elizabeth; and Sarah's eighteen-year-old brother, John Merritt, who also listed his occupation as "moulder." Donnelly had bought property on Big Elk Creek in 1842, two years after his marriage. His purchase, for which he paid $888, included a stone house and eighty-one acres of land. It also included an iron foundry with a working pressure wheel. Since Donnelly listed himself as a molder, he must have tried to make a living from the foundry. Whatever he was doing to earn money, however, it did not go well, since the rest of his time in Chester County was marked by conflicts with creditors and the courts.

Ruins of the house at Pleasant Garden Forge, where the
Donnelly family lived, 1901.
(Photo by Douglas Brinton; courtesy of the Chester County Historical Society.)

By the beginning of 1849 Donnelly owed over $1,000 to forty differ-
ent creditors. One of his creditors, to whom he owed $48.68, sued him.
When Donnelly could not pay that amount, the sheriff seized his farm
and foundry and sold them for exactly $48.68—a loss to Donnelly of
nearly $850. Because the rest of his property was also about to be seized,
Donnelly came up with a scheme: he transferred to a relative most of his
valuables—two horses, a carriage, a wagon, two sets of harness, some
carpeting, and furniture—before the courts and the creditors could get
to them. Not surprisingly, the dodge was discovered, and Donnelly went
to jail for fraud. He was out on bail in a week, and at his trial the jury
found him not guilty on the fraud charge but required that he pay court
costs of over $65. Since there were still forty creditors waiting, to whom
he owed amounts ranging from $3 to $145, Donnelly defaulted. The personal property he turned over to a court-appointed trustee was, by now,
minimal: three bedsteads, nine chairs, ironware, crockery, one cow, two
pigs, some potatoes in the ground, and his molding tools.[23]

The Donnellys' money troubles occurred in 1849, before Elizabeth went to live with the family near the end of 1851. When she arrived, the Donnellys had already lost their farm and foundry but were living nearby, still on Big Elk Creek, probably renting; they might even have rented their old property from the new owners. Elizabeth's move was thus extremely ill-advised—but, of course, at that point Elizabeth had no one to advise her. She came into a household that was in serious financial trouble and surely could not afford a servant. Nor should they have needed one: Matthew Donnelly was not farming, his brother-in-law John Merritt was there to help him with the foundry work, and his wife had only one child to care for. It seems odd for them to bring in a young girl to work for them, especially one who had as spotty a record as Elizabeth did. She had already worked for and left five employers by the time she arrived at the Donnellys'. She left the last one suddenly, while he was away, packing up her few belongings and walking out without notice. Evidently no one else was eager to hire her, since William McCreary had reported seeing her walking the roads during this period, looking for work. In a rural community with a small African American population, where white families were often on the lookout for black labor, Elizabeth would have had a reputation for being unreliable. Donnelly hired her anyway, bringing this difficult, untrained, apparently volatile child into a financially stressed household.

A month later, Elizabeth was abducted, and the first person to be suspected was Matthew Donnelly. In an account of the two Parker kidnappings written for a Chester County newspaper in 1951, one hundred years after the events but drawn from contemporaneous sources, local writer L. J. Ficcio reported that "much criticism was heaped on the head of Donnely [*sic*] from where Elizabeth was taken. . . . There is some evidence to support the belief Donnely hired her to make McCreary's work easier." Ficcio does not cite the "evidence," but the case against Donnelly is strong even without it. Pauli Murray, whose free black great-grandparents bought land and settled in West Nottingham, close to the sites of both Parker kidnappings, uncovered the same suspicions among local residents around Oxford: "According to local legend, [McCreary's] work was carried on by Matthew M. Donnely [*sic*] and there were strong rumors that one of the leading Negro farmers in Upper Oxford township and a pillar of Hosanna Meeting House worked with Donnely as an informer." The black man's son was said to continue the work after his father died. There is no hard evidence of Donnelly's participation in Elizabeth's kidnapping, but it certainly seems that young Elizabeth was set up and drawn into an established network of men, including Donnelly, who had made their plans carefully.[24]

Rachel's early experience was also unsettled but far less dramatic than Elizabeth's, and she seems to have been less troubled by it. Her age is better documented than Elizabeth's; if people remembered Beck's wedding date by the falling stars, they remembered Rachel's birth year, 1834, because it was the year that the seventeen-year locusts appeared. She remained at home until after her father left in 1844, when she was sent out to work for a farmer named James Y. Smith and his wife, who happened to be a niece of Thomas McCreary. Rachel stayed with the Smiths for about a year, taking care of their first child. She was small at that age, though—one person described her as a "smart lump of a girl"—and the Smith baby soon got to be too heavy for her to carry. The Smiths found a sturdier minder for the child and a new employer for Rachel, who went to live with Joseph Miller's family in the very small township of West Nottingham. She remained with the Millers until her kidnapping at the end of 1851. Rachel was originally brought in to help out with the extra work when the Millers decided to take in as temporary boarders some carpenters who were doing a job in the neighborhood. The Millers must have liked her from the start, since she stayed with them for nearly seven apparently untroubled years. Miller's family grew during Rachel's stay; by 1850 he and his wife, Rebecca, had four children, whose ages ranged from four to nineteen. With this many children, some boarders, and a farm to manage, Miller had a more obvious need for live-in help than did Matthew Donnelly. Rachel's compensation for her work at the Miller farm was food, clothing, lodging, and probably a little pocket money.[25]

If Rachel's situation was more stable than Elizabeth's, it should also have been more secure. There were no warning signs of trouble, no evidence of estrangement from her mother, no reason to distrust Joseph Miller or to think that the Miller farm was not a safe place. Thomas

McCreary would later try to implicate Joseph Miller in Rachel's kidnapping, but the people who knew Miller found that claim impossible to credit. Among Miller's strongest defenders was C. M. Burleigh, who called the charge "preposterous and incredible," describing Miller as a "quiet, unassuming, industrious and inoffensive man." According to Burleigh, Miller shared too many characteristics with his rural neighbors, including timidity and a desire to avoid publicity, to risk such an independent and aggressive move as joining up with people he did not even know to carry out a kidnapping:

> It is true that Miller partook of the prejudices of the community around him against colored people, the anti-slavery cause and the abolitionists. He was not a man to lead public sentiment, to discover new truths, or to advocate unpopular reforms; but there is no more reason to believe him capable of the act charged on him by the kidnappers, than any and every other man thus prejudiced through ignorance and popular influence. His action seems entirely consistent with his character and the supposition of his innocence.

(In speaking of the community's dislike of the antislavery cause in general and abolitionists in particular, Burleigh knew whereof he spoke, having suffered his share of abuse in rural Pennsylvania for his own antislavery stance.)[26]

Rachel and the Millers must have gotten along well, for when Rachel was released from jail after spending more than a year there, she immediately returned to the Miller farm. Evidently she found that place, rather than Beck's, the one that felt most like home. All the indications are that Rachel was treated with care and probably with affection by the Millers. The lengths to which Joseph Miller was willing to go to rescue Rachel may offer the strongest evidence of his concern for her, but there is also earlier evidence of her secure place in the Miller household. The doctor who treated the Miller children treated Rachel as well, at Miller's expense. Rachel went to Sunday school with the family at House's Meeting House, a tiny log church near their farm; only a small handful of other black people were regulars at House's during the time Rachel attended. For a period of three or four years Rachel also attended school sporadically with the Miller children at the Pine Grove School, although she reportedly never succeeded in learning to read well enough to be considered literate; her attendance may have been too erratic for that. Rachel was, apparently, the only black child at the school.[27]

The work that Rachel did for the family was varied. Presumably her duties included caring for the younger Miller children, and we know that she did housework: a neighbor of the Millers reported seeing her washing dishes and sweeping. But she also did jobs that took her out of the house and sometimes off the farm. She was entrusted with important errands and allowed to ride one of Miller's horses, and she seems to have been included in the family's social activities as well as their work. Samuel Chambers recalled that, while she was at the Millers', Rachel "used to run about in search of cattle, and enquire of me about them." Rachel Kimbel remembered seeing her at the Millers' "at peach time," and mentioned noticing her "on the road when she was large enough to carry a bucket of water." Others recalled that Rachel ran errands to neighboring farms and to Kirk's store. When Edward Chambers went to the Miller farm to buy oats, it was Rachel who held the bag open while the oats were poured in. Alexander Melrath remembered, in the fall before her abduction, "She came to our house to invite us to a husking at the Millers." On the day she was kidnapped, she had just gotten home from a neighbor's farm, where she had been returning a borrowed sausage stuffer. She must have helped with the stuffing.[28]

Beck seems to have been pleased with Rachel's placement with the Millers. William McCreary, with whom both Jim and Elizabeth Parker lived for a while, tried at one point to bring Rachel to work for him as well, but Beck would not allow it. McCreary recalled, "[I] wanted to get [Rachel] to live with us, but her mother told me she could not let me have her as she lived with Mr. Miller." Rachel herself was evidently content living with the Millers, and it seems that she might have been safe there had the abduction of Elizabeth not gone so well. Elizabeth's kidnapping was clearly well planned in advance, and it went so smoothly that no one even noticed she was gone until Rachel disappeared two weeks later, and

Beck decided that she had better check up on her younger daughter. It was only then that she discovered Elizabeth was missing.[29]

Like other kidnappers, Tom McCreary did not act alone when he took either Elizabeth or Rachel Parker. The reports of other kidnappings in the area generally mention more than one abductor, and sometimes a whole "gang" would be involved. A successful abduction, obviously, needed to be a collaborative project, planned in advance. A likely victim had to be identified, perhaps by a paid informer; the site of the abduction might need to be staked out; if the victim were to be taken by stealth, more than one person would probably be required to overcome the victim's resistance; someone needed to be ready with a getaway conveyance; a temporary hiding place might be required; and a buyer or agent needed to be lined up. One of McCreary's accomplices in both cases was young John Merritt, Matthew Donnelly's brother-in-law, who had already found a niche for himself among a group of gangsters who were irritating the citizens of Chester County. Charles Burleigh, writing to the *Pennsylvania Freeman*, commented on the reputation Merritt had already acquired by the time of the Parker kidnappings. "Though young in years," Burleigh wrote of Merritt, "he is ripe in villainy. He has for years been engaged with a gang of depredators who have infested the lower part of Chester County, engaged in gambling, passing counterfeit money, and other swindling operations." Burleigh does not identify Merritt's "gang," but his description makes it sound as if Merritt had found a place within the well-known Gap gang, a group whose activities included counterfeiting, the theft of property, and eventually the theft of people. Burleigh also called Merritt "McCreary's accomplice and pimp," thereby suggesting a connection between McCreary and the Gap gang, which, although undocumented, would not be at all surprising.[30]

McCreary, an experienced slave catcher and kidnapper, clearly had other accomplices in addition to John Merritt. As some historians of the Underground Railroad, especially those with knowledge of local practices, have pointed out, collaboration in kidnapping could involve much more than the actual abduction of a person: "Underground Rail Road men were greatly annoyed, both by decoys, pretended runaways, sent to them by kidnappers, and by white men who ostensibly came on other business, but were really spies for the slave catchers." Pauli Murray says that her great-grandmother "learned never to trust a peddler going from door to door selling wares [in West Nottingham]. Too often a hired man had disappeared after one of those peddlers came through the village." There were four men involved in Elizabeth Parker's kidnapping, only three of whom have been clearly identified. On that Saturday night in December, Elizabeth was inside the house with Matthew Donnelly and John Merritt; Tom McCreary and the fourth man (a man with long whiskers, according to Elizabeth) were outside. While Elizabeth was clearing the supper dishes, Donnelly went outside for about a quarter of an hour. When he returned, he told Elizabeth to go out and retrieve a bucket, telling her exactly where she would find it. As soon as Elizabeth went outside, following Donnelly's instructions, she was grabbed by McCreary and the whiskered man, gagged with a stick, and hurried off in a wagon driven by McCreary. Donnelly, Merritt, and the whiskered man remained behind.[31]

McCreary took Elizabeth, without stopping and apparently without incident, across the state line to his house in Elkton, Maryland, a distance of about fifteen miles. Since they were too late to catch a Saturday night train and the trains would not run again until midnight on Sunday, McCreary kept Elizabeth, still gagged, in his house that night and all the next day. They took the Sunday midnight train to Baltimore. No one seems to have taken particular notice of the white man traveling with a young black girl in his custody, since this leg of the trip also went without incident. In Baltimore, McCreary took her straight to the slave-trading establishment of the Campbell brothers, Walter and Bernard, on Pratt Street near the wharf. On the train, McCreary had told Elizabeth that, from then on, she must tell anyone who asked that her name was Henrietta Crocus and that she had run away from a family named Schoolfield in Baltimore. Elizabeth was too frightened to do anything but obey McCreary. From that moment, she began answering to the name Henrietta; it would be six months before anyone called her Elizabeth again.[32]

Two weeks after his successful abduction of Elizabeth, McCreary came for Rachel. This time, he made the mistake of not waiting for the protection of darkness. He knocked on the back door of Joseph Miller's house at about eleven in the morning on December 31. When Miller's wife, Rebecca, answered the knock, he asked her for directions. They stood at the door talking until Rachel appeared, curious to see who the visitor was. McCreary pushed past Rebecca Miller, grabbed Rachel, and wrestled her outside, where John Merritt was waiting in a buggy. Joseph Miller was working outside as usual that morning, near the house. The screams of his wife and Rachel brought him running. He reached the buggy in time to grab the harness, but McCreary pulled out his well-used Bowie knife—Rachel called it a sword—and forced Miller back. The buggy then took off in the direction of the Maryland border, less than two miles away.

McCreary and Merritt set out on the most direct route to the Maryland line, which meant heading for the Pine Grove schoolhouse. From there it was a straight shot and a short road to Brick Meeting House, known locally as The Brick, on the Maryland side of the line. The kidnappers had no way of knowing that James Pollock and his son Samuel would be cutting wood near the schoolhouse that morning and that they would be heading up the road by the school with their wagon and team just as the escaping buggy was heading down it. Seeing his way blocked by the Pollocks' team, McCreary jumped out of his buggy and demanded that the Pollocks get out of the way. James Pollock recognized Rachel and saw that she was distressed. Immediately suspecting that she was being kidnapped, he grabbed the axe he had just been using to cut wood. McCreary once again pulled out his knife and held it at Pollock's throat.

What could have turned into a fatal encounter for Pollock was interrupted by Joseph Miller. Anticipating the route the kidnappers would take, Miller, running full tilt, had cut across a strip of rocky grassland to intercept them on the road. Vaulting the wooden fence beside the road, Miller grabbed one of the fence rails and attempted to ram it into the spokes of the buggy. Merritt whipped up the two horses, knocking Miller down and freeing the wheel. The kidnappers were off then, headed for the train depot at Perryville, Maryland, but on a more roundabout route than they had originally planned to take. Since Miller was on foot and the Pollocks were driving a wagon fully loaded with logs, giving chase was out of the question.

Somewhere on the Maryland side of the line, McCreary, Merritt, and Rachel stopped at a tavern, where Rachel managed to tell the landlord she was free. The landlord's wife, seeing how frightened Rachel was, gave her a plate of food and asked the men to leave the distressed girl with her. They refused. McCreary and Rachel continued to the train station at Perryville, while Merritt stayed behind. At the depot, Rachel was able to tell several more people that she was free. Fortunately, among the people to whom she spoke were two young men named Haines and Wiley, who would soon play a vital role in Rachel's rescue. Haines knew McCreary and was aware of his reputation, and he was certain he was witnessing a kidnapping in progress. He spoke with McCreary, advising him that he ought to take Rachel back home, but McCreary instead boarded the train for Baltimore with her. Rachel had never seen a train before, much less ridden on one.[33]

Joseph Miller and the Pollocks immediately began to spread the word about the kidnapping. The reaction was instantaneous. At least two groups of men, and perhaps more, set off on horseback to search the roads heading south, all the way to the depot at Perryville. The searchers would also take a train to Baltimore, arriving in the city shortly after McCreary and Rachel did. Their decision to follow McCreary from Pennsylvania into Maryland turned out to be a momentous one, with consequences that resonated far beyond the borders of those two states, upsetting many lives and ending one. Within twenty-four hours, the abductions of the Parker sisters would no longer be local matters.

4

BORDER JUSTICE

HE UNDERWORLD of trafficking into which the Parker sisters were thrown was large and complex, and its influence reached into all levels of life along the border. Some of those local people, black and white, who provided help to slave hunters and kidnappers coming into the border counties of Pennsylvania were only adding these transactions to illegal or shady enterprises that they already had underway. Other local people, black and white, found ways of resisting the incursions of traffickers as more and more African Americans disappeared from the area. As these efforts—both to assist the traffickers and to frustrate them—became more organized, violence in the area naturally increased. The *Liberator* reported at the end of October 1850 that in Pennsylvania, "the fugitive slaves and the free colored people are arming themselves with pistols, bowie knives and rifles, and learning to use them." Local law enforcement in the rural areas was generally not adequate to cope with the results. State and federal officials had to intervene, and when they did, they brought with them the murky interstate politics of slavery and many opportunities for corruption. Whether or not any irrefutable evidence of official corruption in the kidnappings on the Maryland/Pennsylvania border can be found, there are certainly signs of manipulation of the legal system: favoritism, deal making, cronyism, the triumph of quid pro quo politics. Where such practices did occur, the system of slavery was very likely to be the beneficiary.[1]

Two kidnapping cases that occurred in the Maryland counties of Kent and Queen Anne's, not far south of the Pennsylvania border, suggest how intertwined the interests of slaveholders, kidnappers, slave dealers, and agents of the law could be—and therefore how inconclusive or skewed the outcomes of these cases could be. One kidnapping occurred in late 1850, when a seven-year-old free black child named Jim Brown was taken from the home of William Cahill (or Cahall), near Centreville in Queen Anne's County. This was not the first time that Cahill had been implicated in the kidnapping of children. Two free children, a boy and a girl, who had been bound out as apprentices to Cahill's wife, disappeared in the summer of 1849; the children were never located, and no one was ever charged with the kidnapping. In the 1850 case, Jim Brown's mother, who worked for and lived with the Cahills, had put her son to bed at their house and then gone out to a neighbor's. When she returned, the boy was gone. He was soon found in Baltimore, at the home of a convicted counterfeiter named Thomas "Short Tom" Moffitt, where he was located through the intervention of a Centreville attorney and an unidentified "gentleman" of Baltimore (one suspects he was a Quaker gentleman). Within a few days, five men had been arrested and charged with the kidnapping. The child was brought back to Centreville by John Denning, a Baltimore slave dealer who traded often in the Centreville area. The *Baltimore Sun* reported cheerfully that the reunion between "the little fellow" and his mother was "truly affecting."[2]

After the arrests of the five men, the newspaper in nearby Kent County connected four of them with the earlier disappearance of the two children from Cahill's home, condemning the four as "wretches." The *Baltimore Sun*, almost as steadfastly proslavery in its politics as the *Kent News*, took equal care to distance itself from the boy's abductors—calling them "wretches" as well—and from the whole business of kidnapping. As the *Sun* put it in reporting the Centreville kidnappings, "While we have no sympathy with abolitionists, who seek to disturb our domestic economy, we have just as little for the kidnapper, who would sell a freeman into slavery." Like many other proslavery newspapers, these two carefully positioned themselves in the neutral center of a spectrum that put abolitionists at one end and kidnappers at the other. Whatever the newspapers might have said about their disapproval of kidnappers, however, the courts in Maryland repeatedly refused to convict them of a crime. In the Jim Brown case, the effort to hold someone accountable for taking the boy resulted in a legal fiasco amounting almost to farce. The first trial in the case came up in July 1851. One newspaper reported that Henry Thawley, one of the accused, turned state's evidence and was released; another reported that Thomas Moffitt had also turned state's evidence and "blowed upon some, if not all the rest." The defense counsel for the remaining defendants requested a delay until November, which was granted. Before the trial could resume, Thawley had been shot at and nearly killed by an unknown assailant firing from an alley in the town of Church Hill, near Centreville.[3]

For that or some other reason, the case was once again postponed, this time until May 1852. A trial did actually begin on that date, but only Short Tom Moffitt was tried. His trial attracted crowds of onlookers who packed the courthouse, and the *Kent News* reported that "nearly all of the most able lawyers at the bar were employed in the case"—four attorneys for the state and six for the defense. Moffitt testified that he bought Jim Brown from Henry Thawley for $175, believing Thawley's contention that the boy was a slave. The jury was apparently sympathetic; after five days of testimony and argument, they reached a verdict of not guilty, and Moffitt went free. A year later, the cases against the rest of the men were, according to the *Baltimore Sun*, "abandoned by the state." Evidently, the prosecution simply dismissed several kidnapping charges at once. The newspapers gave no explanation, and obviously no one went to jail.[4]

Tom Moffitt and James Price, meanwhile, were staying busy, undeterred by their indictments in the Jim Brown case. In February 1851, while both were free on bail and awaiting trial, they were named as participants in the kidnapping of a young girl, Rebecca Jane Johnson, from Kent County. Rebecca was the slave of a man named James Spear but had been indentured or rented out to another Kent County farmer and slaveholder, Jonathan Hazle. She was due to be freed when her contracted time with Hazle was up; instead of releasing her, however, Hazle sold her to Moffitt and Price, who in turn took her to Baltimore and sold her to Walter Campbell, the trader, for $425. Rebecca remained in Campbell's slave pen for several weeks before her identity was confirmed and she was returned to James Spear. Jonathan Hazle was arrested and indicted on kidnapping charges, but Moffitt and Price were not. Even the *Kent News* put them into the staple category of kidnapping "wretches" and expressed surprise that they remained free: "These wretches, it is believed, have been engaged in this business for years, and many negroes, supposed to have run off, have, no doubt, been sold by kidnappers."⁵

These three kidnapping cases thus ended, like the Parker case, with some arrests, a few indictments, some long delays, and no convictions. In Maryland, the odds were always so heavily in favor of the kidnappers, even the most incompetent ones, that kidnapping was hardly a risky business, as Tom Moffitt and James Price were apparently aware. The greatest threat seems to have come not from the law but from rivals in the trade, who might be armed and lurking in an alley.⁶

Arresting and convicting kidnappers was comparatively easier in Pennsylvania than in Maryland, but it was not a simple matter there, either. Lancaster County hosted a notorious gang of kidnappers who lived in and around a place called The Gap, in the eastern part of the county, near the Chester County line. The Gap had a history. It was known as early as 1840 as the headquarters of "a numerous gang of thieves and counterfeiters" who were known to burn the barns of anyone who tried to interfere with their business. By the 1850s, with the encouragement of the Fugitive Slave Act, they had expanded their range to include the taking of black people, both fugitive and free. The new enterprise did well. In 1860, the *Philadelphia Inquirer* reported on the gang's ten-year run of successes: "Ever since the passage of the Fugitive Slave law [Lancaster] county has been infested with a set of villains, who steal and sell into slavery free negroes whom they can, either by force or some lying pretext, decoy into their meshes." R. C. Smedley, in his history of the Underground Railroad in Pennsylvania, described the gang as "Land Pirates" who "frequently gave descriptions of [fugitives] to southerners which led to their capture; and when opportunity offered, they assisted in kidnapping free negroes, and carrying them into the Border States to be sold."[7]

The gang managed to remain out of the reach of the law by one means or another, including intimidation. Smedley reports that when three Lancaster County men attempted to have William Baer, the reputed leader of the Gap gang, arrested for kidnapping, two of them had their barns burned and the third saved his only by keeping a guard around it for two months. In January 1851, less than a month after the Parker kidnappings, a free black man named John Williams was abducted from the vicinity of The Gap. Six men rushed into the house where Williams was staying, beat him, dragged him out to a waiting wagon, and fled toward the Maryland border. The *Pennsylvania Freeman* identified the kidnappers as coming from "the 'Gap Tavern,' a notorious place in the neighborhood. They were joined by others outside of the house when they brought the man out. Altogether there were not less than ten or twelve in number." According to the *Freeman*, another man had been taken from the same vicinity just a month previously, and an unsuccessful attempt had been made on a third person. No one was ever arrested or charged in any of the three cases.[8]

The gang acquired some national notoriety when it kidnapped a man named John Brown in March 1860, driving him off in a carriage and then keeping him tied in a tavern garret for more than a day. He was subsequently taken to Baltimore by night and placed in a slave pen. Because of his protests, Brown was eventually identified as a free man and sent back to Lancaster County. The tavern keeper and two of the kidnappers, Francis Wilson and Gilmore Hall, were arrested. Wilson and Hall went to prison for five years, but while they were awaiting trial, the barn of John Brown's employer, who had been instrumental in identifying the kidnappers, was burned to the ground. It was this case that led the *Philadelphia Inquirer* to publish an exasperated exposé of the gang: "A most villainous and desperate gang has infested the neighborhood of the Gap (long celebrated as the harbor of all manner of desperadoes), and when any of our citizens had the courage to prosecute any of them, the torch was applied to his house or barn, thus keeping the neighborhood in terror. Therefore, they could commit crime with impunity, for no one dare inform upon them." The *Inquirer* went on to describe a case from 1852 involving a Baltimore police officer named Ridgely, who had attempted to arrest a lumberyard worker in Columbia, Pennsylvania, by claiming he was a fugitive slave. When the man resisted, Ridgely shot and killed him. At the request of Governor William Bigler of Pennsylvania, the governor of Maryland sent two commissioners to investigate the killing. According to the *Inquirer*, the investigation was rigged: the commissioners were "friends of the accused" who were not about to get Ridgely in trouble. (One of them, Otho Scott, would later be on the legal team that successfully defended Thomas McCreary in his trial for kidnapping.) In their reports to the two governors, the commissioners stated that they were satisfied "that no harm was intended, that the act was purely accidental." The two governors accepted the report, and the matter was dropped.[9]

The *Inquirer* saw two disturbing trends in this episode. First, it marked the beginning of a surge in kidnappings in the area. Second, it was a clear instance of a pattern of "the connivance [in kidnappings] of public officers in high places" that, according to the *Inquirer*, still persisted. The newspaper connected this official corruption specifically with the Gap gang, strongly suggesting that the gang's connections with officials in both Maryland and Pennsylvania had a lot to do with its success in the trafficking of black people.[10]

The Gap and its gang played an important part in the event that, more than any other, crystallized and intensified tensions along the Maryland/Pennsylvania border—the armed resistance at Christiana, on the eastern edge of Lancaster County very near the Chester County line. That section had gradually become a tinderbox, a pairing of armed camps, a catastrophe waiting to happen. Less than five miles separated The Gap and its gang of predators from the small village of Christiana, which had become what local historian W. U. Hensel called a "refuge territory" for fugitives, some of whom had been settled there for years. The proximity of these two groups meant that, according to Hensel, the violence at Christiana "was not a sudden outbreak." The village had been drawing more than its share of attention for a while. "Local incidents, such as escapes, man hunts, kidnappings and other like events had occurred to an extent sufficient to excite popular interest; and by rumor they had been exaggerated enough to further inflame it." The level of tension in the area meant that something serious was bound to happen. What did happen was an encounter that has been called "the Civil War's first battle."[11]

It began with the flight of four men who were the slaves of Edward Gorsuch, a prosperous farmer in Baltimore County, Maryland.[12] Noah Buley, Nelson Ford, and George and Joshua Hammond left Gorsuch's Retreat Farm on a November night in 1849. Gorsuch was convinced (rightly, as it turned out) that the runaways had gone no farther than southeastern Pennsylvania. He was also persuaded (wrongly this time, and probably naively) that if he could find them, they could be talked into returning with promises of leniency. He solicited help from Pennsylvania officials, but they had no interest in assisting slaveholders and offered no cooperation. Gorsuch continued to search for the men, unsuccessfully, for nearly two years. In 1851, his efforts to find them finally began to pay off, for two important reasons. First, the passage of the Fugitive Slave Act meant he would no longer have to rely on unfriendly Pennsylvania law enforcement and could instead expect more willing cooperation from the commissioners appointed under the new federal law. Second, he hired William Padgett, a member of the Gap gang, to find his slaves for him. Padgett, whom a local historian described as a "miserable creature" with a "keen insight into human nature," was a good choice. He was an escaped slave himself but light-skinned enough to pass for white. He knew the area around Christiana well, and he was an experienced informer. Padgett made his legal living doing two jobs: during the fall months he gathered sumac tops used for the dyeing of leather, and the rest of the year he repaired clocks. Both of these enterprises allowed him to move around the county, to "become aware of every cow path and by-road," and even to get inside the homes of strangers, always on the lookout for fugitives or vulnerable free blacks. Padgett did his work for Gorsuch efficiently, locating his fugitive slaves near Christiana. He wrote to Gorsuch with news of his find, asking him to come as quickly as possible and to meet him at The Gap. Taking with him his son Dickinson, two other relatives, and two neighbors, Gorsuch went to Pennsylvania.[13]

His first stop was Philadelphia, where he picked up the proper arrest warrants from one of the newly appointed commissioners, Edward Ingraham. He also picked up more help in the person of a man named Henry Kline, whom Ingraham deputized to help with the capture and arrest of the four runaways. Kline had worked with Padgett before in the pursuit of fugitives. Gorsuch and Kline then rejoined the rest of the Maryland party at The Gap. On the morning of September 11, 1851, guided by Padgett, they made their move on the home of William Parker, near Christiana. Two of the fugitives, having been warned that Gorsuch was after them, had come to Parker's house to consult about what to do. (One local resident theorized that Padgett led Gorsuch's group to Parker's house, rather than to the places the fugitives were living, because the Gap gang hoped Parker himself would be either killed or captured and returned to slavery in Maryland; he had gotten in their way too many times.) Kline entered the house and demanded that the fugitives give themselves up. Parker's wife, seeing that Kline was not alone, ran to a window and began blowing a horn, a prearranged signal that soon brought reinforcements from the neighborhood; witnesses estimated that between seventy-five and one hundred men eventually showed up, some with firearms and others carrying less lethal weapons. Most of those who came were African American, but among them were also a few white men who lived nearby, including the miller Castner Hanway and the Quaker storekeeper Elijah Lewis. Both Hanway and Lewis tried to persuade the agitated crowd not to use their weapons, but in spite of their pleas, gunshots were fired; in the ensuing chaos before the Gorsuch party withdrew, Edward Gorsuch was killed and his son was badly wounded. Dickinson Gorsuch would survive, under the care of local Quakers, but the first press reports declared him "mortally wounded" and certain to die. News of the death of two white Marylanders at the hands of a mob of blacks in Pennsylvania, including fugitive slaves, was guaranteed to get a swift and angry response.[14]

And it did. In the days immediately after the affair, forty-five U.S. marines were sent to the site to begin rounding up suspected participants. They were joined by forty city police from Philadelphia and a large contingent of special constables deputized for the occasion, including about fifty locals from Lancaster and even a few members of the Gap gang. They were also joined by more than one unofficial posse of vengeance seekers from Maryland. A Baltimore County newspaper reported that "a large body of people" from Gorsuch's part of the county had immediately "proceeded to the scene of the outrage." Special excursion trains began carrying the excited and the curious to Christiana. The newspaper in Kent County, Maryland, reported hearing from travelers who had taken the train through Lancaster County that "the greatest excitement prevailed" throughout the county and that "the negroes were fleeing in every direction." Thomas P. Slaughter has described the results: "According to one witness, blacks were 'hunted like partridges' by those deputized for the search. A brief 'reign of terror' ensued, in which, according to a local historian, 'whites and blacks, bond and free, were rather roughly handled; few households in the region searched were safe from rude intrusion; many suffered terrifying scenes and sounds.'" The *Pennsylvania Freeman* expressed its disgust with "the base crew which were scraped up from the drunkeries of Columbia, Lancaster and York, and from Maryland, to harass a quiet Quaker community." As extensive as the search was, it did not turn up William Parker; he had fled in time, and with the aid of sympathizers he made it safely to Canada. Castner Hanway and Elijah Lewis, hearing there were warrants out for their arrest, turned themselves in voluntarily. When some of the dust had settled, forty people—Hanway, Lewis, and thirty-eight African Americans—were in jail awaiting trial.[15]

Officials in Washington, including Secretary of State Daniel Webster, wanted to make a show trial of the Christiana case as a way of warning against any further resistance to the Fugitive Slave Act. The most dramatic way to do that, they concluded, was to charge the defendants with treason: that crime carried the death penalty, which they were prepared to impose. The two judges tasked with securing convictions in the case, John K. Kane of the federal district court for eastern Pennsylvania and Robert C. Grier of the Pennsylvania Supreme Court, were no friends to fugitives, abolitionists, or the antislavery press. Grier had especially angered the *Pennsylvania Freeman* by dismissing its reporting out of hand. "The statements in it," Grier had said publicly, "are always false." The *Freeman* had therefore taken delight in the problems caused for Grier when two U.S. commissioners in Pennsylvania resigned to protest the passage of the Fugitive Slave Act. The first, Col. W. H. Kane (apparently no kin to Judge Kane), found the law "so repugnant to his feelings as a man, that he [could not] act under it." When the second commissioner resigned, the *Freeman* could not have been more pleased: "Since Reade Washington, in Pittsburgh, resigned the office of United States Commissioner on the passage of the Fugitive Slave Law, following the noble example of Col. Kane of this city [Philadelphia], Judge Grier has not been able to find any man in Pittsburgh to take the office."[16]

Before being assigned to the Christiana trial, both judges had stated their intention to enforce the Fugitive Slave Act, no matter how much antislavery resistance they faced. At the first session of the Pennsylvania district court after the passage of the act, Kane gave a stern, finger-wagging lecture to the grand jury, warning them about the dangers of antislavery influence and assuring them that the new law would prevail:

> We know that this law will be enforced here, fairly and according to its terms; and that it will be vindicated, no matter what the personal character of the men who may assail it; or what their profession or position in life, or their just influence on other topics with those who are about them. This law, I repeat it, will be enforced; and if broken, it will be vindicated. The constitutional compact, which was made within these very walls [Independence Hall, Philadelphia], will never be repudiated here.

The Christiana trial put Kane's protestations to the test. The prosecution, fearing they would not be able to get a conviction if they tried all of the defendants at once and that if they did get such a conviction, all hell might break loose, began by trying Castner Hanway, the white miller, by himself. Hanway had attempted to prevent the violence, but he had also refused to help Kline, a federal appointee, in apprehending the fugitive slaves. This refusal, the prosecution argued, amounted to treason.[17]

After days of testimony, argument by the prosecution, and counter-argument by the defense, which was brilliantly led by Thaddeus Stevens, Judge Grier offered a charge to the jury that, predictably, followed exactly the lines of argument being offered by the proslavery press. What happened at Christiana was, he told the jurors, a "disgraceful tragedy" that could not possibly be considered anything else except by "a few individuals of perverted intellect in some small districts or neighborhoods whose moral atmosphere has been tainted and poisoned by male and female vagrant lecturers and conventions." Berating "infuriated fanatics and unprincipled demagogues" without explicitly calling them abolitionists, the judge went on to declare that the guilt for the murder of Gorsuch "rests not alone on the deluded individuals who were its immediate perpetrators, but the blood taints with even deeper dye the skirts of those who promulgated doctrines subversive of all morality and all government." Having gotten these accusations against abolitionists and other antislavery whites off his chest, Grier then gave his charge a remarkable and completely unexpected turn. He advised the jury that while Hanway and others were certainly guilty of murder, they actually could not be considered legally guilty of treason—the crime for which they were being tried. The jury took the judge's charge seriously and deliberated for only fifteen minutes before declaring Hanway not guilty. The charges against the remaining defendants were subsequently dropped, and the trial was over.[18]

The events at Christiana have been called many things. Most often the episode has been called a riot; William Parker's house even became known locally as the "Riot House." But it has also been called a catastrophe, a slave-hunting tragedy, an outrage, a massacre, an insurrection, and an act of resistance. The most politically charged descriptions of the events at the time called them abolitionist murders. The southern press and some of the more cautious northern newspapers were quick to place the blame for the death of Gorsuch entirely on the interference of white abolitionists. The Chester County *Jeffersonian*, which once referred to an Anti-Slavery Society gathering as "the Nigga Meetin'," echoed Judge Grier's charge to the jury and absolved the black participants from most of the responsibility on the grounds that they were the simple-minded, gullible victims of the schemes of radical abolition-ist troublemakers:

> We do not regard them as the really guilty, who should suffer the penalty to its utmost. In this instance as in most cases, those who led them on, encouraged and ensnared them into the dif-ficulty will escape, while the deluded negro will have to bear the punishment deserved by others. It must be apparent to everyone, that the distance between the two races is becoming wider and wider,—prejudice is strengthening—the inevitable result of the course pursued by the abolitionists, in fanning the negro to acts which never can be countenanced.[19]

The Maryland state legislature appointed a special committee to prepare a response to the events at Christiana. In its overheated report, the committee represented the entire population of Maryland as inno-cent victims of abolitionist atrocity, blaming the killing of Gorsuch, the state's "martyred son," for having blasted all of the hopes for a peaceful American future that had been created by the Fugitive Slave Act. The people of Maryland suffered most and most grievously: "All their bright anticipation of future peace and security were in a moment dissipated by a deed of atrocity and bloodshed unparalleled in the annals of crime." The Maryland attorney general was equally alarmist in his response to the verdict in Christiana, declaring that it "practically strikes dead the Fugitive Slave Act, whenever armed bands of negroes, encouraged by white men, may choose to resist the officer of the United States, and he may be unprovided with an army superior to their forces. It encourages and incites these 'black regiments with white allies,' in their work of murdering Southern masters, who dare to pursue their slaves, by pro-claiming that the United States Courts will not convict them."[20]

It was not only Maryland officialdom that could wax hyperbolic over the events. Both the pro- and antislavery press placed the Fugitive Slave Act at the root of the Christiana fiasco, but with completely different justifications. The proslavery *Kent News* took the law's failure to pro-tect Gorsuch and his legal property as a sign not just of worsening relations between Maryland and Pennsylvania but also of the fragility of the entire Union. The North's commendable willingness to obey the law up to this point, according to the newspaper, had been a sign of its "fidelity to the Constitution and the Union." Disregard of the law in Christiana changed that: "We had hoped that the North by this time understood that upon the faithful, rigid, and constant observance of the Fugitive Slave Law, depended the adhesion of the South to the Federal Union. We fear that in this we have been deceived." The antislavery papers, such as the *Pennsylvania Freeman*, argued exactly the opposite position: it was actually the observance of the law, rather than the violation of it, that had led to the Christiana violence. The *Freeman* found the events at Christiana to be the clearest evidence to date of the "enormity" of the law: "Instead of whining and writhing over this 'horrible massacre,' let every citizen, worthy the name, turn to the cause of it and have manliness enough to demand the remedy. Let the demand be, the *Repeal of the Fugitive Law*, that we may rid our records of a statute fit only to be framed and executed in the bottomless pit." Frederick Douglass would later praise William Parker and his compatriots at Christiana as heroes of the antislavery struggle. Parker's "noble band," said Douglass, was "entitled to the honor of making the first successful resistance to the Fugitive Slave Bill."[21]

The Christiana episode, unlike most other conflicts between fugitives and slave catchers, became a flashpoint in the politics of slavery, on the border and beyond. The most important factor in its notoriety was the fact that a white slaveholder had died at the hands of a crowd of black men, in a state already reported to be friendly to fugitives and hostile to those who attempted to capture them. Another, less dramatic factor was the nature of the people involved, especially William Parker, Henry Kline, and Edward Ingraham. Parker, who sheltered the runaways, was the charismatic leader of a group of free and fugitive African Americans who had vowed to resist the incursions of both slave catchers and kidnappers into their neighborhood and had lived up to their vows in several previous altercations. Parker was known locally as tough, fearless, and determined to keep himself and other fugitives from ever being abducted and returned to slavery. It was to Parker that two of the men being sought by Gorsuch fled when news got out that the Maryland posse was approaching; it was Parker's wife, Eliza, who blew the horn to sound the alarm; and it was Parker who responded to Henry Kline's command to surrender by threatening to break Kline's neck if he took another step. If anyone emerged from the fracas with the reputation of hero, it was William Parker. (Sixty years after the episode at Christiana, the Lancaster County Historical Society erected a granite monument to commemorate the events. On one side of the monument was inscribed the name of Edward Gorsuch—with the epigraph "He died for law"—as well as those of his son Dickinson and his cousin Joshua. The name of Castner Hanway was inscribed on the adjacent side, with the epigraph "He suffered for freedom." The monument also included the names of all the men who were indicted, with William Parker's name buried in the list.)[22]

In going to Edward Ingraham for legal authorization to seize the fugitives and to Henry Kline for help in carrying out the seizure, Edward Gorsuch had unwittingly tapped two people whose names were guaranteed to arouse the anger of any Pennsylvanians inclined to sympathize with fugitives and their protectors. Ingraham and Kline had already earned identical reputations in the state, Kline as "a notorious slave-catching constable" and Ingraham as "the notorious slave-catching commissioner." Henry Kline had a history as a lawbreaker before he became a law enforcer: he had been charged with extortion in 1843 and with passing counterfeit notes in 1844. As a slave catcher, he had sometimes used the services of the Gap gang's William Padgett as an informer. In spite of his considerable blustering at the trial of the Christiana participants, Kline apparently spent much of his time during the actual conflict hiding in a cornfield. Even the *Kent News*, which was entirely sympathetic with Gorsuch, acknowledged that Kline "is said to have showed a want of nerve to discharge his duty." In a retrospective article about Christiana written in 1887, a Hagerstown, Maryland, newspaper referred to Kline as "a low, worthless fellow" who met what the paper considered an appropriate end: "Kline was in such bad odor [after the trial] that he was forced to flee the country altogether. He went west, where he got considerable money through some shady transactions. Several years later he returned to Lancaster and drank himself to death."[23]

Edward Ingraham, because his position as commissioner gave him more authority and more visibility, was even more reviled in the antislavery press than Henry Kline. The case that brought Ingraham the most intense public scrutiny occurred in Philadelphia, nine months before the Christiana case. A man named Adam Gibson was brought before Ingraham and accused of being Emory Rice, a fugitive slave belonging to William Knight of Cecil County, Maryland. Ingraham, insisting that the Fugitive Slave Act required "summary" action in such cases, refused to delay the hearing until counsel could be brought in to represent Gibson. In spite of the testimony of two men who said they had known Adam Gibson for years and knew that he was free, Ingraham ruled in favor of the claimant, and Gibson was hurried off to Cecil County. Fortunately for Gibson, William Knight knew immediately that the man who was brought to him was not Emory Rice and refused to accept him. Gibson was therefore allowed to return to Philadelphia, once more a free man.

The damage to Ingraham's reputation had been done, however, especially among the antislavery forces. The Gibson case earned Ingraham the nickname "Mr. Summary Ingraham," brought denunciations from the press, and led the Pennsylvania Anti-Slavery Society to call him one of the "Iscariots" of his day. John Greenleaf Whittier, the Quaker poet, turned Ingraham into the butt of an ironic joke: "Both [Whig and Democrat] parties have made an unqualified surrender to the Slave Power. They are slaves; and any attempt at escape on their part would promptly come under the cognizance of the Fugitive Slave Law and Commissioner Ingraham." Ingraham's negative press did not, however, prevent him from continuing to perform his duties as expeditiously as possible. By the time he died in 1854, "Summary Ingraham" had secured his reputation as a strict and impatient enforcer of the provisions—and the intentions—of the Fugitive Slave Act.[24]

In his personal life, Ingraham seems to have been a kind of intellectual dilettante whose interests set him at a distance (and perhaps were intended to be a measure of his distance) from the slave catchers who were of necessity his professional colleagues and from the detractors who persistently attacked him in the press. He was a collector of rare books and ephemera with a particular interest in U.S. history and French literature. A Philadelphia newspaper commented in 1848 that his "library and drawing room are as full of rare curiosities as his brain is full of rich and merry conceits." After his death the *North American* announced an auction of his library, containing "only the finest and rarest editions of books." Most curiously, Ingraham kept a record of names that struck his fancy or that he found especially amusing. These were actually published posthumously in 1873 under the title *Singular Surnames.* The volume included such entries—which Ingraham found sufficiently comic to save for posterity—as the marriage of Benjamin Bird and Julia Chaff and the success of Dr. Buster. If the publication of the volume was meant to replace Ingraham's old reputation as a severe and merciless magistrate with a new one as a blithe spirit and a wit, it does not seem to have been a great success.[25]

The case of Andrew Gibson scarred Ingraham's reputation indelibly, not only because Ingraham hurriedly and erroneously remanded a free man to slavery but also because Gibson was brought to him by George Alberti, an active slave catcher in the Philadelphia area and a thoroughly unattractive reprobate whose career had already made him an almost legendary figure. In July 1853, Alberti brought another man to Ingraham, William Fisher, claiming that Fisher was the escaped slave of yet another Cecil County owner. Ingraham, as was his wont, quickly decided in favor of the claimant. The association of Ingraham and Alberti in this case brought it to the attention of newspapers such as the *Albany Evening Journal*, which did not hesitate to link the two in a corrupt enterprise:

> The firm of Alberti & Ingraham, of Philadelphia, is largely engaged in the business of consigning alleged fugitives from labor to merchants at the South. Alberti is by profession a slave catcher, Ingraham an [*sic*] United States Commissioner. The one beats the bush, the other catches the bird, in the trap provided by United States statute. Ingraham's fees are $10 per head. What Alberti gets we do not know, as the law has unaccountably omitted to fix *his* compensation.[26]

Among all the people involved in the ugly businesses of slave catching and kidnapping, none had an uglier (or better-deserved) reputation
than George Alberti. He was reported to have two additional occupations: freelance hangman and "resurrectionist," or body stealer. There
were reports of his having been hired as hangman at executions in
Pittsburgh and Philadelphia, and he was alleged to have appeared on
the scaffold in Pittsburgh with his face painted red and wearing a red
wig. A writer for the *Liberator* attested that in addition to serving as
executioner, Alberti was available to supply cadavers to those willing to
pay enough for them. The writer cited "many a vacant grave and many a
dissecting room" as testimony to Alberti's thefts. He went on to make
a seemingly gratuitous connection between two of Alberti's distasteful
vocations: "Of this I have the positive testimony from physicians who,
while they were students, bought bodies of this adjunct of the Fugitive
Slave Law." Alberti probably had no direct involvement in the Christiana affair or the Parker kidnappings, although he did sometimes use
Elkton, Maryland—Thomas McCreary's town—as a place to conceal
his captives temporarily. He was also hired on occasion by slaveholders
in northern Maryland, including Cecil and Kent Counties, who were
looking for fugitives in Pennsylvania. Alberti's name originally became
linked with Christiana, even though he was not involved in the episode,
through his working relationship with Commissioner Ingraham, who
had supplied Gorsuch with his warrant.[27]

The more significant connection between Alberti and Christiana,
however, came in the stormy political aftermath of a completely remarkable action taken by the newly elected governor of Pennsylvania, William Bigler, who pardoned Alberti after he had been convicted and
sentenced to prison for kidnapping. Alberti was tried in 1851 for the
kidnapping of Joel Thompson, the eighteen-month-old child of a fugitive
slave mother. She had run away from James Mitchell of Cecil County in
1845 and was living in New Jersey when she gave birth to Joel. Alberti
found and arrested her in Philadelphia in 1850. Since she had the child
with her and refused to leave him behind, Alberti took both of them to
Cecil County, delivered them to Mitchell, and was subsequently arrested

when he returned to Pennsylvania and charged with kidnapping Joel. He was convicted on the grounds that Joel Thompson, having been born in a free state, was legally free; his sale as a slave therefore amounted to kidnapping. Alberti argued, unavailingly, that in selling both mother and child he was doing a kindness to the mother by not separating her from her child. The Pennsylvania jury sentenced him to ten years, but he had served only one year when Governor Bigler pardoned him in February 1852.[28]

Responses to the pardon came quickly from all sides, and no one, on any side, saw it as a disinterested act of charity. To many, the pardon was obviously linked to Christiana. The *Times-Picayune* of New Orleans openly and approvingly described the pardon as part of a political deal made in the aftermath of the failed Christiana prosecutions, an effort on the part of the Pennsylvania governor to mend fences with Maryland: "The setting free of the Christiana traitors and murderers required some propitiatory act on the part of the new Governor; and none could have been more fitting than this, as Alberti was guilty of no crime according to the laws of this or any other Southern State." The "propitiatory" pardon of Alberti was also applauded by the *Baltimore Argus*, which used its most inflammatory rhetoric to call for the pardon of Alberti's confederate in the Joel Thompson kidnapping:

> It should be enough for Pennsylvania that . . . a Gorsuch, who perished on her soil in pursuit of her runaway slaves, remains unatoned for and unavenged, without adding to the deep and damning wrong by unjustly and cruelly imprisoning two of her citizens, who were so faithful to the Constitution as to aid in capturing a fugitive slave. One of them has been liberated, it is true, but without indemnification for the wrong he has suffered; the other remains in his solitary dungeon without a friend around to sympathize with him in his woe.[29]

Those who defended Bigler's pardon of Alberti on legal grounds contended that, in Maryland and other southern states, a child born of a slave mother *was* a slave and therefore could legally be sold in Maryland, no matter what the laws of Pennsylvania might say. In one published review of the case, P. A. Browne concluded that Alberti had not been convicted because he had committed a crime but only because he had angered those in Pennsylvania who resented his success in "assisting the owners of fugitive slaves in retaking their property." The Pennsylvanians wanted him sent to jail, according to Browne, and they got their way. The Pennsylvania Anti-Slavery Society, on the other hand, called Bigler's action a "flagrant [and] inexcusable abuse" of executive privilege. Because of the governor's action, according to the Society, "the infamous Alberti, to the chagrin and grief of all respectable people, was again turned loose to prey upon society."[30]

George Alberti lost little time getting back to work after his pardon, plunging back into the pursuits that had landed him in prison in the first place. In November 1852 he arrested George Bordley and took him to Commissioner Ingraham, who remanded him to a slaveholder in Cecil County. Astonishingly, Alberti was also again in pursuit of Adam Gibson, the man whose case had originally brought him and Ingraham to the attention of the antislavery press. This time, he was successful: he brought Gibson to Ingraham, who remanded him to Maryland.[31]

The freewheeling exploits of Alberti, combined with the macabre nature of his avocations, led the Philadelphia *Daily Register* to publish a long and thoroughly disgusted account of what Alberti had been up to since he left prison—or, as the *Daily Register* put it, since "the ponderous marble jaws of the penitentiary vomited him out." Asking, "Who has not heard of Alberti? He is the man in the black mask who figures at every gallows scene," the account went on to describe Alberti's ghoulish delight in the job of hangman and his pleasure in "the moral isolation in which he lives." The newspaper's real contempt, however, was reserved for Alberti the kidnapper, who had, according to the *Daily Register*, established a monopoly on the business of man stealing in the Philadelphia area. "No colored man arrives here but Alberti knows it, through his spies. . . . Nothing stops him. Perjury, corruption of officers, legal chicanery—any means are good which enable him to pocket the reward offered for a human being." The paper ended its account with a plea to the citizens of Philadelphia to stop tolerating Alberti. "Why does he go unpunished for his numerous offences? Why, for instance, is he not arrested and tried for kidnapping Adam Gibson? . . . Let him and his gang go elsewhere to play [*sic*] their nefarious traffic—or let them be safely stowed in the Penitentiary, from which Mr. Bigler took Alberti."[32]

The kidnapping of the Parker sisters and the two trials that ensued took place in the very long and dark shadow of the Christiana events. Castner Hanway's trial ended in Lancaster with his acquittal on December 11, 1851. Elizabeth Parker was abducted from the next county two days later, and Rachel Parker was taken on December 30. Christiana had brought national attention to an out-of-the-way corner of Pennsylvania where some comparatively small battles were taking place. The conflicts became immense in their implications, however, because they so clearly and forcibly replicated parts of the increasingly tense drama of national life. The anger of fugitive slaves that could quickly turn into violence directed at white people, especially white slaveholders, was a subject that was obviously on many minds but was not often an open part of the national debate. Christiana brought the shocking reality of that violent anger into public consciousness, exposing what one early historian called "the open exultation of many persons over the killing and wounding of citizens engaged in a lawful undertaking, and the chagrin of many other orderly and law-abiding people that the law of the land had been violated in bloodshed and its officers successfully resisted." Christiana also underscored the animosity and sometimes deadly competition between slave and free states, here represented by Maryland and Pennsylvania. In the aftermath of the death of Gorsuch and the freeing of the Christiana prisoners, proslavery sentiment in Maryland demanded compensation or at least a quid pro quo. The compromises that resulted—the pardoning of George Alberti and, very probably, the failure to convict Thomas McCreary of kidnapping—were as arbitrary and ineffective in preventing greater violence as the congressional compromises that produced the Fugitive Slave Act in the first place.[33]

The proslavery newspapers blamed the abolitionists not only for what happened at Christiana but also for the kind of guerrilla warfare across state borders that was represented by McCreary, Alberti, William Parker, and others. Slaveholders in Maryland contended that if abolitionists in Pennsylvania could provide sanctuary to fugitives and encourage them to claim the *right* of freedom, even by violent means, then the slaveholders had every *right* to enter Pennsylvania and reclaim their human property, even by violent means. There were, of course, many people who were caught in the crossfire and suffered for it—such as the Parker sisters, Castner Hanway, and especially Joseph Miller. Miller lost his life; Elizabeth and Rachel Parker both lost a year of their lives; Castner Hanway lost his livelihood, his health, and something of what might be called his innocence. One of the ironies of Hanway's experience was that he was assumed by the press to be a Quaker because he was a quiet, self-effacing, nonviolent man, antislavery in his sentiments but not abolitionist in his politics. In fact, Hanway was not a Quaker when he rode to William Parker's house to persuade his angry black neighbors not to use their weapons. It was only after he was arrested and tried for treason—and presumably because of that experience—that he became a Quaker and an abolitionist, joining the Progressive Friends meeting at Longwood, Pennsylvania.[34]

The violent confrontation at Christiana was over in a few hours; the aftermath was long and complicated and the publicity inflammatory. The results had significant implications, not only for the national debates about slavery but also for the local people of southeastern Pennsylvania. The "riot" took place only a few miles from the sites where the Parker sisters were taken. The news would certainly have spread quickly from Christiana to the southern parts of Chester County. Talk about "the riot" must have been constant, and it is hard to imagine that it did not make for increased anxiety on the part of all black people in the area, including ones as young as the Parkers. Steven Lubet has written that "thanks to the dynamics surrounding the Fugitive Slave Act, every runaway was in fact a potential political actor—even those who would far rather have chosen a life of peaceful anonymity." The same could be said of victims like the Parkers, whose personal stories became attached to the politically contentious Christiana story, no matter what the victims themselves might have thought or wished.[35]

The most significant and consequential connections between Christiana and the Parker case were made later, following the death of Joseph

Miller, when everyone was looking for something and someone to blame for his death. Many of those who believed that Miller was murdered—and that number included all of his Chester County friends and neighbors—saw his death as an act of revenge for the death of Edward Gorsuch. The Pennsylvania State Anti-Slavery Society took this explanation as almost a given. According to the Society, the abduction of Rachel Parker and the killing of Miller constituted "another outrage, differing somewhat in character from the Christiana prosecution, but in no wise inferior to it in atrocity. It is closely connected with that affair in its history, the evidence being strong to show that it was perpetrated, at least in part, in revenge for the killing of Gorsuch and the impunity extended to the Christiana prisoners." Some of those who believed (or professed to believe) that Miller's death was suicide—most of them on the Maryland side of the state line—speculated that Miller took his life because he feared he would be treated as Castner Hanway had been. Although he and the other Christiana defendants were eventually declared not guilty of treason, Hanway had spent a troubled three months in jail, unable to work. He had been called a traitor, vilified in public, and threatened with hanging, and he emerged from the trial ill and deeply in debt to lawyers and witnesses.[36]

Whatever one thought about its relevance to the Parkers, Christiana had become a touchstone for subsequent episodes of racial violence, especially along the border, and would remain one for a long time. The court's failure to convict anyone for the death of Gorsuch would also remain an extremely sensitive source of conflict between Maryland and Pennsylvania for years, with ramifications showing up in all kinds of unlikely spots. The *Easton Star*, a newspaper from a strongly proslavery area of Maryland's Eastern Shore, published a letter in 1854 complaining about the tonging of oysters in the Chesapeake Bay by oystermen from Pennsylvania and about that state's generally condescending attitude toward the Eastern Shore. The offended letter writer quoted a Philadelphia newspaper's description of the area as made up of "antideluvian [*sic*] villages where everything is dull but the nigger children and the voracious mosquitoes." He eventually managed, with little concern for logical consistency, to bring his argument around to Gorsuch and Christiana: "If a Philadelphia journal wishes to discuss the subject [of oysters] fairly and honorably, their arguments will be weighed and politely noticed; providing they say nothing of their promptness in returning our fugitive slaves,—for whenever a Pennsylvanian has the impudence to mention that subject, the image of poor murdered Gorsuch rises before us and his blood seems to cry for vengeance. The oyster question, however, we are free to discuss." The Gorsuch digression seems to come out of nowhere, but it effectively makes the point that, at least for this Maryland letter writer, any negotiation between his state and Pennsylvania, on any subject whatsoever, was going to take place in the context of the lingering bitterness left by the Christiana affair.[37]

5

ELIZABETH'S STORY

ELIZABETH PARKER told her story for the first time a few days after her return from Baltimore, where she and her sister had been held awaiting trial to determine whether they were slaves or free. Elizabeth had waited nearly six months and Rachel a full year while their attorneys squabbled about court dates. Once their trials were finally scheduled, witnesses had to be collected and brought down from Pennsylvania to Baltimore. Remarkably, seventy-nine volunteers, men and women, all white, eventually made the trip. Among the Pennsylvanians traveling to Baltimore was a Nottingham resident who, writing under the name "Toby," supplied a few eyewitness accounts of the trial to West Chester's *Village Record* newspaper. Back home in Chester County, a few days after the trial was over, Toby was able to get a scoop— an interview with Elizabeth in which she described her experiences from the moment of her kidnapping through her time in New Orleans and her stay in the Baltimore jail. The sisters were released on January 13, 1853; Toby's account in the *Village Record* was datelined January 22, 1853. The same issue of the newspaper also contained much briefer statements from both Elizabeth and Rachel.

My account of Elizabeth's experience in this chapter relies on both *Village Record* stories: the very brief factual account and, much more heavily, on Toby's interview with Elizabeth. (The full text of that interview is given in the Appendix.) The version of her story he recorded and published offers evidence about the Baltimore/New Orleans slave trade that is consistent with other sources. More importantly, it makes some attempt, however clumsy, to reproduce the voice of young Elizabeth, telling her story immediately upon her return. Toby's story also gives us glimpses of his interaction with Elizabeth and Beck, allowing us to hear something of his own take on the story as he shaped it for publication. Toby's is, for better or for worse, the primary voice of white Chester County that has come down to us through his role as a chronicler of the Parkers' story—and that voice, with its mixture of intimacy, curiosity, bemusement, condescension, and admiration, is itself a large part of the story.

According to Toby, he visited the family at the two-story log home that Beck, whom he calls "Becky, renowned Becky," was sharing with her new husband. He received a warm welcome from Beck, now Mrs. Miller (the name Elizabeth would also assume a few years later), who recognized "Mr. Toby" right away. Wanting, as he said, to establish a "friendly and social feeling," he began by making light of the trauma everyone had just been through by joking with Beck about why she did not have to go to court to prove her freedom, as her daughters had done. Beck's rejoinder was that nobody would have wanted to claim her as a slave; she was too old.

Toby's real interest was in Elizabeth. Rachel was not even at home when he visited, but he assured his readers that this did not matter; everyone already knew her story, and it contained elements that did not bear revisiting: "Rachel's history is familiar to us all, there is outrage and murder in it, and sadly and willingly I am silent about her." Elizabeth's story had been subordinated to Rachel's, that is, because hers did not include the violent and mysterious death of a white citizen of the county: "outrage and murder."[1]

Elizabeth's story had not yet been told, and for Toby what it lacked in outrage it made up for in other ways: "She has had adventures." His reporting of Elizabeth's "adventures" contains some revealing tensions and contradictions. One comes away from Toby's account with the sense that in the interview Elizabeth probably did not say exactly what he wanted her to say or what he thought his readers would want to hear about her time as a slave. The story she told does not fit a familiar, comfortable narrative pattern, especially in its conclusions. There are lessons Toby wants to draw from her experiences, moral certainties he would like to find confirmed there, but they can be attached to her story in only what is ultimately a strained and unconvincing way. For Toby, that is, Elizabeth's story requires his explanation and interpretation if it is to find its way to the right conclusions. He describes Elizabeth as "smart and intelligent" and suggests that she has been changed by her experiences in an unexpected way: she "seems to have improved very much by her travels. Her airs are very much like those our country girls assume after being a year in town. She is often slightly sullen; and not disposed to be communicative." In the case of this interview, however, Toby insists that Elizabeth "spoke freely," although he acknowledges that she did not volunteer information but spoke only in answer to his questions. She talked rapidly and "gets her words out with an air, and tries to be a little stilted." Toby does not quite seem to recognize the changed Elizabeth. To the white man who knew her before her "adventures," this bright but sullen girl with her airs and stilted talk seems somehow affected. She is not the plain, rural, servant girl, grateful to be home, that he expected to find. From a contemporary reader's perspective, however, the Elizabeth that Toby describes does not seem inconsistent with the image of the girl who emerges from accounts of her before the kidnapping—difficult, at odds with her mother, independent, diffident, walking the roads alone, never staying with any employer for very long, finally making a disastrous choice: "She got down there to Donnelly's," Toby says, "and among them she was carried off" into slavery.

Toby struggles to accommodate this incommunicative, probably resentful girl within the sentimental, highly rhetorical, and formulaic framework he brought with him to the interview. In writing about the consequences of slavery in this mode, he is putting himself, perhaps deliberately, in the company of the best-known contemporaneous moralist on the subject of slavery. Stowe's *Uncle Tom's Cabin*, published a year earlier, had worked the sentimental mode to such remarkable effect that the book and its author had become an international phenomenon. Stowe had also written effusively about slaves who found freedom—in her case, a couple with an infant child who made a successful flight to Canada:

> Who can speak of the blessedness of that first day of freedom! Is not the *sense* of liberty a higher and a finer one than any of the five? . . . Who can speak the blessings of that rest which comes down on the free man's pillow, under laws which insure to him the rights that God has given to man? How fair and precious to that mother was that sleeping child's face, endeared by the memory of a thousand dangers! How impossible was it to sleep, in the exuberant possession of such blessedness![2]

Toby's language is sometimes as fulsome as Stowe's, and his emphasis, like hers, is on the emotionally charged image of mother and child. Elizabeth and Rachel are now, he says, "restored after many a weary day of sorrow and confinement, of suffering and adventure, to that blessed refuge and rest for all abused and stricken ones—the cottage of their mother. What a long, long aching, terrible year of absence from both these loved objects, the past one has been to them."

Unlike Stowe, however, Toby is not writing a novel, and he does not have the liberty to shift things about to make language and event match up. His opening, with its sentimental hymn to home and mother, sits very uneasily with the closing paragraphs of his story. Only at the end, after he has finished transcribing Elizabeth's narrative, does he admit some discomfiting facts into his account. He acknowledges that "Elizabeth was never a favorite of her mother's," that Beck and Elizabeth fought and that once Beck drove Elizabeth out and told her never to come home again, and that Beck's only comment in response to Elizabeth's recounting of her experiences was almost a rebuke: "This 'ere trip of her'n will do her good. She'll be settled now." In light of this knowledge, as well as the knowledge that Beck sent Elizabeth out to work when she was a very young child, it is difficult to believe that her mother's "cottage" was much of a "blessed refuge" for Elizabeth, a place where she could feel "restored." The "three great blessed boons of life," Toby writes, are "Home, Love, and Liberty." He implies that Elizabeth was deprived of all three when McCreary kidnapped her and that all were restored when she was returned to Beck's log house in Chester County. In fact, what we know of her life before her abduction suggests how little she had known of any of these. Had she known them, McCreary might never have found her.

The most striking contradiction between Elizabeth's experience and Toby's rendering of it comes in the final paragraph of his story. What he has to report here comes out grudgingly, hedged with qualifiers ("appears," "pretty well," "rather," "I do not suppose," "I heard," "I believe"), in a style that has none of the flourishes of the opening sentiments:

> Elizabeth, by her story, appears to have been pretty well treated during her absence, and had rather a pleasant, easy life of it, and I do not suppose, as far as the matter of usage and labor was concerned, that she cared very much whether she returned or remained. Indeed, I heard that she stated in Baltimore that she did not want to come back, but she said to us that she was very glad to get back, and I believe that to be the truth, for to all of us, high and low, rich and poor, black or white, *Liberty* is very, very sweet.

Toby chooses the ending he wants for this story ("I believe that to be the truth"), and he rushes to it after he gets through the sticky business of Elizabeth's reluctance to come home. The ending he chooses is the one that restores the abused Elizabeth to home and mother and confirms a simplified, safe, and reductive version of the antislavery message: liberty is always sweet, even to those who are low, poor, and black.

The platitudinous conclusion Toby supplies for his slavery story is overshadowed by his startling acknowledgement that this girl, who was mistreated in multiple ways in the course of her kidnapping and enslavement, actually might not have *wanted* to exchange that rough life for the "freedom" of home. With the advantages of hindsight and more objectivity than a contemporary observer like Toby could be expected to have, it makes sense that Elizabeth's experiences in Baltimore and New Orleans, even as a slave, might have seemed preferable to her experiences as a child worker, living in white households on the isolated farms of rural Pennsylvania, where no one even noticed when she disappeared. She was not a slave in Pennsylvania, but neither was she free. She probably had more "liberty" in New Orleans than she had in Chester County. She was probably safer. She was certainly less isolated. She lived among other black people, some of them her age. She was in a cosmopolitan city, with all its distractions. She went to dances and visited the theater. Her work was not physically demanding. It is likely that she was better fed, and she may have been more comfortably housed. Even Toby acknowledges that Elizabeth seemed at least ambivalent about which life was the better one: "The novelty and adventure, I imagine, pleased her a little." We will never know what Elizabeth really thought about her time in New Orleans, but it would certainly be understandable if, at least for a moment, she "did not want to come back."

In answer to Toby's questions about her experiences, Elizabeth supplied him with details, beginning with the night she was kidnapped. She told him that McCreary kept her gagged from the time he seized her in Donnelly's yard until they boarded the train for Baltimore more than twenty-four hours later. When they arrived in the city, she said, she was taken straight to a place McCreary was familiar with from previous sales, Walter Campbell's slave pen. Elizabeth was thus thrust into the heart of a thriving, noisily busy, extremely profitable, multistate enterprise. Walter Campbell and his brother Bernard ran what was probably, by 1851, the largest slave-trading operation in a major slave-trading port. They had opened their business in 1844, when Baltimore was emerging as the leading exporter of slave labor to markets farther south. The Campbells bought and sold slaves and also provided "pen" or "jail" space to other dealers who needed to board slaves temporarily. Their business was modest to begin with. In their first four years, the brothers shipped only 271 slaves to New Orleans. Their business increased markedly in 1848 when Bernard and Walter bought the old premises of Hope Slatter, one of the most well-known and successful of all the Baltimore dealers, who did an extensive trade with New Orleans. Their new site, the one to which Elizabeth and Rachel were both brought, consisted of two brick buildings: a three-story building in front that housed the offices and a two-story building behind, with barred windows, that housed the slaves being boarded or waiting for sale. Adjacent was a paved yard where the "stock" could attempt to entertain themselves during the day. The Campbells were quick to capitalize on Slatter's name and reputation: "Persons having slaves to sell will hereafter find us located at the extensive establishment formerly owned by Hope H. Slatter. We have purchased his entire possessions on Pratt Street No. 244, at which place all who have slaves to sell will be sure to get the highest price, when the negroes are young and likely.—The place is now open to receive on Board, negroes which are for sale, at 25 cents per day." This advertisement, which ran in a number of Maryland newspapers, carried an endorsement by Slatter, who "cheerfully recommend[ed]" the Campbells to his old customers.[3]

Like Slatter and several other Baltimore dealers, the Campbells became specialists in the New Orleans trade, opening their own branch in Louisiana. Between 1844 and 1853, they sent fifty-nine shipments to New Orleans, carrying a total of 1,279 slaves. Bernard, who took on the Louisiana end of the business, oversaw a slave pen in New Orleans and a farm eighty miles outside of the city, where any slaves not sold by the beginning of the hot New Orleans summer could be worked and acclimated to the conditions of Deep South slavery. When the opening of the Civil War began to slow down the profits from slave trading, the Campbells were able to keep their Baltimore business going by continuing to rent out space, sometimes to slaveholders who wanted to protect their property from being confiscated by Union soldiers. Even that business, of course, finally had to end. In July 1863, one of the Union officers, Colonel William Birney, was sent to liberate the slave jails of Baltimore, including the Campbells' pen, and provided a brief account of what he found. Birney described the establishment as including "a brick paved yard, twenty-five feet in width by forty in length. . . . In this yard no tree or shrub grows—no flower or blade of grass can be seen." In the pen Birney found twenty-six men, twenty-seven women, one young boy, and three infants. Later excavations in the area uncovered the remains of a tunnel, apparently built by Slatter before he sold the property to the Campbells, which covered the short distance from the pen to the area of the docks.[4]

It was to this Pratt Street pen that McCreary brought Elizabeth, where Walter Campbell was waiting for them. According to Elizabeth, while she and McCreary were on the train, McCreary had told her, at gunpoint, that she must from then on tell anyone who asked that her real name was Henrietta Crocus, that she and her mother and sister had been the slaves of a Mrs. Hannah Dickehut of Baltimore, and that she was a runaway. Early in her first morning at the Campbells' pen, she was taken into a room where Mrs. Dickehut's son-in-law, Luther Schoolfield, was waiting. Because she was terrified of McCreary and his rifle, Elizabeth said to Schoolfield what she had been told she must say: that she was Henrietta Crocus, a slave, and that she had run away. The following morning, Luther Schoolfield's wife appeared, along with several other women whom Elizabeth could not identify, and Elizabeth again confirmed that she was Henrietta Crocus, a runaway. These identifications were apparently sufficient to convince Walter Campbell either that Elizabeth was indeed a slave or that the story was airtight enough that no one would ever know she was not. He purchased Elizabeth from McCreary, who was acting as the agent of Luther Schoolfield, for $600.

McCreary, the Schoolfields, and Mrs. Dickehut, having disposed of Elizabeth and collected their money, then pass out of Elizabeth's story—but only temporarily. The kidnapping of Rachel and the death of Joseph Miller, the trial of McCreary, and Rachel's freedom trial would bring them all back, into court this time, and subject them to more public scrutiny and controversy than they could ever have bargained for.

Hannah Dickehut claimed that she had lost three slaves: Juno Crocus and her two daughters, Eliza and Henrietta. She had purchased them from her daughter, a Mrs. Hynson, but because she had no immediate use for the women she had bought, she allowed them to remain with her daughter. In April 1847, Juno and the girls ran away. Luther Schoolfield, acting on the authority of his mother-in-law, produced a handbill describing the three runaways and offering a reward for their capture:

> $200 reward:—Ran away on Sunday night, April 25th, three negroes, mother and two children: the woman's name is Juno Crocus, aged 28 years, of a yellow or light chestnut color, about five feet high, round face and person: Eliza, aged 13 years, of a shade darker than the mother, lively appearance, bright eyes: Henrietta, aged 11 years, nearly the same color. The woman's husband, (named Allan Crocus, and father of the children), a free man, is supposed to have gone with them: The above reward will be paid for the recovery of the negroes, or proportionate for any of them.[5]

Nothing came of the advertisement for the Crocus family until nearly five years later, when Thomas McCreary approached Schoolfield to report that he had found Henrietta, the youngest daughter, living with the Donnelly family in Chester County; the person he had actually found was Elizabeth Parker. According to Luther Schoolfield, he believed McCreary's claim and gave him "verbal authority" to seize Henrietta/Elizabeth, which McCreary proceeded to do. Presumably, he also collected the "proportionate" share of the reward promised in the handbill. Having delivered Elizabeth to Baltimore, McCreary then asked for a power of attorney to allow him to arrest Eliza/Rachel, saying that he had learned her whereabouts from the sister he had already captured. Schoolfield granted his request.[6]

We may never know the full truth about all these stories, nor do the later court testimonies help to make things much clearer. Thomas McCreary swore, under oath, that he believed the Parker family was actually the Crocus family. Luther Schoolfield swore, under oath, that he believed McCreary had found the runaways belonging to his mother-in-law and that he sold Elizabeth to Walter Campbell in good faith, believing her to be Henrietta Crocus. Elizabeth, of course, never got to swear or even to speak in court, although dozens of Chester County residents eventually did speak in her behalf. If it is impossible to know whether McCreary and Schoolfield were telling the truth, it may not be possible, either, to determine for certain anyone's motives in this case, especially given the biases in the original reporting. In Pennsylvania, McCreary was considered a thuggish kidnapper who was coddled by Maryland authorities; in Maryland, he was defended as a slave catcher who was harassed by Pennsylvania abolitionists in the course of carrying out his entirely legal business. In taking the Parker sisters, was he consciously kidnapping, or did he believe he was catching slaves?

We do not have the answer, but we do have clues, patterns, and consistencies. It seems very likely that McCreary was following an elaborate plan of the kind he had been successful with before and that it was, in fact, immaterial to him whether or not the Parkers and the Crocuses were the same. He would have known about the Dickehut slaves from the handbill that was circulated, and he had ample time and opportunity to scout out three women who could plausibly pass for the three runaways. If it turned out that they actually were the runaways, then so much the better. His regular trips into Pennsylvania to deliver the mail, as well as his network of relatives and accomplices there, gave him plenty of chances to do the scouting. The fact that nearly five years had elapsed since the slaves ran away was actually an advantage for McCreary, since any quibbles about whether the Parkers looked convincingly like the Crocuses might be explained by the passage of time.

Luther Schoolfield was compliant—maybe because he believed the Parkers really were the Crocuses, or because he was intimidated by the genuinely intimidating McCreary, or because he needed money and the scheme seemed workable, or perhaps for all of these reasons. In covering the story, the New Orleans *Times-Picayune* referred to Schoolfield as "a responsible and wealthy citizen," but that newspaper had ideological reasons to spin the story to the advantage of the slaveholder, and there are some indications that the paper might have exaggerated Schoolfield's financial status. Schoolfield ran a downtown Baltimore lottery business that McCreary might even have patronized, although Schoolfield evidently had significant competition for customers in the market for a lottery ticket. A new arrival in Baltimore in 1846 noted that "the traffic most obtrusively and flauntingly carried on" in downtown Baltimore "was the traffic in lottery tickets." In addition to newspaper ads and circulars, the lottery managers scattered "big posters in colored letters . . . in every square and at every corner." Whether McCreary knew Schoolfield personally or not, the advertising for his lottery had at least made Schoolfield's name visible for years, beginning in 1843. This snappy ad from the *Baltimore Sun* in 1844 was typical: "To secure the capitals, be sure and find the ever fortunate SCHOOLFIELD & CO., No. 1 North Calvert Street, sign of the big window glass, and revolving lights." The ads ran frequently in the *Sun* into 1849, then became scattered, and finally ended in 1852. By 1856, Schoolfield was trying other ways of making a living: the partnership of Pierce & Schoolfield was advertising oysters for sale at Schoolfield's home address, and the 1860 Baltimore city directory listed Luther A. Schoolfield as a real estate broker. During these years, when the sources of his income were shifting, he had an ever-growing family to support. His household in 1850 included his wife, eight children (there would eventually be twelve), and his mother-in-law. His heavy domestic responsibilities, seen in conjunction with the erratic trajectory of his career, suggest that he might have welcomed the prospect of selling three slaves in 1852 (the year his lottery business seems to have ended) and might thus have found McCreary's overtures especially attractive.[7]

Whether or not Schoolfield was eager to get in on McCreary's deal, it is clear that, once in, he was in no hurry to get out. The arrest and sale of Elizabeth went smoothly, but McCreary's effort to kidnap Rachel—and sell her as Eliza Crocus—ran into unexpected resistance and turned into a major and well-publicized fiasco. Joseph Miller was killed and McCreary was charged with kidnapping, a charge he would escape only through some preposterous testimony that almost no one believed. Despite the verdict, practically all the testimony at his trial pegged him as a kidnapper. Still, Schoolfield held his ground, continuing to insist that Rachel and Elizabeth Parker were really Eliza and Henrietta Crocus and that they were his family's property. Because Schoolfield refused to yield, even in the face of strong evidence that he was wrong, Rachel and Elizabeth both had to remain in one kind of custody or another until their case could be tried in court.

Elizabeth would end up spending almost six months in the Baltimore jail, but she had already spent much of the previous six months in other kinds of confinement. Her first incarceration was in the Campbells' slave pen, where she remained for almost two weeks, waiting for the next boat to New Orleans. Her account of this time in Baltimore is typically sketchy and dispassionate. The information she gives shows signs of being supplied as terse answers to the kinds of questions Toby would have been likely to ask: How many other people were in the pen with you? What did you have to eat? Where did you sleep? How long did you stay? About thirty other people were in the pen with her, she says. She was given corn cake, rice, and potatoes to eat, and the beds were "pretty good." She stayed about two weeks. And that is the extent of her report. No one came to look for her, and she did not leave the pen.

On December 18, 1851, the schooner *Henry A. Barling* left Baltimore for New Orleans carrying fifty slaves. The shippers were Bernard M. and Walter L. Campbell. Among the names on the ship manifest is that of Henrietta Crocus; her age is given as fifteen. Elizabeth's departure on that ship, with the wrong name and probably the wrong age, marks the beginning of what must have been a completely disorienting and bewildering period for her. It might also, however, have been at the same time oddly exhilarating. Henrietta Crocus had replaced the isolated and unhappy Elizabeth Parker. Who would Henrietta turn out to be? What would her life be like? In his informative study of antebellum slave markets, Walter Johnson offers a theory about the psychological transformations experienced by free people who were kidnapped and sold—that is, people like Elizabeth Parker. Kidnapped people, Johnson points out, could not be sold as slaves if their true histories were known, so they had to have new ones provided for them. "Just as kidnapping made slaves of free people, the traders' packaging created slaves who did not previously exist out of the pieces of people who formerly did. By detaching slaves from their history and replacing human singularity with fashioned salability, the traders were doing more than selling slaves: they were making them." When Elizabeth boarded the ship, her own process of refashioning was begun. She was no longer within reach of anyone who knew that her name was Elizabeth, that she was born in Pennsylvania, or that she was free. From that point on she was Henrietta, she was a slave, and she was for sale.[8]

Johnson contends that people who were already enslaved when they entered the markets of New Orleans began a process of establishing an identity and a community for themselves there: they "soon set about reconstructing the communities and social identities that had been fractured by the trade." They were able to produce a new version of the slave culture they all brought with them, a version that was adapted to the landscape of Deep South slavery. Elizabeth's response to being enslaved in New Orleans was different. Because she was so young and because she arrived in New Orleans with very little experience of either slave or free black communities and cultures, Elizabeth went through a process that was more like constructing than reconstructing. Her time as a slave was very brief, and her experience was obviously not representative of the general experience of U.S. slavery with all its attendant horrors. Still, as brief as it was, her slave life would make her seem changed to Toby. She came home putting on airs, he concluded. Toby's reaction suggests that Elizabeth did not return from New Orleans feeling that she had been robbed of her identity; rather, she gave the impression that she had found a more confident self in New Orleans, a self that would forever have trouble feeling at home in her mother's rural, predominantly white world. She apparently hated Thomas McCreary intensely for the rest of her life, but in her public comments she never expressed resentment of anyone she encountered in her life in New Orleans.[9]

Elizabeth complains that the beginning of the trip from Baltimore on the *Henry A. Barling* was cold; the ice in the harbor had to be broken before the ship could get underway. She has no complaints, however, about the rest of the trip, which took about a month. She speaks of herself as part of a group, the "we" that consisted of the slaves on board: "We were very well accommodated," she says. Being surrounded by other black people who were sharing the same experience would have been new for Elizabeth, whose short life had been spent largely in white households. She speaks of her comparative freedom on the ship as if it were also a new condition for her, or at least one that she did not expect to encounter as a captive headed for slavery. "We" were allowed to move around on the ship, she says, had plenty to eat, and had "first rate" beds. "I liked the voyage right well," Elizabeth concludes.

The *Henry A. Barling* arrived in New Orleans on January 12, 1852. Elizabeth did not comment to Toby on her first impressions of the city, but she must have been overwhelmed. With just under 120,000 residents, it was not at that time an especially large city, but the booming slave trade made it an unusually busy place. By 1850 the city had about two hundred registered slave traders, and this number does not include the brokers, auctioneers, and others who were needed to keep the trade going. The slave selling was constant. The pens of traders like the Campbells, where most of the sales took place, were open long hours for buyers who wanted to browse; there were frequent auctions in the large venues, such as the St. Louis and St. Charles Hotels; and until 1852, slaves could be, and were, sold openly in the streets. According to Frederic Bancroft, the variety of sales opportunities allowed for the marketing of all sorts and conditions of people, including people like Elizabeth: "There were always in this market many kidnapped free negroes, stolen slaves, unclaimed runaways, vagrants, drunkards and general good-for-nothings, recently sold for jail dues—all gathered, one or a few at a time, by speculators, thieves or cheats and brought here where they could best be disposed of and where even the riffraff, infancy and decrepitude had a price."[10]

Elizabeth and her companions from the ship were taken directly to the slave pen operated by the Campbells, located on Esplanade Street just outside the French Quarter. While auctions were allowed inside the Quarter, slave pens were not; the streets bordering the Quarter were therefore prime territory for slave traders. Walter Campbell advertised his Esplanade Street establishment as "due west from the St. Charles Hotel, and . . . convenient to all the merchants and hotels." By 1860, at least twenty-five other traders were also doing business within a few blocks of the St. Charles. (A local resident observed in 1850, perhaps with some exaggeration, that five hundred to eight hundred slaves might be displayed along the sidewalk in front of the slave pens on Esplanade Street, where they would stand from nine in the morning until late afternoon.)[11]

As they had done in Baltimore, the Campbells had taken over the premises of Hope Slatter in New Orleans. Once again taking advantage of Slatter's reputation, Walter Campbell signed his newspaper advertisements "Walter L. Campbell, Successor of Slatter." Like many other slave-dealing businesses in New Orleans, the establishment occupied by the Campbells consisted of both showroom space for sales and living quarters for those waiting to be sold. The majority of slaves bought in the city were purchased not at auctions but at salesrooms like the Campbells', where slaves were on display daily, buyers could shop at their leisure, and deals might take days. The Campbells' property included a single-story house with four large rooms and a gallery that extended the full length of the building and could be used for display and sales. The property also included a store, an adjacent open area or yard, and a two-story brick building that probably served as living quarters.[12]

Elizabeth arrived in New Orleans in the middle of the busy season for slave trading in the city. Prices for slaves tended to be highest in January, and the Campbells kept their salesroom well stocked during the winter months. A January 1851 advertisement from Walter Campbell announced that he would be receiving shipments of slaves from Maryland and Virginia "every fifteen or twenty days during the season." By this point, the Campbells were concentrating their buying in those two states, since slaves from that area were highly valued. The Eastern Shore of Maryland, in particular, was considered to produce slaves who were accustomed to field work in hot, humid weather and were therefore especially well suited to Louisiana plantation labor. The brothers made their focus clear in their advertising. In the fall of 1852, a Campbell advertisement announced, "A first shipment of over a hundred thousand dollars worth of slaves will be received from Virginia and Maryland about the 1st of November. . . . During the trading season large shipments will be received from the above States, and a complete assortment kept up."[13]

Even if the Campbells inflated their numbers for advertising purposes, they still processed a large number of people and kept their pen well supplied with what they called "stock." Elizabeth recalled that there were already forty or fifty people being kept at the Campbell house when she arrived. They would have been maintained carefully: it was standard

practice in New Orleans for slaves in the pens to be fed well and provided with new clothes while they waited, to make them more attractive
to buyers. During the day, Campbell's slaves were all kept together in
one room, seated on the floor, with men and women on separate sides.
When a prospective buyer came in, all had to stand and present themselves for inspection. As Elizabeth described the process to Toby, "The
buyer would walk along, and when he found some person he liked the
looks of, he would get them out in the middle of the floor, and make 'em
jump backwards and forwards, and run and swing themselves about, and
then he would look at their teeth and examine their backs."

Elizabeth's account of the slave shopping she witnessed is very similar
to those of other eyewitnesses, such as the version recorded by Ebenezer
Davies, an English minister who visited New Orleans in 1849. Davies
registered his astonishment when one of the very first things he saw
when he disembarked in the city was a slave market:

> We came upon a street in which a long row, or rather several rows,
> of black and coloured people were exposed in the open air (and
> under a smiling sun) for sale! There must have been from 70 to
> 100, all young people, varying from 15 to 30 years of age. . . . The
> whole were arranged under a kind of verandah, having a foot-
> bench (about six inches high) to stand upon, and their backs rest-
> ing against the wall. None were in any way tied or chained; but
> two white men ("soul-drivers," I suppose) were sauntering about
> in front of them, each with a cigar in his mouth, a whip under his
> arm, and his hands in his pockets, looking out for purchasers. . . .
> It was between twelve and one in the day; but there was no crowd,
> not even a single boy or girl looking on,—so common and every-
> day was the character of the scene.

Perhaps Davies was expecting high drama and obvious physical cruelty;
at any rate, as it turned out, the sheer ordinariness of the process was a
large part of what he found so disturbing.[14]

Elizabeth says little else about the circumstances of her time in the
slave pen, except that after a few days she was allowed to go out into the

streets, under the supervision of an overseer, with a few others who were waiting to be sold; that the beds, unlike the ones in the Baltimore pen and on the ship, were hard; and that everyone had to sleep in a row, head to toe. Unlike many slaves awaiting buyers in New Orleans, Elizabeth, being young and healthy, waited only a short time before she began to draw attention. Slaves could be held for months while they were fed and generally polished up in order to bring the maximum price. Elizabeth attracted a buyer after only about two weeks: a "man from the country" who checked her back and her teeth and was evidently interested in a purchase. (When Elizabeth recounted to Toby the story of having her teeth checked, her mother Beck, who was listening in, offered an explanation: "That was to see if she was a good feeder.... [T]hat was the reason they would not have anything to do with me in Baltimore, I hadn't teeth enough.") However, according to Elizabeth, Campbell rejected the man's offer: "He wouldn't sell me to go into the country at all."[15] Elizabeth does not explain why Campbell refused to sell her to the country buyer, and she may not have known why, but probably it was because the price he was offered was not good enough. He must have seen the possibility for a more lucrative sale to a city buyer, sizing up Elizabeth as a suitable prospect for a house servant or a street vendor—the job she was ultimately given. Campbell could afford to be choosy, since girls of Elizabeth's age were scarce in the New Orleans slave markets. In his study of the New Orleans trade, Michael Tadman estimates that girls in Elizabeth's age group, ten to fourteen, made up only 2 percent of the imports between 1850 and 1859. The majority of slaves imported in those years were males aged ten to nineteen and females aged twenty to twenty-nine.[16]

The Campbells sold to both the city and the plantation markets. Some of their advertisements were directed specifically to the sugar planters, offering for sale large groups of field hands or what one of their 1851 ads referred to as "heavy men and women . . . all of whom are young, athletic and efficient." Other advertisements were aimed at urban buyers; another 1851 ad announced that among the slaves imported from Maryland and Virginia then on hand in the Campbells' pen were "an Engineer, 26 years of age, [who] has had seven years' experience; and his wife, a choice house woman in every respect, a cook, washer, and ironer." Keeping Elizabeth out of the "heavy" group meant that the Campbells probably intended her for the market for urban servants, but they might even have imagined finding a buyer for her as a "fancy girl." These young women, or even young girls, who were intended as mistresses for their white purchasers, could bring among the highest prices in the New Orleans market, sometimes going for over $2,000. That possibility might have been a long shot, however, since fancy girls were generally light-skinned and Elizabeth was described as fairly dark.[17]

The right buyer did come along soon, a black man acting as agent for someone who could have been either his employer or his owner, a woman whom Elizabeth described as a Mrs. Chero or Churo, a "creowl." Since the slave sales areas were considered inappropriate places for women to come on business, a woman who wished to purchase a slave would need to send a male agent. Walter Johnson reports the case of another Creole woman, Polyxeme Reynes, whose husband purchased slaves for her beginning in 1833, using her money. Like Elizabeth's purchaser, Reynes used her slaves to establish a business, selling clothes and bonnets on the street. In Elizabeth's case, the agent and Campbell struck a deal after an examination of Elizabeth and some questions. Elizabeth thought the man paid $900 for her. If that was indeed the price, then Campbell surely did well not to take the first offer.[18]

Slave prices in New Orleans varied so widely as to make it very difficult to determine anything like an average or median price (the attempt to come up with reliable figures has engendered a long and sometimes contentious academic debate). As one historian has noted, "Prices were what the slave trade was all about." Gender, age, physical condition, and place of origin could all make a difference in the price a slave brought. House servants and skilled workers brought more than field hands, and those with no marks of punishment were worth more than those with scars from beatings or confinements.[19]

We can get some idea of the significance of Elizabeth's price, however, by comparing it to a few other figures. William Jay generalized in 1853 that an able-bodied black man sold in the South for $800 to $1,000. (For Jay, this was a sufficient explanation for the frequency of kidnapping; it could be a very lucrative business.) In their study of the economics of slavery, Robert W. Fogel and Stanley Engerman estimated the average price for a fifteen-year-old girl in the Old South in 1850 as between $500 and $600. In Richmond in 1850, according to Michael Tadman, girls between the ages of ten and fifteen were bringing anywhere from $375 to $650. In New Orleans specifically, Walter Johnson cites an average price of about $600 for girls between twelve and twenty sold by one New Orleans trader in 1858. Fredric Bancroft reported on the sale, in the 1840s, of a young girl who was bought in South Carolina for $600 and sold in New Orleans for $1,500. As unspecific as these numbers are, they suggest at least that Campbell probably did reasonably well on the sale of Elizabeth. If her sale prices in Baltimore and New Orleans were both reported accurately, then McCreary and his accomplices shared $600 and Campbell cleared a profit of $300.[20]

Once she was sold, Elizabeth was put to work immediately. She recalled her time with the woman who purchased her as more pleasant than otherwise: "She was a Creowl, sir, a creowl, she kept a flower garden and kept some sows and made molasses candy. The man who bought me took me in to her, she told me she liked my looks, and all she wanted of me was to sell milk and candy and flowers, and that if I was honest and done the best I could, she would treat me well, so I set into work in the morning." When Elizabeth entered this working household, she joined a group of slave women who already had an established routine. Along with the other women, Elizabeth took milk to a market in the early mornings and sold it by the pint and the quart; in the late morning she sold "long platted sticks" of molasses candy on the streets. In the late afternoons and evenings she sold flowers in the theaters and at dances. On Saturday nights she went to what she (or perhaps Toby) called the "colored" or quadroon dance parties, where her flower selling went especially well. She and, presumably, the other women were allowed to stay at the dances or the theater until ten o'clock. They were given rice, bread, and meat to eat, although Elizabeth said that she and the other women often bought their own food when they were working on the street. These women formed part of an established contingent of female slaves who for years had been working the streets and the entertainments of New Orleans, selling a variety of goods.

According to Elizabeth, she did well in her new life. She seemed proud of her success in negotiating this strange new world and pleasing her employer. Mrs. Churo, she reported, was good to her and gave her the responsibilities of a house servant in addition to her sales duties. She sold a "heap" of Mrs. Churo's molasses candy on the street and another "heap" of flowers at the Saturday night "colored" dance parties. Her accommodations were a pleasant surprise: "We had fust-rate feather beds there and we all slept in her house where she was herself." Sometimes Elizabeth's duties even included dressing Mrs. Churo. Her narrative, as transcribed by Toby, conveys a sense of wonder at the newness and strangeness of it all: the theater performances and the balls; the two pampered daughters of the house, who did not get up until midmorning; the businesswoman who needed someone to help dress her; the good feather beds. She never says directly that she enjoyed her life in New Orleans, but she comes close, saying that she got along well with Mrs. Churo, who was "nice," and that she did not see "anybody have very hard times of it." Even Toby acknowledges that, according to Elizabeth, life in the city was fairly easy and extremely interesting.

That life lasted only about five months. It ended suddenly one night when she was stopped on the street and challenged by a watchman because she was out later than usual. When the watchman doubted her claim to be one of Mrs. Churo's slaves and seemed about to make trouble for her, Elizabeth decided to tell him the truth—that she was free and had been kidnapped from Pennsylvania. As it turned out, Elizabeth may have been lucky, comparatively speaking, in this encounter with the night watchman. Slaves in New Orleans were required to get off the streets at eight o'clock at night unless they had a special permit; a cannon was fired in the Place d'Armes to let them know that they were no longer allowed outdoors. If a slave was caught out after eight without a permit, he or she could be taken to jail by a watchman to spend the night and await the next morning's punishment. Often that meant a whipping, but for women, it could mean being sent to the workhouse, put on what amounted to a chain gang, and set to work cleaning the streets and markets of the city.[21]

In this case, the watchman did with her what he would have done with any slave who was out too late: he put her into custody—into the "calaboose," according to Elizabeth—until the next morning, when she was taken before a magistrate. Bernard Campbell was summoned to identify her and produce a bill of sale, which, as it turned out, he did not have. The magistrate then sent Elizabeth back to Mrs. Churo's. What happened next is sketched only briefly in Elizabeth's report: "The magistrate afterwards called on Mrs. C., at her house, and had a long talk with her in the parlor. I do not know what he said, as they were by themselves. About a month afterwards, I was sent back to Baltimore."

Since Elizabeth could not have known what transpired in that parlor conversation or what other kinds of transactions went on in the weeks while she waited to see what would become of her, we can know little of them, either. However, it seems likely that the story she told to the watchman and the magistrate created a small crisis, especially after Bernard Campbell could produce no evidence that he had purchased her legally. Here was a young girl who insisted she was a kidnap victim, and the man who bought her in Baltimore and sold her in New Orleans had no documentation that would counter her story. The missing "bill of sale" is a minor detail in Elizabeth's account, but it is surely an important factor in the story of what became of her. The Campbells must have dispensed with a receipt when they purchased Elizabeth from McCreary because they suspected (or perhaps knew) that Elizabeth was free, and they did not want to leave a paper trail by which she might be traced. As for McCreary, he would certainly not want to put his name on the receipt for a girl he had taken by stealth and without a legal warrant.

The magistrate, needing to be cautious in dealing with one of the most important slave traders in his town, apparently took the necessary steps to resolve a problem that he must have encountered many times before. He talked with Mrs. Churo and with Bernard Campbell, arrangements were made to return Elizabeth to Baltimore, and no one got into trouble. Presumably, Mrs. Churo got her money back.

Elizabeth's kidnapping had gone unreported back in Chester County. The man from whose house she was taken, Matthew Donnelly, was apparently part of the abduction scheme and would obviously have kept quiet about her absence. No one else even noticed that she was gone until after Rachel was kidnapped; Beck then decided to check up on her other daughter and discovered that she, too, was missing. In time this news reached Baltimore, where a group of interested Quakers connected the girl missing from Pennsylvania with the girl found in New Orleans, a connection that must have resulted in the magistrate's visit to Mrs. Churo's parlor. And here the trail begins to become clearer. Confronted with the charge that he had sold a kidnapped free girl, Walter Campbell agreed to bring her back to Baltimore, on condition that a bond of $1,500 be posted to compensate him in case it turned out that she really was Henrietta Crocus and not Elizabeth Parker. The funds were raised and provided to Campbell. Just how the money was raised became, like most things connected with the Parker case, a matter of contention: John Miller Dickey would later be credited with finding the money, although a Chester County newspaper wrote at the time that the funds were guaranteed to Campbell by "seven or eight citizens of Baltimore." These would most likely have been Quakers from the city, since they had done exactly this kind of thing before. Whoever was responsible—and it seems probable that both Baltimore and Chester County had a hand in the transaction—Campbell cooperated and arranged to have Elizabeth sent back to Baltimore.[22]

Elizabeth waited in the Campbell pen in New Orleans until the end of June or the beginning of July before there was a ship available to take her back to Maryland. Finally, after a two-week voyage on which her companions were six slaves who were being sent back from New Orleans because, according to Elizabeth, "they were sickly," she arrived in Baltimore. Her return did not, of course, mean a restoration of her freedom or a ticket back to Chester County. No matter what the Quakers, the friends of Joseph Miller, or the New Orleans authorities thought, Luther Schoolfield was still claiming that Elizabeth was his mother-in-law's runaway slave who had been legally apprehended by Thomas McCreary. She was, therefore, immediately sent to the Campbells' Baltimore pen, where she was put to work helping with the cooking: "The table was set out in the yard, and there we had to eat; I had no shoes, and working over a hot stove in the house, and then out on the cold ground in my bare feet gave me a bad cold." Evidently Elizabeth was ill at the time of Rachel's trial, since a Chester County resident who was present commented that she looked "bad—like she had been dragged through a sick cow." Her cold was still troubling her when she was interviewed by Toby.[23]

When news of Elizabeth's arrival reached Chester County, a delegation hurried to Baltimore to confirm her identification. They were able to persuade Campbell to release her to the authorities, who placed her in the city jail, where she joined her sister. Elizabeth said nothing about her reunion with Rachel, but the Philadelphia Female Anti-Slavery Society described it in language worthy of Toby or Mrs. Stowe: "These two sisters, thus parted, met in circumstances so highly tragic, so deeply pathetic, that, were they the theme of a romance, they would thrill the soul of every reader."[24]

While she was in New Orleans, Elizabeth would not have known that Joseph Miller had been killed or that Thomas McCreary had been tried for kidnapping Rachel and found not guilty. (McCreary's trial ended in acquittal on the very day Elizabeth arrived in New Orleans.) She would have been unaware of the many negotiations that had taken place on her behalf. She would not have known that her chance encounter with the night watchman in New Orleans would lead to a series of communications among Baltimore, New Orleans, and Chester County, nor would she have known that dozens of people had become involved in the effort to bring her back to Maryland and restore her freedom. She probably would have been staggered, and presumably pleased, to know how much money had been spent just to get her onto a return ship. She would never have met most of the people involved, and the money that had been changing hands since the day of her abduction would have made little difference to her own immediate comfort or well-being. She would probably not have known exactly why she was being moved around from one kind of jail to another. She certainly would not have known where the next move would take her. She would have had no role to play in any of the negotiations that would determine her fate. All she would know to do, one imagines, was wait and see where she was sent next.

6

BALTIMORE

DECEMBER 31, 1851, was a busier and more stressful day for Francis S. Corkran than he could have imagined, even though he was no stranger to stress.[1] He had gone to the office at his Baltimore lumber business early on that Wednesday morning, perhaps expecting a light day's work on New Year's Eve. By 8:15, his day had become very complicated. Lewis Newcomer, a young fellow Quaker who worked at the post office in Baltimore, showed up at his door saying he had urgent business with Corkran, a story Corkran needed to hear right away. The story Newcomer told was about the kidnapping in Chester County of a girl named Rachel Parker. She and her kidnapper had been spotted at the Perryville train depot by two young men who lived nearby, Eli Haines and his friend Wiley, as they waited to catch the train to Philadelphia.[2]

Eli Haines had known immediately that something was wrong when he saw McCreary at the Perryville depot with a young black girl who was trying to explain that she was free and not a slave. It is possible, even likely, that Haines knew McCreary, or at least recognized him, and knew of his reputation. At any rate, he and Wiley immediately determined to help the distressed girl. They abandoned their Philadelphia plans and instead boarded the same Baltimore-bound train on which McCreary and his captive were traveling. When the train reached the city, they followed McCreary to Campbell's slave pen. With their suspicions about a kidnapping confirmed, they returned to the train station on the assumption that a search party might be following close behind McCreary. They were right: Joseph Miller and his companions arrived on the 5:00 A.M. train.

The seven men who accompanied Miller to Baltimore were an accidental and somewhat ill-assorted posse. None of them suspected when they left home in an attempt to stop a kidnapping that this chase would take them all the way to Baltimore, or that they would not get home again until late the next day. Most of them were Joseph Miller's relatives and neighbors from West Nottingham. Three of them, Lewis Melrath, Jesse Kirk, and Samuel Pollock, had gathered at Miller's house immediately after the kidnapping—angry and determined to do something. Melrath and Kirk were Miller's brothers-in-law. Samuel Pollock and his father, Thomas, were neighbors and, in Nottingham terms, relative newcomers to the county: Thomas was a native of Ireland who had been in West Nottingham for twenty years, for much of that time operating a tavern called the Christiana House. It was the Pollocks who had put up the first resistance to McCreary, just minutes after Rachel was abducted. Melrath, Kirk, Pollock, and Miller consulted briefly and then set off on horseback to find McCreary and Rachel.

Another of Miller's brothers-in-law, Abner Richardson, joined a second group that was gathering at the nearby home of the Quaker farmer Hart Coates. Richardson had gone to the Coates farm to meet William Morris, a neighbor who owed him some money and had come to pay his debt. The news of Rachel's abduction reached the three men at Coates's home. Richardson, Morris, and Coates were soon joined by twenty-five-year-old Benjamin Furness, a Quaker acquaintance of Coates's, who had also heard about the kidnapping and had come to offer his aid. Furness, who lived five miles away in Lancaster County, was in many ways the odd man among the pursuers. He was the only one who was not from Chester County and the only one who was not a friend or relative of Joseph Miller. He also probably had the most personal experience with slave catchers and kidnappers of any in the group. His father, Oliver, had given enough aid to runaways in Lancaster County to earn a reputation as "the fugitive's friend," although he was so quiet about his antislavery work that no one was ever able to document it. But his reputation in the neighborhood was solid. In his history of the Underground Railroad, R. C. Smedley said of Oliver Furness and his family that "theirs were good works quietly accomplished." On that late December day, Benjamin kept up the Furness family tradition of responding to calls for help with no questions asked. He had never heard of Rachel Parker until the day of her kidnapping, and he had never met Joseph Miller until he caught up with him and his party on the road. News of the abduction was brought to him at his home in Little Britain, and that was enough for him. He rode to Hart Coates's farm, where he found Coates, Morris, and Richardson excitedly talking, like everyone else in the neighborhood, about the kidnapping. With Furness now willing to join them, the men set out in hopes of intercepting Rachel and her kidnapper. They rode as far as the train depot at Perryville, a distance of about twelve miles, before deciding to turn around and abandon the search. As they approached Battle Swamp Tavern, however, Coates and his group, heading north toward home, met Miller and his group heading south toward Perryville.[3]

Since Miller and his group were not ready to give up, the men who met at the tavern determined to join forces and press the search farther. Now eight strong, they rode to Perryville (four of them retracing their steps), where the innkeeper told them that they had just missed McCreary; he had been there and had already taken a train for Baltimore. That information was surely frustrating, and it left them with another difficult decision to make. The next train would not leave until 2:00 A.M.; they were in their work clothes; they had brought nothing with them; they were expected home soon. They consulted and agreed that, as much as they wanted to go home, they could not just give up and let the kidnapper go, especially after such a near miss. Had they lost McCreary's trail at this point, surely no one would have blamed them, nor could they have blamed themselves if they had thrown up their hands and considered that they had done all they could. But now they knew McCreary was on the train headed for Baltimore, just ahead of them, and this made a great difference; they had to go, too. They waited for the two o'clock train and boarded it, leaving their horses behind at Perryville.

They were met in the city three hours later by an excited Haines and Wiley with their news about Rachel's whereabouts. The men, most of them new to the city and to the business of chasing down kidnappers, were uncertain what to do next; they had a common purpose but little sense of how to carry it out. Benjamin Furness came up with an idea: he recommended that they enlist the aid of his wife's cousin, Lewis Newcomer, another Quaker from Chester County who had moved to Baltimore not long before. Newcomer might help them find their way around the city, Furness thought. More importantly, Newcomer had brought his strong Pennsylvania Quaker connections with him to the city, and he might know people who could be useful.

Newcomer had recently married Esther Anne Brosius, daughter of Mahlon Brosius, an important Underground Railroad agent in Chester County. Like many others in the county, Brosius made his living as a potter, taking advantage of both the rich clay deposits in the area and a local tradition of Quaker pottery making. He was described by one local historian as typifying "the Chester County trilogy of Quaker, Abolitionist, and Potter." The three attributes were frequently found together for a good reason: potters sent their wares around to country stores in southeastern Pennsylvania and in the northern counties of Maryland's Eastern Shore, and the wagonloads of pottery belonging to Brosius and other members of the "trilogy" sometimes concealed fugitives, hidden in the hay used to protect the pots, who were being sent on to the next agent. (At one point, Brosius and his wife, Mary, accomplished a feat of rescue that became legendary in the county. They received a group of thirty-three fugitives at once; the whole group was fed, bedded in the barn, and successfully guided by night along the twelve miles to the next Quaker refuge.)[4]

The Pennsylvanians were right in thinking that Newcomer, with his Quaker connections and credentials, would be willing and able to help. As soon as he had heard their story, he took it straight to Francis Corkran. Like Newcomer, Corkran was a smart choice and a logical one. He had been called on to help fugitives and kidnapping victims before, and he knew his way around the slave-trading pens and the jails of Baltimore. He had earned his *bona fides* as an antislavery activist in Cambridge, Maryland, on the state's Eastern Shore, where his aid to fugitives had apparently gotten him into deep enough trouble that he thought it prudent to move his family up to Baltimore. In his 1898 account of Underground Railroad activity on the Eastern Shore, William T. Kelley, a fellow Quaker, reported that Corkran had left Caroline County in 1841, when he was twenty-six or twenty-seven, because he was suspected of being an agent and had learned that his life was consequently in danger. Considering Corkran's later antislavery career in Baltimore and the "severe persecution" Kelley says he suffered there, Kelley was willing to declare Corkran "Maryland's greatest Abolitionist," although he gives no specific examples of Corkran's activities. Of his "persecution," Kelley mentions "mobs, clothing torn from his back, loss of many thousands of dollars in costs, and perhaps imprisonment," although again he offers no details. One recent biography of Harriet Tubman identifies Corkran as someone on whom Tubman "relied heavily" for help on her routes around Cambridge. The authors cite no evidence for the identification, however, so their account remains as tantalizing as Kelley's.[5]

After moving to Baltimore, Corkran joined forces with other activist members of the Baltimore Monthly Meeting, including John Needles, Eli Lamb (who would become Corkran's son-in-law), Samuel Townsend, and Elizabeth Townsend Turner. Before the war, while the slave trade in Baltimore was still a thriving business, these and other Quakers were active in policing the traders' pens in search of anyone who had been kidnapped or otherwise did not belong there and needed help in getting out. After emancipation, they were all founding members of the Association in Aid of Freedmen of Maryland; Corkran was its first chairman and probably the moving spirit behind its formation. The Association was organized in 1864 in response to the sudden emancipation of thousands of people in Maryland who were likely to have few resources and no place to go. As their founding document put it, the organizers were concerned that many of these newly freed people "hitherto unaccustomed to provide for themselves will be thrown upon their own resources, and the sudden assumption of the responsibilities attendant upon this new phase of life together with the helplessness of the very young and of the aged may occasion distress, for the relief of which there is no provision made by law." The group ended its activities in 1867, when the stream of indigent and sometimes desperate families was no longer overwhelming. By that point, members of the Association had given hundreds of hours to the work. They had met with nearly two thousand freed persons, distributed two thousand pieces of clothing, and given out $3,000 in aid.[6]

Those numbers represented a significant commitment of resources, including money, which was typical of this group of Baltimore Quakers. The Parker case alone would become very expensive before it was over: the amount of money required to bring Elizabeth Parker home from New Orleans and to provide lawyers and witnesses for the trials of McCreary and Rachel Parker—witnesses who needed food and housing for several days—would have been considerable. The *Baltimore Sun* took note of the significant local contributions at the time of McCreary's trial and shook a finger at the Pennsylvanians: "The costs of prosecution [of McCreary], it may be proper to state, are sustained by a few citizens of this place; those from abroad disavow the least connection with the *financial* department." The *Sun* was only partially right; some of that money was apparently raised in Chester County and a large chunk came from the state of Pennsylvania, but much of it was Baltimore Quaker money. The *Oxford Press* explained that "the costs of the trial were divided, these amounting to $1000, besides $3000 expended by the state of Pennsylvania and heavy outlays by friendly citizens of Baltimore and Chester County." Francis Corkran may have contributed a healthy share of the costs himself, given William Kelley's mention of the "many thousand dollars in costs" he contributed to the antislavery cause. Also typical of these Quakers was their wish to make it clear, in describing the Association in Aid of Freedmen, that their sole object was to supplement the law, not to break it or even to circumvent it. Similarly, when they entered the charged force field around the Parker kidnappings, it was only to help Rachel, Elizabeth, and Joseph Miller and his friends to negotiate within the law.[7]

Corkran and other members of the Baltimore Monthly Meeting generally kept their antislavery activism quiet, for understandable reasons.

Most accounts of the Parker kidnappings, or of antislavery activity in and around Baltimore, do not mention him. He became something of a known figure later, and a largely unpopular one in the city, through his public support for Abraham Lincoln, who was generally detested in Maryland. Corkran was one of only seven voters in his Baltimore district to cast a vote for Lincoln in 1860, and when Lincoln rewarded him for his support by appointing him Collector of the Port of Baltimore in 1861, Corkran became Maryland's first Republican appointee to public office. The appointment did not sit well at home. The *Baltimore Sun* editorialized against it, warning: "If Mr. Lincoln appoint a republican partisan to any office in slaveholding States, it will be inconsistent with his remark that he would make no appointments in such States that would not be generally acceptable to the community." When Corkran's appointment went through anyway, it provoked enough local outrage that Corkran apparently had to make himself scarce once again; according to the *Sun*, he "thought best to leave the city for a few days."[8]

Corkran's political convictions continued to put him in difficult and even dangerous situations. As a member of the Baltimore Republican Committee, he was one of the group who planned to escort Lincoln partway on the ceremonial train journey to Washington for the 1861 inaugural. The Committee traveled to Harrisburg, Pennsylvania, intending to meet Lincoln there and accompany him as far as Baltimore. A huge crowd had gathered to meet Lincoln's train, partly out of curiosity but mainly, according to the (fervently anti-Lincoln) *Sun*, as a show of resistance to Lincoln and especially to "his friends here, whose unpopularity with the great mass of the people is so notorious." As it turned out, unbeknown to everyone including the Republican Committee, Lincoln had been quietly whisked to Washington on an earlier train because of assassination threats in Baltimore. The crowd, deprived of the president, turned its resentment on his reception committee. Corkran and one other committeeman were the primary targets, but "they were protected by the police, and neither of them were injured further than knocking their hats over their eyes." Corkran remained a steadfast supporter of Lincoln, although he and the president would butt heads on the issue of emancipation in Maryland. Since the Emancipation Proclamation applied only to states that had seceded from the union, as Maryland had not, slavery was not abolished there until the state revised its constitution in 1864. Lincoln was determined not to make unpopular appointments in the state that would further alienate his political opponents, which meant he resisted appointing any additional antislavery Republicans. Corkran was frustrated with this policy because he felt it encouraged opposition to the emancipation of Maryland slaves.[9]

Interestingly, Corkran insisted that the real reason for the resistance of local officials to emancipation was that they conflated it with abolitionism, which they despised, considering abolitionists "not worthy of the confidence of any gentleman." It is hardly surprising that Corkran, who had a business to run and a family to support in Maryland, always denied that he was an abolitionist himself. In spite of William Kelley's eulogizing of him after his death as Maryland's greatest abolitionist, Corkran was always careful to distinguish between his efforts on behalf of free blacks on the one hand and, on the other, the aid to fugitive slaves that helped to make abolitionism so reviled in slave states like Maryland. When he was called as a witness in the kidnapping trial of Thomas McCreary, Corkran made a point of distancing himself from abolitionism. This might have been a smart, calculated move, since he knew that admitting to an association with the movement could seriously compromise his credibility with a Maryland jury. More likely, however, Corkran was making an honest statement of the principles that guided his antislavery actions. Acknowledging that he was a member of the Society of Friends, Corkran went on to deny that his Quakerism meant that he was in favor of encouraging slaves to run away or protecting them when they did run—that is, that he was an abolitionist:

> [I] am not nor never was a member of any society formed for the purpose of aiding slaves to obtain their freedom; am decidedly opposed to any interference or clandestine interruption, or any other kind of interruption of the rights of slave-holders in the property of slaves. . . . I have never, to my recollection, doubted the authority of this government to enact such laws as will conduce to its preservation, and in the passage of the Fugitive Slave

Law; regarding it as a step deemed proper by the government, as a good citizen thereof, I could not call, nor did I, such a measure in question.[10]

When in 1863 Corkran was still charged with being an abolitionist, he was defended by a supporter who based his denial of the charge on the implicit assumption that the project of abolitionism required breaking the law. In a letter to the *Daily National Intelligencer*, which he signed as "Baltimore," the supporter explained why Corkran could not be called an abolitionist:

> While he has accomplished perhaps as much as any other man of his age in Maryland, by recourse to law, in rescuing from bondage those who were unjustly deprived of their freedom, he defies the world to prove that he ever interfered by word or act with the legal rights of slaveholders, or gave the slightest encouragement to others to engage in anything of the kind. So uniform and consistent has been his course in that respect that he has secured the friendship and esteem of some of the largest slaveholders in the section of the state in which he resides.

Even Corkran's obituary, written in 1886, paused to straighten out his racial politics for the reader: "Mr. Corkran always showed an active interest in the anti-slavery cause, though not an extreme abolitionist." His wariness about being identified with abolitionism was not unique to him. When Lucretia Mott visited John Needles, Rebecca Sinclair Turner, and others of Corkran's Quaker colleagues in Baltimore—all of whom were active in the antislavery cause and in aid to freedmen—she remarked that the visit was encouraging in every way but one: "All are afraid of too much abolition."[11]

The denials of Corkran's abolitionism were made, by him and others, to protect his reputation and clarify his role in the antislavery effort. No one, including Corkran, denied that he had devoted much time and energy to visiting the slave markets in search of kidnap victims and working to free them before they could be sold. He had a reputation in the city. He knew Walter Campbell and the other traders, and they knew him. Corkran must, in fact, have had a sense of déjà vu when he learned that he was needed to help in the rescue of a Pennsylvania free black girl who had been abducted by McCreary and brought to Baltimore. He and McCreary had very likely crossed paths before. When McCreary had abducted Tom Mitchell from Chester County two years earlier, he had been pursued to Baltimore by two Quakers from the county, one of whom was Mitchell's employer, George Martin (see Chapter 2). Finding himself detained by the authorities in Baltimore, Martin had sent word immediately to two Quakers in the city that he knew would be ready to help: John Needles and a man identified by the *Cecil Democrat* only as "a notorious abolitionist, from somewhere Down East." Given Francis Corkran's origins on the lower Eastern Shore of Maryland, his close association with John Needles, and his reputation in some quarters as a "notorious abolitionist" and in others as a reliable friend to kidnap victims, it is very probable that he was the second man on whom Martin called for aid. It is also probable that Corkran was instrumental in having Mitchell returned to Chester County.[12]

It was a logical decision, therefore, for Lewis Newcomer to come straight to Corkran's office early on that Wednesday morning with news of a kidnap victim who had just been brought to the city. He had learned from Haines and Wiley that the kidnapper was Thomas McCreary, that McCreary claimed Rachel was a slave belonging to Luther Schoolfield, that a group of eight men had also arrived in Baltimore that morning in pursuit of Rachel and McCreary, and that, once they were in town, they had no idea what to do next. Corkran knew at once what they should do: nothing. He wanted first to have a conversation with Schoolfield; it was possible, he thought, that things could be settled quickly and easily before the Pennsylvania farmers got themselves in trouble.

Corkran set off in search of Schoolfield, taking Lewis Newcomer with him. They went first to Schoolfield's lottery office; not finding him there, they tried his home and then walked through the market area near his office, finally locating him at Walter Campbell's slave pen. Corkran calmly proposed a deal to Schoolfield, a way of getting everything settled quickly. If Schoolfield could direct him to "a respectable citizen of Baltimore" who could swear that this girl who had just been brought to Campbell's pen was really Eliza Crocus, a fugitive slave, he would drop the matter entirely and everyone, including McCreary, could go his way peacefully. "I told him I thought, from his countenance, that he would not do that which he thought wrong," Corkran later explained, "and hence my willingness to have this matter amicably adjusted without taking it to court." Corkran then left Schoolfield to consider the challenge.[13]

Corkran's next stop on this frenetic morning was the office of Augustine Pennington, justice of the peace in Baltimore's fifteenth ward. He found a tense group gathered at Pennington's office: Joseph Miller, Thomas McCreary, the trader Walter Campbell, and a fourth man named John O. Price, who would play an obscure but significant role in the events that followed. Price enters this story briefly and then leaves it again, unless he is one of the unidentified figures who later hover in its shadows. He appears to have had several careers, including one as a horse and mule breeder and one as a slave catcher. He must have done well at one or all of his professions, since in 1865 he hosted a fundraiser for a church in Cockeysville, Maryland, which the newspaper described as being held at the "mansion of John O. Price, Esq." He seems to have been a character to be reckoned with; his record invites some comparison to Thomas McCreary's own history. Back in the 1840s he had been charged at least twice with assault, and in the 1850s he was acting as an agent for slaveholders in search of fugitives. Whether Price and McCreary actually worked together in the slave-hunting business is not clear, but the fact that Price was there on the day McCreary was charged and was willing to help supply his bail suggests that their relationship, whatever its nature, was a close one.[14]

If Corkran had hoped to head off trouble by forcing Schoolfield's hand and circumventing the courts and the press, he was too late: by the time he reached Pennington's office, Miller had already filed kidnapping charges against both McCreary and his accomplice John Merritt, and McCreary had been arrested. Getting him arrested had been no easy matter; the report that traveled back to Chester County was that no officer wanted to invite trouble for himself by executing a warrant for the dangerous and apparently well-connected Tom McCreary. Finally one constable agreed, reportedly saying that "he would do it at the risk of his life." Walter Campbell and John Price each put up, on the spot, $300 of the $900 that Pennington set as bail, with McCreary paying the remaining third himself. Pennington also required bond money from Joseph Miller to guarantee that he would show up in court to testify against McCreary. Although Corkran had never met Miller before, he and Lewis Newcomer put up the money for him, probably drawing on Quaker funds. And then things began to heat up in the justice's office. Both Campbell and Price were infuriated by the kidnapping charge against McCreary. Price was especially outraged and angrily accused the Pennsylvanians of being "perjured villains." Francis Corkran did his best to calm the two men, but with little success.[15]

Joseph Miller, by all accounts a shy and unassertive man, must have been bewildered and more than a little anxious by this point. Less than twenty-four hours earlier he had been following a familiar routine, working outside on his farm, while his wife, Rebecca, and "their girl," Rachel, worked in the house. Now he was in a city he did not know, in a state where resentment at the death of Edward Gorsuch still ran high and where Pennsylvanians were generally disliked; he was among furious strangers who were accusing him of lying, with another stranger, a reputed abolitionist, as his only guide through the morass he encountered. He must have wondered more than once whether he made the right choice in getting on the train for Baltimore and bearding the dangerous McCreary in his den. Chasing a kidnapper on the familiar roads of West Nottingham, in the company of family and friends, was one thing; being raged at in a Baltimore magistrate's office was another thing altogether. He would later confide to Abner Richardson that "if he ever got home he would never get in such a scrape again."[16]

At some time in the late morning or early afternoon of that Wednesday, Corkran and Newcomer went back to Campbell's pen to find Rachel. They had been joined by the Quakers John Needles and Samuel Townsend, both of whom were also familiar visitors to the Baltimore slave pens. Needles was known for being especially vigilant toward the slave traders; the memorial published at his death noted that "he would go to the slave pens and ask permission to go through to look for those legally entitled to their freedom; and through his efforts many were set at liberty, to their great joy and his satisfaction." The group of Quakers arrived at the pen just in time to see McCreary leaving with Rachel in a carriage, heading for the Baltimore jail. Since Corkran did not want to let McCreary out of his sight, fearing he might take off with Rachel again to try his luck farther south, he and his colleagues followed McCreary to the jail and waited to see that Rachel was safely deposited there. Corkran then returned to his office, presumably thinking that he had done all he could for Rachel and Joseph Miller and that the sequel was out of his hands. He was wrong.[17]

McCreary had taken Rachel to the jail on Walter Campbell's instructions. On learning that there was a kidnapping charge against McCreary, Campbell had refused to keep Rachel on his premises and demanded that McCreary remove her to the city jail for safekeeping until the charges could be clarified. He recited a familiar mantra: slave catching and kidnapping were very different matters; he fully approved of the former and detested the latter. He would not knowingly accept a kidnap victim for sale. Campbell's cooperation with the law and his denunciation of kidnapping might seem admirable, but they need not be taken as a sign of any particular sensitivity or honesty on his part. He and other Baltimore slave traders were in a highly profitable and highly visible business that required careful attention to their relationship with the public. Slave trading was tolerated in places like Baltimore, and the trader was obviously patronized by enough of the public to keep him in business; on the whole, however, the trader himself was what one Baltimore observer called "a sort of Pariah," one whose profession was useful but generally disliked. Most slaveholders preferred to sell directly to another slaveholder whenever possible, thereby maintaining the fiction that this was a personal rather than a business transaction; going through a "nigger trader" would mean implicitly acknowledging that their slaves were commodities. The traders therefore used as many avenues as they could— cooperating in the return of kidnapped free blacks, fitting out their slaves in new clothes, advertising (truthfully or not) that they did not split up families or sell slaves out of the state—to gain the public goodwill they needed. As a highly successful trader, Campbell would have been practiced in the techniques.[18]

At midafternoon on this confusing day, Joseph Miller appeared at Corkran's office, seeming very nervous. The last twenty-four hours had taken a toll on the whole Chester County party, but especially on him, and he still faced the ordeal of going to the jail and identifying Rachel. He told Corkran that he was afraid of being attacked by proslavery mobs if he went there. The Christiana case was very much on his mind; he worried aloud that, at the least, he might suffer Castner Hanway's fate and be charged with treason. Corkran did his best to calm Miller and put his fears to rest. He tried to assure him that the people of Baltimore were not likely to turn on him for what he had done. As for treason, he could see no grounds for such a charge. Miller just needed to be calm and cautious when he went to the jail. Corkran even got Miller to joke a little about his nervousness. In spite of his reassurances to Miller, however, Corkran was secretly also nervous, as he admitted later. He worried about the safety of these strangers who had put themselves in his hands and about the mood of McCreary and his friends. He thought that Miller needed to get out of Baltimore and back to Pennsylvania as soon as possible.

Corkran thought it best to accompany Miller and the other Pennsylvanians to the jail, where Miller identified Rachel as the young girl who worked for him. By this time, news of McCreary's arrest had spread and, as Miller had feared, a small crowd had gathered outside the jail. Lewis Melrath recalled hearing one of the onlookers say, "There goes them damned abolitionists who murdered Gorsuch." Abner Richardson reported that he heard someone else say he hoped they would all be mobbed before they left. Seeing the possibility for real trouble, Corkran and Newcomer faced the hecklers, and Corkran—Marylander and reputed abolitionist or not—gained the admiration of the local Chester County press by what he did next. The West Chester *Village Record*, identifying Corkran as an "opulent and influential merchant of the city," described him as standing between "our philanthropic band" from Pennsylvania and "the rising tide" of angry threat in Baltimore. Corkran told the excited crowd that "he was a Marylander, but a Dan Webster and a Compromise man all over, and wanted to see justice and law prevail on every side of the line, and advised them to do likewise." Maybe all it took was for Corkran to declare his loyalty to Maryland. At any rate, the conciliatory speech seemed to work, and the trouble that had been brewing did not happen.[19]

When the tense visit to the jail was over, Corkran invited the eight Pennsylvanians to have supper at his home and to stay the night if they wanted. He knew they were exhausted and worried. He also thought they might not have enough money to pay for food at a hotel, much less lodging, and besides, it had begun to rain. The men accepted the supper but declined the invitation to stay overnight; what they all wanted most was to get back to Perryville and their horses and then go home. The entire company seemed to Corkran relaxed and cheerful over supper; they must have felt that their ordeal was over, that they had done well by Miller and Rachel, and that home and a warm bed were within hailing distance. Even Miller struck Corkran as more relaxed than he had been earlier. When his guests' clothes were dry and they were refreshed, Corkran quietly sent an assistant to find an omnibus that could take them, in a group, to the station. He was not at all sure they were as safe in Baltimore as he had protested; he thought it best for them to stay together and keep off the streets as much as possible. Being "mobbed" was a real possibility in this city that had a well-deserved reputation for rowdyism and public violence. In the twelve months of 1849, there had been 566 arrests for mob actions, including disorderly conduct, resisting arrest, and inciting riots. Anger at the Pennsylvanians was already smoldering, and it would not take much to set it off.[20]

Corkran even arranged for the omnibus to take the group by a roundabout way to the train station, where Hart Coates bought the tickets for everyone. They made the trip without incident. The sense of relief they had felt when they were guests in the security of Corkran's home, however, gave way to a return of anxiety once they were on their own. William Morris recalled that, as they were waiting for the train, Miller again looked depressed; he worried that he was going to be charged with treason and hanged. No one tried to interfere with the Pennsylvania party, but Abner Richardson did hear someone comment, as they boarded, that it was "damned well they got in the cars when they did." Even more disconcerting, Thomas McCreary boarded the same train, although he entered a different car. Abner Richardson and Benjamin Furness also noticed a large man boarding, who did get into the same car with them. The man went in and out of the car several times before taking a place by the stove, where he seemed to be watching them. Joseph Miller felt threatened by him. "Do you see that large man there?" he asked Samuel Pollock nervously. "He intends no good for me." The large man on the train joins John O. Price and the bearded man who took part in Elizabeth's kidnapping as shadow figures in this story, McCreary's probable accomplices or partners who managed to avoid both prosecution and public scrutiny. Presumably there were others like them, perhaps many others.[21]

The party had just boarded the train when Miller, who was a heavy smoker, took out a cigar and lit it. The large man then moved over to Miller and tapped him on the shoulder. According to one report, he reminded Miller that smoking was prohibited on the train; another witness thought the man asked Miller to come outside with him. Whatever was said, Miller moved out to the platform, in spite of his friends urging him not to leave the car. William Morris called out to him not to go, but it did no good. After about two minutes, Abner Richardson and Jesse Kirk, feeling concerned, followed him out to the platform. Miller was nowhere to be seen. Very shortly after, the train began to move. Miller's friends, by now very concerned, decided they should search the whole train. They sent Eli Haines's friend Wiley to do the searching, since he might not be recognized; because he had the least connection to the kidnapping and the arrest of McCreary, he was believed to be in the least danger. Wiley returned to report that Miller was not on the train.

When the train reached Havre de Grace, a ferry ride across the river from Perryville, the worried Pennsylvania party searched the train again, with no success. The best they could imagine, and hope, was that the train had left without Miller and he had been stranded in Baltimore. They decided that someone had to go back to Baltimore and try to reconstruct Miller's moves; the rest would go home and wait for news. No one knew what else to do. Jesse Kirk and Abner Richardson, two of Miller's brothers-in-law, agreed to go back to the city. They boarded the next Baltimore-bound train. To their distress, so did McCreary and the mysterious large man—together, this time.

Kirk and Richardson arrived in the city very late at night; because they were both exhausted and frightened, they went straight to the first hotel they could find and locked themselves in a room. They had not seen McCreary and his ominous companion again, but the presence of those two on the train must have been deeply unsettling, especially since they seemed to be following the Pennsylvania group. The next day, Thursday, January 1, not knowing what else to do and fearing for their own safety, Kirk and Richardson sought out Francis Corkran first thing. This time, Corkran found himself not knowing what to do either, and he was worried. Hearing that Miller was missing made him rethink their conversations of the previous day, when Miller had admitted that he was afraid for his life and Corkran had tried to jolly him out of his fears. What had happened after he saw Miller off? Corkran ran through all the possibilities he could think of. Maybe he had panicked at the thought of getting on the train with McCreary, or had feared traveling all the way home at night and had decided to wait for a day train. Or, possibly, someone had decided to separate him from his companions and had found a reason to have him arrested. He might even have let his fears make him a little crazy, and run off or hidden himself somewhere. Given these possible scenarios, the only two places where it seemed logical to search were the jail and the train station. Corkran sent Kirk and Richardson to the jail, and he went off to the station. Once he was there, all he could do was ask around. Had anyone seen a man wandering around the depot after the train left last night? There had been someone, a man wearing spectacles. Miller did not wear spectacles. No one else had been seen.

Kirk and Richardson did not turn up any information, either. Miller had simply disappeared. With no more places to search, Corkran sent the two men back to Chester County and an anxiously waiting community with the bad news that Miller still could not be found. The word spread quickly around West Nottingham; now everyone wanted to do something purposeful, to stop waiting, worrying, and rushing from house to house. Meetings were held that same Thursday night; they drew crowds.

At one meeting, the recommendation with the most support was that a posse should be organized, armed, and sent to find Thomas McCreary and lynch him on the spot. It was with some difficulty that the sentiment for a lynching was toned down and a new plan formed, to send a group of men back to Baltimore to exhaust every possibility in a new search for Miller. Twenty men quickly volunteered to go. They met at Lewis Melrath's house on Friday, intending to travel together to the city.

Before they could leave, however, the stagecoach driver from Perryville arrived with a letter that changed everything. It was from Francis Corkran, addressed to Abner Richardson:

> Esteemed Friend: I have to convey to thee the melancholy intelligence that the body of Joseph C. Miller was found this morning, about two miles from Stemmer's Run, near the Philadelphia Railroad landing. It was interred at the place it was found; but by all means his friends should come on and have it taken up and examined so as to know how he came to his death. I hope this will be attended to at once.—They should labor under no fear as to bodily injury by any persons here. I can assure thee they will not be molested. Please move in this matter at once.[22]

Miller's friends and family had feared for his life, but they had not imagined anything like this humiliating, lonely death and burial. It was worse than even Miller had feared. One county resident who was with Miller's wife and children when the news was brought to them reported that "such a scene of distress I hope it may never again be my lot to witness; it was heart-rending in the extreme."[23]

The men who had been planning to travel to Baltimore to search for Joseph Miller now had other, even more distressing reasons to go. They needed to retrieve his body and bring it home, they needed to find out what happened to him, and they needed for someone to get started making sure that justice was done. They were certain Miller had been murdered, and they were fairly certain Thomas McCreary was the man responsible. So a delegation did go to Baltimore, on the same Friday that the body was found, but if they had expected to find sympathy in the city and support for their outrage and their grief, they were wrong. The news about Miller that had reached them in Chester County had also reached Baltimore, and it was news indeed. The report that the body of the man who turned in Thomas McCreary for kidnapping had been found at Stemmer's Run produced what the newspapers liked to call "great excitement." No one knew yet exactly what had happened, but everyone was interested, and people definitely had opinions. The *Baltimore Sun* immediately declared the death a suicide and almost automatically invoked Christiana. Miller's death, the paper explained, was due to the "rashness and temerity" of a "most remarkably timid man" who had been spooked by the possibility of treason charges, "of which so much has been lately heard in Pennsylvania." The Chester County men, all of whom lived almost within shouting distance of Christiana, knew as soon as they reached the city that they had best keep their presence as quiet as possible, get their business done, and go home.[24]

Whether or not the threat of violence against them was real, their fear of it was. Whether or not they wanted to be drawn into the bitter interstate conflict that had been intensified by the Gorsuch killing, they were smack in the middle of it. Baltimore had become for them a frighteningly foreign place, as Francis Corkran clearly understood. Keeping their presence quiet meant tucking themselves into a hotel and staying there, off the streets of Baltimore. That much they were able to do. But how would they get their business done? This time their primary local contact was another Pennsylvania Quaker who had recently moved to Baltimore, Levi K. Brown. Born in Lancaster County, where he recalled going to school occasionally with Rachel and Elizabeth's mother, Brown had spent much of his working life in Chester County and retained many attachments and loyalties there. He ran a store in Oxford, owned a store and a temperance hotel in West Chester, and was postmaster of Oxford for a while.

Like Lewis Newcomer, Brown quickly became part of the Baltimore Quaker network once he moved to the city. When the group from Chester County called on him for help, he was there to steer them through what turned out to be an extraordinarily difficult and vexing time. In true Quaker fashion, Brown appears to have done his work both quietly and efficiently. However, because he was never required to give detailed testimony to any of the juries investigating the kidnapping of Rachel or the death of Miller, there is little evidence of exactly how he went about helping the Pennsylvanians get through their grim business. The newspaper in Oxford, praising local residents who took an active interest in Rachel's welfare, noted only that "Levi K. Brown of Lancaster County was also active in the matter and rendered much valuable assistance." Given the amount of help, both financial and practical, that was provided to the Parker sisters and to Joseph Miller's friends, and given the organizational strength of the Baltimore Quakers, it seems certain that there were other Quakers who helped out but whose names are even less in evidence than Levi Brown's. A Chester County resident who followed closely the kidnappings, the murder, and the various outcomes remarked years later that "the Society of Friends in Baltimore took the matter in hand and many other worthy citizens belonging to the Presbyterian Church and others lent their aid and influence." The clear implication is that Corkran and Brown had significant help from other Quakers in the city, but their names and their contributions remain unspecified.[25]

Brown may have urged the Pennsylvanians to remain out of sight of Baltimore's "rowdies," or they may have made that decision themselves. Either way, they stayed inside their hotel until after dark, when Brown led them the nine miles out to Stemmer's Run. There they found Miller's body buried two feet deep, in a wooden box with a badly fitting lid that had allowed the dirt to sift in around the body. By this point, they must have learned at least something of how and why the body had undergone that crude burial, but they could not know the full story until sometime later, after they had done all they could to get Miller home to Chester County and bury him properly. The story, as it turned out, was just the kind the newspapers could hardly get enough of.

When Miller's body was first found on that Friday morning, January 2, he was tied to the branch of a small tree by two handkerchiefs knotted together, one around his neck and the second around a branch of the tree. The branch from which he hung was no more than five feet high; both of Miller's feet rested on the ground. As soon as the men who found him realized that he was well beyond being revived, they sent for the county coroner, William H. Gittings (critics of the proceedings would later make a point of noting that Gittings was a tavern keeper, as if that information cast doubt on his reliability). It was about midday when Gittings got the summons; he had just returned from Baltimore and eaten his dinner when he had to set out on the seven-mile trip from his house to Stemmer's Run. He found the body still tied to the tree—a sapling, really, only about two and a half inches in diameter—by two handkerchiefs. Miller's feet were on the ground, his knees bent; he had a small twig in his mouth. The coroner could see no signs of a struggle in the area. The local constable had already summoned a jury for an inquest, so Gittings had the body cut down and proceeded immediately with his examination of the body and the site. He found that the teeth of the corpse were closed on the twig, but not very firmly. There was no blood, the tongue was not protruding, and the face appeared natural. The entire weight of the body, he thought, seemed held by the handkerchief about its neck.

It was getting late by the time the jury was assembled and sworn in. Coroner Gittings presented his findings to them, describing only the appearance and the situation of the body as he found it. There was no mention of marks on the body. Nor was there any mention of how Miller came to be at Stemmer's Run, and apparently no contesting of the coroner's explanation that Miller had somehow managed to hang himself from a small branch five feet from the ground. It was late in the evening when Gittings reached his astonishing conclusion: Miller had committed suicide by tying himself to the tree—by the neck, five feet off the ground—and throwing his feet out from under him. The jury, in obvious disregard of the evidence, returned a verdict of death by suicide, and the body was hastily buried in a makeshift coffin, a few feet from where it was found. The coroner and the jury then went home.[26]

Sometime even later that evening, Levi Brown and the men from Pennsylvania arrived and began digging up the body. They took it, in its rough box, back to Baltimore, where they intended to procure a proper coffin and then transport the body back to West Nottingham. However, they could not find an undertaker in Baltimore who would agree to accept the body, even long enough for a coffin to be built. Apparently, no undertaker or coffin maker wanted anything to do with the man who had turned in Thomas McCreary or with his friends and relations, who were from Pennsylvania and traveled with Quakers. The Pennsylvanians were learning that they were not going to find much help in Baltimore, not after Christiana and Gorsuch. The Quakers in the city were able, somehow, to provide a temporary vault for the body and then to secure a coffin, allowing William Morris and Abner Richardson to start for home, on the train, with the body. When they reached Perryville they found, once again, that no one was willing to help them. They were forced to leave the coffin in an abandoned sawmill at Perryville and set out on foot, on a January night with snow on the ground, looking for a way to get themselves and their burden home safely. They had no choice but to walk the five cold miles to Port Deposit, where they were finally able to procure a horse and sled.

That is what happened. It took a while, however, for West Chester's *Village Record* to sort out what happened from what was rumored to have happened. The first stories published by the paper were truly disquieting. It initially reported that Morris and Richardson had found Miller's grave, but that Miller was not in it. The paper had an explanation that reflected the inflammatory stories making their way around the county: "It is the prevailing opinion that [the body] has been dug up by these black-hearted wretches and sold to the doctors for dissection." In fact, Morris and Richardson returned home safely with the body, which was buried in the cemetery at House's Meeting House in West Nottingham, the Millers' family church.[27]

The body remained in House's cemetery less than a week, however, before it was disturbed. The governor of Maryland made the surprise announcement that a second examination needed to be held, one that he promised would be more thorough and more official than the first, hasty one. A requisition was therefore made for the body, and the inquest was set for Saturday, January 10, at Starr's Tavern in the north of Baltimore County. Miller's family and friends complied very reluctantly with the governor's request. They were far from satisfied with the first results and thought a second examination of the body was needed. At the same time, they had understandable questions about why the governor of Maryland would take an action that seemed, at first blush, so friendly and accommodating to Pennsylvania. There was widespread suspicion in Chester County that the second inquest was a put-up job, probably instigated by Thomas McCreary, to confirm the first results and quiet any rumors about murder.

The antislavery press in Pennsylvania agreed that it was very hard to explain the new inquest unless it was part of a plan by Maryland officials to make sure the truth about Miller's death remained hidden. The *Pennsylvania Freeman* refused to accept the verdict of suicide from the first inquest but was not prepared to trust any subsequent inquest that might be held in Maryland, "well knowing from frequent observation of similar investigations, the degree of thoroughness . . . which such cases get in slaveholding communities, when our 'peculiar institution' (to say nothing of Southern reputation) happens to be involved even indirectly." The Baltimore newspapers were equally puzzled but, being reluctant to second-guess the governor, were more cautious in their statements. The *Argus* commented only that the second inquest was being held because "there are some who suspect the agency of murderous means in bringing about this fatal result." The *Sun*, which had originally called the death a "distressing case of suicide," now concurred that the results of the first inquest had not satisfied everyone, for admittedly good reasons: "There is a mystery connected with [Miller's] death and the circumstances attending it, which we would gladly see resolved satisfactorily." Even the *Cecil Whig*, which had steadfastly blamed McCreary's legal troubles on the meddling of Pennsylvania abolitionists, found this a perplexing case. "Some think that, fearing the consequences of the false oath which they allege [Miller] took, like the conscience-smitten Judas, he went away and hanged himself. Others that he was seized and hung by the avengers of the murdered Gorsuch." The *Whig* did not find either theory convincing and, like the *Sun*, could conclude only that "much mystery" still surrounded the case.[28]

Miller's body was disinterred and sent to Baltimore on Friday, January 9. It was accompanied by James Mullen, one of Miller's farmer neighbors, who stayed with it overnight at the Baltimore train depot. On Saturday morning the body was taken to Starr's Tavern, a psychologically significant site chosen specifically because of its location not far from Edward Gorsuch's farm. The inquest was presided over by George M. Hiss, a justice of the peace who was serving as acting coroner. Dr. Benjamin Woods was designated to perform the examination; a jury was summoned and sworn in, and witnesses were called, from Chester County and from Baltimore. Those who made the trip from Chester County included five of the original group that had accompanied Miller on that first determined dash to Baltimore in pursuit of McCreary, including Abner Richardson and William Morris.

At two o'clock on that Saturday, George Hiss got things going. The body was produced and removed from the coffin, in front of the jury and the onlookers. It was not a quiet proceeding. The *Pennsylvania Freeman* reported that some of the crowd that had pressed into the room had to be ejected by the coroner because of their "threats of violence towards the Pennsylvania witnesses, and their ungentlemanly bearing towards even Baltimoreans!" An account of the inquest written years later by an anonymous resident of Chester County, who was clearly still outraged by the proceedings, added that "a great crowd of rowdies attended, who occupied their time drinking whiskey and cursing the Pennsylvania abolitionists." These stories, however, did not appear in the coverage provided by the *Baltimore Sun*, whose reporter focused on providing the graphic details of the proceedings followed by the moral reflections that justified sharing such grisly information with the public. Opening the coffin revealed what the reporter called "one of the most revolting scenes which we have ever beheld." The body was frozen, covered in mud and dirt, and the clothes were tattered. Things only got worse when the clothes were removed to reveal the "stiffened and haggard corpse," the sight of which must have "proven a most solemn and impressive lesson regarding the shortness and vanity of the present life to those who gazed upon it."[29]

Dr. Woods then began his examination of the body. As he worked, he kept assuring the jury that he could see nothing that indicated violence to the living person. The examination was thorough but, like the one performed by Coroner Gittings, only external; no attempt was made to examine any internal organs. When the doctor had finished, he and

James Mullen wrapped the body in clean linens furnished by the proprietor of the tavern and replaced it in the coffin. Hiss took the jury into another room and gave them some unusually pointed instructions. He wanted them to sift the evidence very carefully because, as the *Sun* explained, "it was obvious that there was a strong sectional feeling concerning the case; the citizens of an adjoining state entertained ill feelings in the matter: and he therefore would again caution them as to the verdict they would render."[30]

The jury then began to hear testimony, beginning with Dr. Woods. The appearance of the body, he said, was natural; there was nothing unusual about it, internally or externally. The neck was not broken, which indicated that he probably died from strangulation. There were bruises on the hips, but those were probably caused by the handling of the body after death. Other marks on the body could have been the result of the chafing of clothes on the frozen flesh. The only suspicious marks that Dr. Woods could see were on the wrists: two similar indentations, one on each wrist, that could have been produced by handcuffs. They could also, however, have been produced by the victim himself, if he had instinctively thrown his hands back against the tree when he fell forward. The marks were only suspicious, the doctor warned the jury, and not conclusive evidence of anything. In short, while Woods instructed the jury—with the press present and taking notes—to be especially conscientious and objective because of the political significance the inquest had taken on, he also came very close to instructing them to find no evidence of foul play.

William Gittings next reported on his prior examination of the body and repeated his conviction that Miller's death was a suicide. The Pennsylvania witnesses were then asked, one by one, to recount the events of the Wednesday evening, from the time they boarded the train with Miller to make the return trip from Baltimore to the time they reached Havre de Grace and concluded that Miller was no longer on the train. All gave their version of the events, concurring that Miller had walked off the train only minutes after the group had entered it. Francis Corkran also testified, detailing his conversations with Miller and his activities on the day Miller spent in Baltimore. The final witness called was

The cemetery at Union ME Church in West Nottingham,
formerly House's Meeting House, showing the graves of Joseph Miller;
his wife, Rebecca; and two of their daughters.
(Photo by the author.)

Luther Schoolfield, who was asked to confirm or deny a rumor making
the rounds. According to the rumor, Schoolfield, on hearing of Miller's
death, had gone straight to the offices of the *Baltimore Sun*, where he
told a reporter that Miller had left the train at Stemmer's Run. That
version of things contradicted the testimonies of the witnesses from
Pennsylvania, who placed Miller's departure from the train back in Baltimore. But Schoolfield's story provided convenient support for the suicide theory. It might make some sense if Miller had gotten off the train
at Stemmer's Run and immediately killed himself. It was a lot harder to
believe that he got off in Baltimore, walked nine miles along the tracks
to Stemmer's Run, and then tied himself to the tree. Schoolfield, not
surprisingly, vehemently denied that he had told anyone from the *Sun*
anything about the case. (No one in Pennsylvania would believe him.)

George Hiss then dismissed the jury until Monday, cautioning them not to discuss the case with anyone. When they reconvened, the jury rendered the verdict that would confirm the suspicions in Chester County about a put-up job: death by suicide. No one, including Thomas McCreary, would be charged with murder. Joseph Miller's body was taken to West Nottingham and reburied in the churchyard at House's Meeting House. It was his third burial. It would not be his last.

7

LEGAL JUSTICE

WHILE THE ATTENTION of the press was focused primarily on the question of how Joseph Miller died, Thomas McCreary's kidnapping trial was being prepared for in Baltimore. There was no question that McCreary had taken Rachel Parker, by force, from Joseph Miller's home. There were plenty of witnesses to confirm the abduction. The important questions, for both the prosecution and the defense, were less easily answered. Was the girl now in the Baltimore jail Rachel Parker, a free person, or was she Eliza Crocus, an escaped slave? If she was Rachel Parker, as she claimed, did McCreary take her knowing she was free, in which case he was guilty of kidnapping? Or did he really believe that in taking Elizabeth and Rachel Parker to Baltimore he was actually returning Henrietta and Eliza Crocus to their legal owner? The first matter to be settled at the trial before any other determinations could be made was whether Rachel was slave or free—that is, whether she was Rachel or Eliza.

Eliza and Henrietta Crocus and their mother, Juno, were roughly the same ages as Rachel, Elizabeth, and Rebecca Parker. Like the Parker sisters, Eliza and Henrietta Crocus had been separated from their mother when they were quite young. All three of the Crocus women had been slaves in the family of Hannah Dickehut, the mother-in-law of Luther Schoolfield.

Hannah had purchased them from her daughter, a Mrs. Hynson, who died in 1847. When Hannah Dickehut moved in with the family of her other daughter, Elizabeth Schoolfield, she took Juno with her but bound out the two girls to other people. Eight-year-old Eliza went first to a Mrs. McGinnis and after that to an older woman named Susannah Martin. She remained with Mrs. Martin from December 1844 until April 1847, when she and the rest of her family ran away.

The girls' father, Allen Crocus, was a free man who worked for many years maintaining the lights at the North Point lighthouse in Baltimore. Both he and Juno came to visit Eliza frequently while she was living with Susannah Martin. Eliza also visited her mother three or four times a year at the Schoolfields' home. One Sunday night, Juno came to Susannah Martin's door with the story of an emergency: Allen Crocus had broken a blood vessel and was dying, and Juno wanted to take Eliza to see him before he died. The sympathetic Martin immediately gave her permission for Eliza to go with her mother, and that was the last she saw of either of them. Allen and Henrietta Crocus also disappeared, the whole family apparently making a successful escape from Maryland. Like many other fugitives, they simply vanished. Now, four years later, Thomas McCreary and Luther Schoolfield were claiming that Eliza had been found and was back in Baltimore, safely sequestered in the city jail.

McCreary's trial for kidnapping was set to begin on January 7. The question of Rachel's identity—slave or free—was at the top of the agenda for both prosecution and defense, since McCreary's fate hinged on that question. Because Maryland law did not allow blacks to testify against whites (although they could testify *for* them), what Rachel said about her identity or her freedom or her treatment by McCreary did not matter; it was not admissible in court. Rachel had no recourse, either, when Schoolfield decided that she should remain in the Baltimore jail until McCreary's trial was over and her legal status was determined. Her Quaker supporters in the city, who had become accustomed to speaking and acting on behalf of black people who were silenced or immobilized by the laws of the state, first asked that she be released on bond, which they offered to pay. When that request was denied by the magistrate, they asked Schoolfield if, since he was claiming that Rachel belonged to him, he would at least remove her from jail and take her to his home until she could be tried. Schoolfield refused, offering a reason that might not have been very persuasive but that was politically canny for that particular moment in Baltimore: he was afraid, he said, that the abolitionists from Pennsylvania would come and steal her. She would be better off remaining in jail.

So began Rachel's year-long acquaintance with the Baltimore city jail, a facility that was used primarily for holding persons like the Parkers—Elizabeth joined her sister six months later—who were awaiting trial. Unlike the Parkers, however, most of the detainees waited only a short time for their court date. The turnover rate was generally high; during the year the Parkers were confined (1852), over 2,000 people were admitted to the jail, whereas the average daily occupancy rate was just over 100. The coming and going of inmates was therefore constant. Those admitted during the year included 148 black women and 4 black girls. Three of the 4 girls, including Rachel and Elizabeth, were being held for "safekeeping." Sixteen white men were also held on this charge, as well as 8 black women. In their annual report for 1852, the jail's Board of Visitors noted that the facility had only twelve rooms to accommodate the prisoners, whose numbers occasionally rose to as many as 140. The Board decried the overcrowded conditions, as it had done in previous reports, remarking that anyone who visited the jail would find it "debasing and demoralizing," especially in a city whose citizenry were "proverbial for their generous philanthropy and for Christian zeal." Members of the Board were especially concerned about those people who were being confined until they could be tried and who might be entirely innocent; they were bound to be "degraded" by their close and prolonged contact with the more "vicious" inmates. The specific cases of Rachel and Elizabeth apparently troubled the Board, since their report called attention to the plight of inmates who had been awaiting trial for an inordinately long time, "some as long as 12 months [such as Rachel], and others from 5 to 10 months [such as Elizabeth]." While hundreds of people came and went over the course of the year, the Parkers stayed and waited.[1]

Luther Schoolfield spent a lot of time at the Baltimore jail in the days before the trial. It was at the jail that Francis Corkran had found him, on the day Joseph Miller and his companions had first arrived in the city, and it was there that Corkran had challenged Schoolfield to find one respectable citizen of Baltimore who would swear that Rachel was actually Eliza Crocus. The day after the challenge, January 1, Schoolfield set out to find that person. That was also the day that Jesse Kirk and Abner Richardson came back to Corkran to report that Joseph Miller had gone missing from the train. While Corkran was busy helping the men from Chester County in their search for Miller, therefore, Schoolfield was busy with his own search, looking for that respectable citizen who would confirm his claim to ownership of the young woman he called Eliza Crocus.

Schoolfield went directly to the jail on that Thursday morning, to request that he be allowed to take Rachel out so that he could have her identified more easily. The warden thought it was an unusual request but granted it on condition that Schoolfield bring a deputy along. Schoolfield, agreeing with the condition, took Rachel to the home of Susannah Martin, the woman for whom Eliza Crocus had worked. Seven or eight other women were gathered there when they arrived, evidently having been summoned by Schoolfield. He stood Rachel in front of the parlor full of women and asked Mrs. Martin if she knew the girl. The elderly Martin hesitated; she could not be sure. Schoolfield tried again, this time asking Martin if Rachel *looked* like Eliza. Martin acknowledged that there was a resemblance, especially about the forehead, but again she dithered. She could not swear that this was Eliza Crocus. Martin's granddaughter, Jane Needles, then spoke up. She had been living with her grandparents when Eliza worked for them, and she remembered the girl clearly. The person Luther Schoolfield brought in to her grandmother's parlor, she said, was not anyone she knew. It was not Eliza Crocus. She was sure.

Schoolfield turned next to another woman in the room, Mrs. McGinnis, in whose home Eliza had lived before going to Susannah Martin's. Mrs. McGinnis said she thought the young woman with Schoolfield was Eliza Crocus. When pushed to say how she knew her, McGinnis mentioned her prominent mouth, her pigeon-toed walk, and the fact that one shoulder was higher than the other. The other women in the room then began to offer their opinions. Some of them had not even known Eliza, but all had known her mother, Juno. Some said they *thought* Rachel was Eliza; others said they *thought* she was not. No one was really sure either way. Schoolfield, who must have been very frustrated and annoyed by the waffling of his potential witnesses, then took Rachel away. Before he left, he alerted the women that some of them would probably be summoned to testify in court. Their response to his announcement was unanimous: no. They would not go to court. There would be no point, they said, since they could not swear to anything. (As it turned out, both Susannah Martin and Jane Needles did end up testifying at McCreary's trial, but not for the defense. They were called by the prosecution and both swore that Rachel was not Eliza.)[2]

The trial was set to begin less than a week after Schoolfield's interviews. Since most of the women gathered at Susannah Martin's house refused to swear that Rachel was really Eliza, Schoolfield and the defense had work to do: they needed more, and better, witnesses. Before the trial was over, they had found eight, including three members of Schoolfield's family and two people who had never seen Eliza Crocus in their lives but knew her mother slightly. The prosecution would produce fifteen witnesses, eleven of them Chester County residents who would testify to having known Rachel and her family for years.

After his failure at Susannah Martin's, Schoolfield's next strategy was taking people to the jail to ask them to identify the girl he called Eliza Crocus. A total of seven people went at his request, including his wife, Elizabeth; his son, William Henry; and his mother-in-law, Hannah Dickehut. The others were Sarah Johnson, a dressmaker who had lived with Mrs. Hynson while Juno worked for her; Patrick Lynch, who knew Allen Crocus well and Juno slightly but had never seen Eliza; and William Blandel, who sold shoes to Juno and her children at his shop, which had been closed for more than eight years. There was an eighth visitor to the jail, who was not brought there by Schoolfield. William Hopkins, a Quaker, had known Allen and Juno but had never seen Eliza before. He had read about the case in the newspapers and decided to find out the truth about this Eliza-claiming-to-be-Rachel for himself. He went to the jail without prompting from anyone, viewed a row of eight or nine girls who were brought to him, pointed to one, and asked the warden if that was Eliza. The warden said it was. On the basis of that identification, and this time in defiance of the work of the other Baltimore Quakers on Rachel's behalf, Hopkins agreed to testify for the defense.

Fifteen-year-old William Schoolfield seems to have been dragged kicking and screaming to the jail by his father. Luther Schoolfield had taken him into a room where a group of female inmates had been gathered; he told his son to pick out Eliza from the group. William examined all of the women and reportedly chose Rachel. When asked about that jail visit at the trial, William was, in good adolescent fashion, somewhat surly and generally uncooperative. He testified that he had said nothing to the rest of the family about his experience at the jail, either that evening or the next day, and he recalled no conversation at home about the kidnapping or the trial. William saw nothing unusual about his diffident attitude; he had not talked about his visit to the jail, he explained, "[because] I did not feel any particular interest in the girl's arrest, and I did not tell them when I got home, because I knew that father would tell them if he wanted them to know." Young William was obviously a reluctant witness, but at least he could claim to have identified Rachel as Eliza, without—according to William—any prompting from his father.[3]

Elizabeth Schoolfield, Hannah Dickehut, and Sarah Johnson also visited the jail, also accompanied by Luther Schoolfield. In each of their cases, Rachel was brought to them alone, rather than as part of a group. Schoolfield asked each of the women if she recognized the person before her as Eliza Crocus, and each said she did. Sarah Johnson later explained that, in her profession as a fashionable dressmaker, she was particularly attuned to the "shapes and forms" of people. When she saw Rachel at the jail, she "was confident" that she was seeing Eliza: "Her shape and manner of standing strengthened my belief as to her identity." Rachel explained to each of the women that her name was Rachel Parker, that she had been born in Pennsylvania, and that most recently she had been living with Joseph Miller in West Nottingham. It did not matter: all three continued to insist that she was Eliza Crocus. Schoolfield also brought to the jail William Bandel, the shoe seller, and Patrick Lynch, who had known Allen Crocus. Bandel "looked at the girl in the jail some time" and became increasingly convinced that he was seeing Eliza, "especially when she walked across the floor." Patrick Lynch, according to his own testimony, requested that he be shown a "number of girls together" so that he could try to pick out the right one. When a group was brought to him, he pointed to Rachel; the warden told him he had got it right.[4]

By the time the case came to trial, it had become freighted with so much political, especially sectional, significance that the real issue for the interested public was not whether justice would be done or the truth established but which side would get revenge on the other. Both sides brought the heaviest hitters they could find to the contest. Rachel's supporters had secured the services of two prominent Baltimore lawyers, William Henry Norris and Davis H. Hoopes, both of them strategic choices. Norris had acquired some immunity from political attack in Maryland by virtue of being a slaveholder and having earned the respect of the proslavery *Baltimore Sun*, which called him a man of "personal and professional honor, purity, independence, fearlessness, and incapability of corruption." Davis Hoopes also brought a conveniently balanced résumé to the trial. He was a native of Chester County but had spent years living and working in Mississippi, one of the most committed slave states in the Union, where he had been a judge and a state senator. Both lawyers would therefore be hard to discredit on the grounds of antislavery bias.[5]

To face off against the two prosecuting attorneys, the defense brought in no less than five of its own, in addition to the state's attorney: William P. Preston, William P. Maulsby, Otho Scott, Philip Thomas, and Charles H. Pitts. They made an imposing team, especially the first three. Preston, Maulsby, and Scott all had high-profile political careers in addition to their legal ones, and all three had worked together in the past. The *North American* called them "old political and personal friends, as well as eminent talent." Maulsby and Scott were both members of the Maryland state senate in 1843, and Maulsby, who declined an attempt to get him to run for governor in 1849, would go on to become president of the Chesapeake and Ohio Canal in 1856. Scott was put in charge of arranging and systematizing the Maryland code in 1861. Preston would become a Democratic candidate for the U.S. Congress from Maryland's third district in 1859. (His candidacy would give him firsthand experience of Baltimore's notorious "rowdies": when he visited the polls on election day, he was seriously injured by a blow on the back of his head from a slingshot and another blow to his nose from a pair of brass knuckles.)[6]

The trial opened on January 7, with Justice Pennington presiding and the courtroom packed with onlookers. As the *Baltimore Sun* put it, the trial "attracted a crowded auditory." The first three days produced testimony from eleven Pennsylvania witnesses, whose combined accounts affirmed that the girl in the jail was Rachel Parker, the daughter of Rebecca and Ned Parker—both free—and that she had been born in Chester County, Pennsylvania, had grown up there, and had most recently worked for Joseph Miller. Several of these witnesses had visited the girl that McCreary had brought to the Baltimore jail and were willing to swear that she was Rachel Parker. The prosecution also called as witnesses two of the Baltimoreans whom Schoolfield had tried to recruit for the defense, Susannah Martin and Jane Needles. Needles swore that the girl Luther Schoolfield asked her to identify as Eliza Crocus was in fact a stranger; she had never seen her before. Susannah Martin got off to a bad start when she took the stand. The *Sun* explained that she was "a most respectable and venerable lady" who was "much trepidated at the commencement of her testimony." Evidently because of her trepidation, Martin began by saying that Eliza Crocus was bound out to her by Hannah Dickehut about 1801. The obvious error in the date sent the lawyers for both sides into a huddle that lasted for an hour, as they debated whether the testimony of this addled witness could be allowed. It was finally allowed, and Martin went on to say that she could not see any convincing likeness between the girl who had worked for her—and run away from her—and the girl that Luther Schoolfield had brought to her house.[7]

The defense began calling witnesses on the third day, beginning with Schoolfield's son and wife as well as Sarah Johnson. These three witnesses put in motion an obviously prearranged argument that would be picked up and carried on by nearly everyone who took the stand to claim that Rachel Parker was actually Eliza Crocus, whether they had any recollection of Eliza or not. They all testified that the girl they saw at the jail bore such a strong resemblance to Juno Crocus, whom they did remember, that she had to be Juno's daughter. William Henry School-field testified that Eliza used to come and visit Juno occasionally when Juno lived with his family. He did not remember Eliza well at all, but he recognized her because "she has a rather funny mouth; it sticks out like her mother's," and she sounded like Juno: "Her manner of speaking was like her mother; she talked very fast also, like her mother." Elizabeth Schoolfield offered a similar testimony. She admitted that although she had glimpsed Eliza when she came to visit Juno, "I never noticed her particularly" at that time. She did, however, take particular notice of the girl at the jail: "The resemblance between the child and her mother is remarkable; she also resemble[s] her father in a measure, but more partic-ularly her mother; her mother had a peculiar way of walking and stand-ing; I can scarcely describe it; the child or girl at the jail has the same peculiarity exactly." Sarah Johnson, the dressmaker with the good eye for form, saw several resemblances between the girl at the jail and Juno Crocus, especially in their posture: "Her mother was peculiarly shaped in the back, and I recognized the same peculiarity in the girl.... When I went to the jail, I was struck with her manner of standing, so much like her mother; her complexion was rather darker than Juno's, pretty much the same, however."[8]

The sworn testimonies of most of the Baltimoreans were so com-pletely irreconcilable with those of the Pennsylvanians that the *New York Herald* prefaced its report on the trial by acknowledging that "every step seems to be involved in deeper mystery. There is either a singular mistake on one side or the other, or else a great quantity of very hard swear-ing." The contradictions only continued as the trial progressed. Han-nah Dickehut took the stand and swore that Rachel Parker and Eliza Crocus were the same person. She did acknowledge, however, that she remembered Juno much better than she remembered Eliza. In fact, she admitted that like her daughter Elizabeth, she "took no particular notice of the girl" because, in general, she "did not notice colored people much." She was still confident of her identification, however, because of the resemblances she noticed between Juno and the girl her son-in-law had taken her to see at the jail. Her evidence: their voices were similar, and they both had high cheekbones. These two resemblances, Mrs. Dickehut testified, "induced me to think it was the same girl." Luther Schoolfield followed his mother-in-law to the stand and echoed her testimony. He admitted that, like the rest of his family, he barely remembered Eliza, but he seemed to consider that fact irrelevant: "My personal recollection of the girl does not assist my identification of her." He was still certain: "From the strong resemblance to the parents, I believe her to be Eliza Crocus."[9]

The defense argument—that Rachel resembled Juno and Allen Crocus so closely that she had to be their daughter—was so weak that even the *Cecil Whig*, McCreary's hometown newspaper, confessed that "the weight of the evidence" was running "in favor of the freedom of the girl." Chester County's *American Republican* argued for closing the trial without calling any further witnesses: "The evidence already produced appears to be conclusive that the girl was free, and the forcible capture and carrying off being admitted, we can see no necessity for prolonging the examination." In Baltimore, however, the trial continued, in spite of the views and advice of the press, with even more testimony identifying Rachel as Eliza on the grounds of her resemblance to one or both of Eliza's parents. Both William Hopkins and Patrick Lynch declared that they did not know the girl they saw in the jail, but that she had a strong resemblance to both Juno and Allen Crocus, whom they did know. William Bandel admitted under questioning that he saw Eliza Crocus no more than five times, and the last time was at least eight years previous, but still he was sure: he "knew the whole family, and by the looks of the girl at the jail was convinced she was one of the family." Lyle Goodwin testified that he knew the Crocus family but had known Eliza only as a small child. He could identify her, however, because of certain resemblances to her parents. Her face was a dead giveaway: she looked like her father from the cheekbone down, Goodwin said, and like her mother from the cheekbone up.[10]

It seemed that the fifth day of the trial was not going to produce any surprises. Much of that day was taken up by the testimony of Francis

Corkran, who was called to the stand by the defense. He was asked to give a detailed account of the day he spent in the company of Joseph Miller and the other men from Chester County. McCreary's lawyers pressed him, throughout his testimony, to comment on the behavior of Miller. Did he seem rational? Was he distraught? Was he acting crazy? Corkran offered the defense no foothold. He gave a thorough account of his day, reiterating his opinion that Joseph Miller had appeared apprehensive on the day they were together but that he had never seemed irrational or suicidal. In between questions from the defense team, Corkran managed to slip in his opinion of the case: although he had no hard evidence to offer, he told the court, he was persuaded that McCreary knew Rachel was free when he took her, and for that reason he thought that "all good citizens should endeavor to place the offender in such a position that he might learn a lesson and not do so again." Corkran was the last witness scheduled to be called. When his testimony was over, Justice Pennington declared the evidence closed. All that remained was for him to make a ruling, and it was hard for anyone to imagine how the ruling could go in McCreary's favor.[11]

What happened next, however, turned the case upside down and electrified the courtroom. As the onlookers were gathering their belongings and preparing to leave the court, Philip Thomas, one of the defense lawyers who had been quiet during most of the proceedings, rose to his feet and announced that a very important witness had just arrived in Baltimore, a witness whose testimony would solve all the remaining mysteries and answer all the remaining questions. Not surprisingly, given that preamble, Justice Pennington agreed to hear the new witness. With that, the onlookers took their seats again, the hearing resumed, and John Merritt, McCreary's accomplice, took the stand. The testimony he gave soon had the courtroom in an unholy uproar.

The story Merritt told was all about Joseph Miller, who was, according to Merritt, entirely complicit in the kidnapping of Rachel. Merritt said that he sought out Miller, whom he had never met before, because he had heard that the girl working for Miller was one of the slaves who had run away from Luther Schoolfield four years ago. Miller at first denied that he knew anything about the runaway slaves, according to

Merritt, but then admitted that, yes, in fact he did know that the Parkers were really the fugitive Crocuses, and he knew how to locate all three. Furthermore, he was interested in a deal; he asked Merritt what he would give to get all three of the Crocuses back—mother and two daughters. Merritt said he did not know how to put a price on them; he would have to consult with a man he knew about in Elkton. Miller agreed but warned Merritt that he would like to be well paid for his part in the plan. Before they parted, Miller told Merritt that if the plan went through and if he was at home when they came to get the girl, he would have to pretend to protect her; he would have to "make a big fuss" so no one would suspect him. Merritt then, according to his narrative, went to Elkton to talk with Thomas McCreary, whom he vowed he had also never met before. He did not explain why he sought out McCreary, nor did anyone ask him that, as if it were assumed that anyone looking for runaways in the vicinity of Cecil County would go first to Tom McCreary. Merritt's story jumped then to the actual kidnapping—or arrest, in his version—which was carried out by himself, McCreary, and another man from Elkton named Alexander, who was also a stranger to Merritt. When they took Rachel, Miller was at home, and he did, as promised, make "a great fuss," although, as Merritt put it, he mostly ran around and "did not do much and did not appear as though he wanted to do much." When asked why he did not try to arrest Rebecca Parker as well as Rachel, Merritt answered that he was afraid of the abolitionists: "It would have been as much as his life was worth to have attempted that."

And there his story ended. Merritt had some trouble getting his tale out because of the mayhem it caused in the courtroom. For McCreary's sympathizers, Merritt's "hail-Mary" testimony was perfect; there could not have been a better way to end the trial. According to the *Baltimore Sun*, "It was difficult at times to preserve order: the large crowd in attendance repeatedly manifesting their gratification in shouts and general rounds of applause. It was a scene, indeed, which beggars description, and needs it not, for the extraordinary character of the sequel in itself is sufficiently startling without comment."[12]

Justice Pennington rendered his opinion the following day: the charges of kidnapping against Thomas McCreary were dropped, and he was discharged. In making his decision, Pennington issued a prepared statement designed to counteract the rowdy and unrestrained victory celebration that took place in his court and to preempt the charges of partisanship that were bound to come from Pennsylvania and other places north. It was an unusual case, the justice acknowledged, one that had already attracted a lot of public attention, but the careful, professional way the case was handled by everyone was a matter for congratulations all around. The justice took particular pains to draw the attention of the Pennsylvanians involved to the fairness with which they and their case had been treated in a Maryland court. In a grand rhetorical flourish that combined obsequiousness with more than a hint of gloating, Pennington expressed his hope that the case would remind the Pennsylvanians of something important:

> that there exists in Maryland, upon the subject of slavery, as upon all other subjects, a solemn and sincere determination scrupulously to respect the rights, feelings, and peculiar views of our brethren and friends of [Pennsylvania], however they may differ from our own, and to establish in their minds the fact, that they may with confidence enter the territory of Maryland and prosecute what they conceive to be right, without an apprehension of being molested by individuals or riots, the danger of bloodshed and death—and that justice, calmly and dispassionately, through a legal medium, will be fairly meted out.

For Pennington, John Merritt's testimony had wrapped up almost everything, including the question of how Joseph Miller died. Miller's responsibility for the kidnapping of Rachel Parker, which Pennington obviously fully accepted, implied his responsibility for his own death. The Pennsylvanians were wrong, therefore, to fear "bloodshed and death" if they came into Maryland looking to prosecute, no matter how wrong-headed or misbegotten their case. Miller came into the state making false charges against a Maryland citizen, and no one harmed him. He was done in by his own guilt, which he had brought on himself. What Pennington left open was the fate of the kidnapped girl whom he clearly believed to be a fugitive slave. "Eliza alias Rachel," as he called her, was to remain in jail "subject to the order of her owner."[13]

The *Cecil Whig* agreed with Pennington that Merritt's testimony explained the death of Joseph Miller; having made his deal with Merritt, Miller must have later begun to fear that his part in the kidnapping plot would be exposed: "His mind was preyed upon, until in an evil moment, he left the cars and hung himself." The *Whig* found reason to trust the rest of Merritt's testimony as well, even while admitting that the whole case, "taken in all its bearings and results, is a strange—a mysterious affair." Mysteries or not, the *Whig* was more than ready to call this case closed and see the antislavers sent back to Pennsylvania, having learned a lesson about meddling in Maryland's business. The *Whig*, seemingly grasping at straws, found one strong bit of evidence in the fact that Rachel Parker was taken in broad daylight, whereas McCreary usually made his slave-hunting forays into Pennsylvania at night. The daylight raid, the paper concluded, must have been arranged so that Miller could make that "fuss" in front of his neighbors, to disguise his part in the scheme.

The presence of all those witnesses from Pennsylvania who swore that Rachel had been born and raised in Chester County obviously presented a sticky problem for the *Whig*, one that it struggled to explain. No matter how one looked at it, the newspaper admitted, their testimony was "a remarkable thing." The *Whig* could not credit the theory that all of those plain, honest farmers had deliberately gone to Baltimore planning to perjure themselves. But if they were not liars, neither were they "fanatics" (i.e., abolitionists) who might have sworn that Rachel was free on the purely theoretical and irrational grounds that all people are born free and therefore none are slaves. The only explanation that made any sense to the newspaper was one its northern contemporaries might have called pharisaical: all of the Pennsylvanians just "supposed themselves to be certain" that they had known Rachel for all those years. The paper pointed out that it is easy for anyone to become confused about dates, and those farmers could easily have been given misinformation about Rachel that they came to believe as the truth. More than likely, they saw a black girl around "without noticing her particularly," and they accepted the stories they were told about her. In short, they made a mistake.[14]

On the other hand, the *Whig* was not entirely comfortable with the fact that it was John Merritt who offered the crucial testimony. His part in the taking of Rachel, and therefore the likelihood that he would be arrested if the charge against McCreary was sustained, threw some suspicion on the story. But the *Whig* reminded any Pennsylvanians who doubted Merritt's testimony that Merritt was himself from Pennsylvania, and that they needed to keep that in mind when they accused him of sectional bias. Besides, no matter what one thought of his story, there was one good reason to accept it: it was the "only key to the death of Miller."[15]

The *Pennsylvania Freeman* found the *Whig*'s conclusions not just groundless but absurd. The *Freeman* reasoned that to believe John Merritt's story was to charge with perjury "a whole community of farmers, mechanics, teachers, physicians and clergymen." The *Freeman* also refused to accept the alternative to perjury offered by the *Cecil Whig*— that the same community was just confused or mistaken, or both. Rachel was known to be "a girl of unusual intelligence and sociability," one who would be noticed and known in her neighborhood. "No one who had ever seen her, even for a few hours, would be likely to mistake her afterwards, and it is not possible that such a mistake could be made by men and women who had seen and conversed with her almost daily for years." As for Merritt's testimony, the *Freeman* found it preposterous—a desperate attempt by a confederate of the accused man to save him, made at the very last moment when there was nothing else left to try; an impartial judge would not have given it any weight at all. The major argument put forward by the *Freeman*, however, was a defense of the character and integrity of Joseph Miller. In contrast to Merritt, "a man of worthless and abandoned character, who might be expected to commit almost any crime," Miller was known to be a "quiet, unassuming, industrious and inoffensive man, unusually timid and remarkable for his tenderness of feeling and warmth of sympathy." It was inconceivable to the *Freeman* that such a man would league himself with John Merritt, who was "the pimp of a professional kidnapper" and a complete stranger to him, or that he would agree to sell into slavery the girl who had lived in his family for years and cared for his children. The *Freeman* stood firmly with Miller's friends and relatives, finding that "the conviction in and around Nottingham is universal that Miller was murdered by the kidnappers or through their instigation" and expressing its hope that the community would not rest content with the Maryland court's wildly irresponsible conclusion.[16]

Indeed, the Nottingham community did not rest content with the conclusions reached by the courts and the press in Maryland about either the guilt of Thomas McCreary or the reasons for the death of Joseph Miller. Nor did the community's Quaker allies in Baltimore; one of their first actions was to file a "petition for freedom" in Baltimore City Court to secure the release of Rachel Parker from jail. Since her release required a court hearing, the Baltimore allies, along with Henry Evans, editor of West Chester's *Village Record* and a member of the Pennsylvania legislature, persuaded Governor Bigler of Pennsylvania to appoint a legal team to represent her case. In the meantime, the Quakers had also been busy trying to locate Elizabeth Parker and bring her home. That process took months, but with the cooperation of Walter Campbell, Elizabeth was eventually found and put on a ship for the return voyage to Baltimore. The plan was to get through Rachel's trial first and then initiate procedures for declaring Elizabeth free as well.[17]

Around West Nottingham, distrust of the findings of the two Maryland postmortem examinations was so deep that Miller's friends and sympathizers decided to organize their own examination, this time in Pennsylvania. Two physicians were enlisted: James Hutchinson, the Millers' family doctor, and Ebenezer Dickey, a member of one of the most influential families in the county and brother of John Miller Dickey, who would play his own part in the long effort to free Rachel. Shortly after McCreary's trial ended, therefore, Miller's body was exhumed for the third time and given its third examination. This time, the two physicians performed a full autopsy, opening the body to examine the brain, stomach, and heart. They found none of the injury to the blood vessels of the neck or damage to the tongue that would have resulted from strangulation. The stomach and intestines were empty and inflamed.

The blood vessels in the brain were slightly congested. The muscles on the backs of the wrists were bruised. Given these findings, the physicians concluded confidently that Miller had not died by hanging, as the first two postmortems had found. Instead, he had been handcuffed, given a generous amount of poison which caused violent vomiting, and then hanged after he was dead. He had, in short, been murdered.

Miller's ravaged body was buried again, back in the cemetery at House's Meeting House. It was still not the final interment, however. The findings of the autopsy had answered some questions, but they had also created "anxiety and excitement" in the neighborhood. People wanted to know more; they especially wanted to be sure about the poison. The body was therefore exhumed for a fourth time, and a fourth examination was performed, again by Hutchinson and Dickey. This time, they ran several tests on the stomach and intestines; what they found, each time they tested, was arsenic. The *West Chester Register* announced, in its own homespun terms, the conclusion that Hutchinson and Dickey reached: "It was the unanimous opinion of the physicians that Miller did not hang himself, unless he done it after he was dead." After the autopsy, the body was buried—for the fifth time.[18]

The discovery of the arsenic was the clincher for Miller's friends and their allies. The *Pennsylvania Freeman* summed up the arguments that, in addition to the presence of arsenic in the body, could be arrayed to make the case for murder. First, Miller was found tied to a tree by two handkerchiefs, only one of which belonged to him; someone else had supplied the second handkerchief. Second, it would be unthinkable for him to swallow a fatal dose of poison and then tie himself to a tree, by the neck. Third, it was said by a "reliable authority" that Miller was wearing mittens when he was found, which would have made it almost impossible for him to tie the knots in the handkerchiefs. Fourth, there had been a heavy rain on the night Miller went missing, but his clothes were dry when he was found, indicating that he had not left the train to go straight to the tree to hang himself. More likely, he had been taken somewhere, given the poison, and then brought to the tree after he was dead and the rain had stopped. Finally, the train ticket Miller bought in Baltimore was still in his pocket. If he had ridden the train all the way to Stemmer's Run, his ticket would have been taken by the conductor before he disembarked. He must therefore have left the train before it departed from Baltimore or soon after, when it was still miles from the place where his body was found. The *Freeman* was satisfied: "The circumstances all point to but one conclusion, and that is, that Miller was foully murdered."[19]

One would think that the *Freeman*'s carefully reasoned conclusion was close to incontestable. However, confidence about Miller's murder stopped at the state line. The *Baltimore Sun* also totted up all of the evidence, including the discovery of arsenic in the body, and remained unmoved in its conviction that the death was a suicide: Miller used the arsenic to kill himself. He had been complicit in the kidnapping of Rachel Parker and feared being caught out. There was no reason, the *Sun* argued, to distrust the findings of the "searching and thorough" examinations given the body in Maryland. And there was every reason to believe that Miller had sufficient motivation to take his own life: "The utter ruin of his reputation was staring him in the face. He had not properly estimated the consequences of his act, and impelled to the encounter, his nervous system turned him aside, and prompted him to seek relief in death."[20]

The *Sun* was definitely not alone in taking this stand. A letter to the *Germantown* [Maryland] *Telegraph* from a Maryland resident living near Stemmer's Run stated succinctly an attitude that could be found in print in other parts of the state as well. The letter writer professed no respect for McCreary and his occupations, although he wished to make it clear that McCreary was not a "noted kidnapper," as he was known in Pennsylvania, but a "noted slave-catcher." There was an important difference. Still, no one could esteem such a person: "I assure you such characters hold an unenviable position even in Maryland." On the other hand, McCreary was at least open and shameless about his distasteful business, while Miller had been underhanded and hypocritical about his part in the capture of Rachel: "Such as Miller, and I believe them to be numerous in Pennsylvania, are much more despicable than those that proclaim to the world their profession."[21]

For the residents of Chester County, the Parker case was far from over. As they saw it, Maryland officials had done nothing to answer their questions and everything to cover up the whole matter. Joseph Miller had died from arsenic poisoning and no one had been charged with his murder; Rachel Parker was still in jail, waiting for a legal determination that she was free; Elizabeth Parker was, at that point, still missing; Thomas McCreary, John Merritt, and Matthew Donnelly were all free men. As for the trial, West Chester's *American Republican* newspaper was sure that there had been "false swearing on one side or the other," and the paper had little doubt about which side it was. The Chester County men who testified were "men of unimpeachable truth and integrity, and anything but Abolitionists or opponents to the execution of the Fugitive Slave law." The witnesses for the defense, on the other hand, included "several of whom we know nothing, except that many of them were interested and the principal one . . . was McCreary's fellow and aid in the perpetration of the crime, and when swearing for McCreary, was swearing for himself." And yet the defense had won.[22]

Back in Elkton, local resident James McCauley noted in his diary on January 10, the second day of the trial, that there was "much excitement about McCreary and the negro case in Baltimore." On January 17, two days after the verdict was rendered, McCauley noted, simply, "McCreary at home."[23]

8

FREEDOM

THE KIDNAPPING of Rachel and Elizabeth Parker had been troubling enough to the people of Chester County, but the unexplained death of Joseph Miller was something unprecedented and truly shocking. Black people had been hustled out of the county by slave catchers and kidnappers for years, and white people had been chasing after them to bring them back, sometimes successfully and sometimes not. But for one of those white people to die—in the process of doing what most in the county considered the right thing—was another matter altogether. Maybe most galling of all, Pennsylvania was being humiliated by its neighbor state. The kidnapper came from Maryland, and now a Maryland court had refused to convict him; Joseph Miller died in Maryland and, according to Chester County opinion, he was most likely murdered by someone from Maryland. Given the sectional bitterness in which this case was drenched, the three miles separating Joseph Miller's farm from the Pennsylvania/Maryland border might as well have been three thousand.

The anger and frustration caused by the outcome of McCreary's trial moved the "Parker case" to a new place in the public consciousness; it also produced a new set of local citizens ready to act on behalf of their fellow Pennsylvanians. Until this point, the people directly involved in the case had been largely county farmers, men who were uncomfortable in the city or in the limelight, wherever it might find them. The acquittal of McCreary and the results of the Nottingham autopsies on the body of Joseph Miller motivated a different and more likely group of activists, some of them urban and most of them accustomed to some form of public life and to the languages and methods of politics—local, sectional, or racial. Included in this group were Henry S. Evans, the West Chester newspaper editor and state legislator, and John Miller Dickey, pastor of the Oxford Presbyterian Church. As these and other prominent names began to appear in the press in connection with the Parker case, the names that had become familiar through reports of the kidnappings and the McCreary trial (such as Richardson, Kirk, Coates, and Furness) receded from sight for a while, to reemerge only when Joseph Miller's friends and relatives were once again summoned to court.

John Miller Dickey was a county aristocrat, a member of one of the most prominent and influential families in Chester County. His father, Ebenezer, had served for many years as pastor of the Oxford Presbyterian Church and was a strong advocate of both temperance and education, producing several pamphlets on the subjects. A former slaveholder, he became an early member of the local colonization society. Ebenezer's two brothers, Samuel and David, were successful businessmen in the county, Samuel founding a cotton mill at Hopewell and David establishing a textile mill in lower Oxford. Their operations made Hopewell and its vicinity the center of a cotton-weaving industry in the county; the mills also allowed the Dickey family to flourish economically until the early 1860s. Ebenezer's duties as a pastor and reformer did not prevent him from joining his two brothers as an active partner in the family textile business. He also remained close to the farming life of the county; he invented and patented an improved butter-working machine, and he liked to say of himself that he "preached lime and religion." By 1862, however, the family businesses had declined enough that the brothers were forced to close the mills and sell off most of their property. In that year, the family listed for sale seventeen different properties in or near Oxford, including at least eight farms, a grist mill, two cotton factories, and a store.[1]

Ebenezer's three sons—John, Samuel, and Ebenezer—managed, like their father, to combine careers in the professions with active business, political, and civic interests. John succeeded his father in the pulpit at the Oxford Presbyterian Church in 1831, where he remained for twenty-five years. Samuel also began as a Presbyterian minister, serving a church in Lancaster County. When a throat problem forced him to give up the ministry, he returned to Chester County and found plenty of other things to occupy the Dickey entrepreneurial spirit: he became president of the National Bank of Oxford, was active in bringing the Baltimore Central Railroad to the town, and partnered with John in the founding of the Oxford Female Seminary—all of this before his early death at the age of thirty-seven. The third son, Ebenezer, was the physician who assisted at the two autopsies performed on Joseph Miller's body after it was returned to Chester County. A local historian, Gilbert Cope, noted that Ebenezer took part in two "exciting events" in 1852: the Miller autopsies and "an extinction and exposure of some local alleged spiritualistic manifestations." His public life, even without the excursions into the disruption of séances, may have been the most varied and energetic among the three brothers. In addition to practicing medicine, he was president of the Octoraro Bank in Oxford, president of the Baltimore Central Railroad, and, after 1856, a member of the Pennsylvania legislature.[2]

John Miller Dickey and his brother Ebenezer followed their father's example not only in their advocacy of education but also in their promotion of the colonization movement. John's support for colonization led Gilbert Cope to declare that he "was noted for his strong antislavery principles." There were many in the antislavery camp, however, who would have taken issue with Cope's characterization. Charles Burleigh, the abolitionist who had butted heads with Dickey in the course of his speaking tours through the county, considered Dickey a "clerical ruffian" who, rather than working to advance the antislavery cause, was determined to throw as many obstacles as he could in the way of the real antislavery activists. Both Cope and Burleigh may have been partly right: Dickey, like many others in his time and place, hated slavery but probably hated abolitionists even more—especially the ones who were not local. For him, colonization was a more sensible and peaceable answer to the slavery question than abolition, and it was certainly more genteel. Dickey was also a great believer in universal education, as evidenced by his role in founding a number of Sabbath Schools for children in the county and his close work with the Oxford Female Seminary, a teacher-training institute. These combined interests in colonization and education led to Dickey's major role in the establishment of Ashmun Institute (which would later become Lincoln University), just outside Oxford. The school, chartered in 1853, was publicly dedicated to the general education of young black men but privately intended as a recruiting ground for Liberia. That intention was reflected in the choice of a name for the school: Jehudi Ashmun was an agent of the Colonization Society and a former administrator of Liberia. (The name was changed in 1867, the president of the school at the time explaining that the change reflected the school's belief that prior to emancipation, the only future the founders could envision for blacks was in Liberia, whereas after Lincoln, it had become possible to envision a future for them in the United States.)[3]

Years after the Parker affair was all over, Gilbert Cope wrote admiringly about Dickey's participation in the events with a boosterish disregard for evidence or fact. According to Cope, when Rachel Parker was kidnapped, "no one dared to pursue or attempt her recovery. All were intimidated by threats of personal violence if they should presume to enter a slave state for any such purpose. Dr. Dickey formed a party of a few interested men and started for Baltimore." In another place, Cope wrote that Dickey "became the leader in the twelve months' contest for the recovery [of the Parkers], a service attended with such great bodily danger that, when leaving home in connection with the case and the subsequent trial, he bade farewell to his family, uncertain that he would live to return." In fact, Dickey was not part of the party that originally went to Baltimore in search of Rachel, and it is doubtful that his life was ever in as much danger as were the lives of those men who did go—certainly including Joseph Miller. Whether he intended to or not, Cope, by making an epic hero of Dickey, succeeded in diminishing the roles of those local citizens who, quietly and fearfully, took genuine risks, encountered genuine danger, and were genuinely brave.[4]

The important role that John Miller Dickey did play in the ultimate release of both of the Parkers hardly needed Cope's exaggerations and distortions (which, let it be said in Cope's defense, probably did not originate with him but with Dickey's son). Dickey stepped in after the autopsies on Miller's body and was instrumental both in keeping the outrage alive in Chester County and in preventing the Parker case from simply fading away in Baltimore. The two autopsies, with John's brother Ebenezer participating, had been held on January 17 and 20, 1852; by February 3, John Miller Dickey was in Baltimore. He joined forces with another Presbyterian minister, William S. Plummer of Baltimore, and the two met with Luther Schoolfield, reminding him of all those sworn testimonies to Rachel Parker's freedom offered by "men of veracity and honor" at McCreary's trial and trying to convince Schoolfield to agree to release her. When Schoolfield refused, insisting that there had to be a trial to determine her status and that she had to remain in jail until the trial was over, Dickey returned to Chester County and immediately got busy there. He was one of the organizers of a meeting, held on February 6, with two announced purposes: first, to let Drs. Hutchinson and Dickey give the details of the two autopsies on Miller's body and, second, to organize a search for Elizabeth, bring her home, and move her legal case and Rachel's along as quickly as possible.[5]

The meeting, held on a wintry, wet night at the schoolhouse in the small village of Hopewell, drew a crowd of at least fifty and probably more.[6] Miller's neighbors and relatives were there, but so were others who were not farmers or laborers but lawyers, doctors, and businessmen. West Chester's *American Republican*, reporting on the professional men who attended, hinted proudly that they were the sort who would give a new caché to the Parker support. The newspaper assured its readers "at home and abroad" (presumably meaning in Maryland) that the men at the meeting were "among the most intelligent and respectable citizens of our county,—lawabiding and Union-loving men," who were not partisans or abolitionist radicals but had the good of all people and all states at heart. At the meeting, the announced business was completed efficiently; Drs. Hutchinson and Dickey reported on their autopsies, and funds were subscribed to help return Elizabeth Parker from New

Orleans. While these discussions were going on, a committee was set to work on a list of resolutions to be endorsed by the meeting. The committee emerged with a document that left no doubt as to the sympathies of those attending. The ten resolutions, all voted on and approved, set out the meeting's convictions about a number of things: that Rachel Parker was a free person, that Joseph Miller had been murdered by the administration of arsenic, that the testimony of John Merritt was perjured and motivated by "a most unhallowed desire to steep in infamy the memory of murdered innocence," and that the "humanity and benevolence" of Joseph Miller must be honored. The statement also expressed abhorrence of the careless burial of Miller's body after the first Maryland postmortem and appreciation to those hospitable Baltimoreans who had been helpful in the "cause."

These resolutions passed quickly and easily. How could good citizens argue about kidnapping, perjury, infamy, disrespect for the dead, or thanking one's hosts? The real excitement came from a resolution made just at the end of the meeting, as the company was breaking up. Precisely what happened is hard to determine, since no one seemed willing, in the aftermath, to go on record with a good account. Certainly nobody was about to volunteer the name of the author of the resolution, which declared, in effect, that any man who shot Thomas McCreary and/or John Merritt "like a common cur" would not only be entirely within his rights but also have the thanks of the entire community. No one who had attended the meeting was ready to admit to supporting such a suggestion, either. Some protested afterward that they had left before the resolution was made and heard rumblings only later; some said they heard the resolution, made by an unknown person in the crowd, but did not think a vote was ever taken on it; others insisted they did not hear a thing. All were positive, however, that no more was said about the resolution after the meeting dispersed.[7]

The Hopewell meeting and the publication of its resolutions had an effect, although it was not at all what the attendees had hoped for; the hardening of resolve in Chester County met with a similar response in Baltimore. The meeting had taken place on February 6; by the middle of that month, Luther Schoolfield had requested that Rachel's freedom trial, in which he was the defendant, be moved from the Baltimore city court to the Baltimore County court, on the grounds that he could not get a fair and impartial trial in the city. To the friends of Miller and the Parkers, this reasoning seemed entirely specious. The *Village Record* published an angry letter from Baltimore, probably from Francis Corkran's Quaker colleague Samuel Townsend (it was signed simply S.T.), which assumed purely political motives behind the change of venue for the case: "It is passing strange, indeed, if in a contest between a little negro girl, claiming her freedom, and an old and respectable resident of this city, the latter should not be able to obtain justice from a jury of his fellow townsmen." Strange or not, Schoolfield's request was granted. The case had been first on the docket in the city court; in the county court, it had no place on the docket at all until the lawyers and the judge could agree on one. A Baltimore resident, writing to West Chester's *American Republican* to express his suspicions about the motives for the change, echoed what many in Chester County were already thinking. The move, he wrote, was obviously made for the same reason that the second examination of Joseph Miller's body had been held in Baltimore County, near the Gorsuch farm—that is, "for the purpose of enlisting in this case the sympathy prevailing [in Baltimore County] for the late Mr. Gorsuch." The failure to convict the Christiana defendants, he reported, "is regarded here as an outrage on the feelings of our citizens, and it will undoubtedly have its effect in this trial." About Christiana, he was right.[8]

The *National Era*, an African American newspaper, raised an even more basic question about the trial: why was it being held in Maryland rather than in Pennsylvania, where Rachel had lived and where she had been abducted? A long and detailed answer was offered in a letter to the newspaper written by J. E. Snodgrass, a Baltimore physician, who saw the refusal to move the trial as a way of keeping potential black witnesses out of the courtroom. "The testimony of persons guilty of the crime of being clothed in a dark skin," Snodgrass wrote, "is never tolerated in the courts of this or any other slaveholding State, where one of the parties is of the white race, unless the testimony is favorable to the latter's cause." Given the failure of their efforts to move the trial out of Maryland, Rachel's supporters had to fall back on what Snodgrass saw as a risky and racist legal procedure: "The tardy and expensive process 'petition for freedom,' adopted by the counsel for poor Rachel, was appealed to . . . as the only remedy for the colored race in this State; and it throws the *onus probandi* on the victimized, instead of the victimizer, where slavery desires it thrown—for the darkened color of the skin is evidence presumptive of servitude in all cases; and the proving of a negative is the anomalous requirement made of every person accused, or even suspected, of running away with himself!" In spite of his frustration with the obstacles that Maryland law had put in the way of Rachel's freedom, Snodgrass predicted that her case would be strong enough to overcome them.[9]

Finding a trial date turned out to be, for the plaintiffs, a maddeningly complicated process. The shift from one court to another meant that efforts to get the case scheduled could not even begin until the county court session opened in mid-April. By then, Rachel had been waiting in the city jail for three months. When one of the lawyers representing her, William H. Norris (who had also represented her at McCreary's trial), was finally able to ask the court to put her case on its calendar, the legal jockeying began. The prosecuting attorney insisted that the case would have to wait until after all the previously scheduled criminal business of the court had been taken care of. Having accepted this provision, the attorneys for the two sides agreed on a date in July—a full three months in the future—that seemed safely past the time needed to finish the cases already scheduled. That compromise was scrapped, however, when one of Schoolcraft's lawyers, William Schley, predicted that Rachel's case would take at least ten days and might even last two weeks. At that point the judge intervened, pointing out that, if Schley was right, the case could run on into August, which was harvest time, and he would *never* summon a jury in a rural county in harvest time. The trial would have to wait until after the crops were in. And there the discussion ended. Rachel would have to wait.

Everything connected with the case, from beginning to end, was thoroughly infected with politics of all kinds, even the personal kind. After their frustration with the scheduling negotiations, Rachel's supporters were dealt another unexpected blow in late April. The second Baltimore lawyer engaged to represent Rachel, Davis H. Hoopes, suddenly resigned from the case. In making his departure, Hoopes did not go quietly. He took the opportunity of his resignation to make it clear that his legal feathers had been well and truly ruffled. Hoopes said he had accepted the engagement in the hope that the case would develop calmly, "without creating any unnecessary excitement." He had assumed that the case rested entirely on a question of identity; if it should turn out that Rachel Parker was in fact a slave, then he "had no wish to interfere with the rights of the owners." Hoopes's statement, as conveyed by the *Baltimore Sun*, then turned coy and somewhat cryptic, as he rhetorically lifted his skirts, tiptoed away, and removed himself from the mess he claimed others had created:

> He had been particularly anxious that the case should be tried precisely as any other case, avoiding every thing that might give undue importance to it, or tend, even remotely, to add any thing to the ill-feeling, which unfortunately a certain recent and most melancholy circumstance has created in the minds of some of our citizens against the State of Pennsylvania. That upon this and some other subjects, however connected with the case, his sentiments were not concurred in by the worthy gentlemen who now claim the right to control the case. Under these circumstances, he would now respectfully ask of the court that his name be withdrawn from it.[10]

Hoopes clearly thought he was losing control of the case to others who were pushing an agenda he did not like. At the heart of that agenda must have been the death of Joseph Miller and the deep suspicion in Pennsylvania that Thomas McCreary was behind it. To allow that issue to shape Rachel's freedom trial would assuredly produce another ugly Maryland/Pennsylvania political brawl, one that could do serious damage to a lawyer's reputation. Although Hoopes was practicing in Baltimore, he was a native of Chester County, which made him vulnerable to charges of antislavery bias. He seemed especially concerned, therefore, to make it clear that he did not want to further unsettle the people of Maryland, who were still smarting from the "melancholy circumstance" of the death of Edward Gorsuch. Hoopes must have recognized that, given the nature of the case and the inflamed feelings surrounding it on all sides, a Baltimore lawyer from Chester County was not going to come out smelling like a rose, no matter how the verdict went, and any talk of murder could only make things worse. Better to get out before the trouble started.

After Hoopes's April announcement, progress on the case was excruciatingly slow throughout most of the rest of the year. Two events important to the case did occur in July. First, the Pennsylvania legislature authorized the state to employ lawyers to represent both of the sisters at their trials. Second, Elizabeth Parker arrived back in Baltimore after her six months as a slave, having spent most of that time in New Orleans. She was taken straight to the Campbells' slave pen. In order to be sure that the right girl had been brought home, the Baltimore friends of the case sent to Chester County for witnesses who could confirm her identity. James Mullen, Robert Hughes, and James Hutchinson, all longtime residents of the county who had testified at McCreary's trial in January, returned to Baltimore and made their visit to the pen. When they arrived, they were shown into a yard where about twenty-five women and girls waited. The men surveyed the group and announced, with more than a little puzzlement, that Elizabeth was not among them. Walter Campbell, evidently having set up a bit of a test for the men, then ordered a smaller group, including Elizabeth, to be brought into the yard. By all accounts, Elizabeth and the men recognized each other immediately and greeted each other warmly.

The meeting was sufficient to convince Walter Campbell that Elizabeth should be released—not into freedom, of course, but into the Baltimore jail, where she joined Rachel, who had by that point already been held for six months. Together, the sisters would wait nearly another six months, "among thieves and murderers," according to the *Pennsylvania Freeman*, before their case was finally heard. Elizabeth had little to say about her time in the jail, but her "release" from slavery in New Orleans into imprisonment in Baltimore was in fact a move from relative freedom and mobility to complete confinement and isolation. Like Rachel's, her future was now dependent on the political jousting of politicians, lawyers, and judges on both sides of the state line, most of whom had never even seen either of the two girls.[11]

The Parker case nearly dropped out of sight during the sisters' long spell of waiting. Back in February, local Chester County newspapers had been reporting regularly on the "high excitement" caused by the ongoing story of the kidnapping, the murder, and McCreary's trial. The Miller autopsies had been commented on at length, as had the Hopewell meeting. By July, however, any advances in the case were taking place in Baltimore or Harrisburg and not in Chester County. West Chester's *Village Record*, which had kept county residents fully apprised of the course of McCreary's trial and of other events related to the case, was having to search for news in August. Life in town was deadly dull, the paper reported, since all the farmers were busy and no one had time to come to town. "The local news is uncommonly dull, too. . . . Will nobody perpetrate something, to get up an excitement—matrimony, for instance?" What the paper presented as a complaint was in fact a boast, as another story in the same issue made clear. The country person's quiet dullness could be the city person's serenity, and Chester County was eager to attract the city person: "Many of the citizens of Philadelphia have sought health and comfort, during the warm weather, in the quiet shade of Chester and Delaware Counties. Almost daily, families visit our borough, and wend their way to our quiet farm houses where they luxuriate on fresh milk and sweet butter." The *Village Record* was understandably happy for the epicenter of the Parker agitation to move out of the county and into the hands of lawyers and legislators in the cities, making room for less divisive and more amusing "excitements" that could attract tourists and their money.[12]

Rachel's trial did not begin until January 4, 1853, more than a year after her kidnapping. It was listed officially on the court docket as "Rachel Parker, by her next friend, Francis Corkran, vs. Hannah Dickehut, a petition for freedom."[13] Dickehut's lawyers (hers in name only; they were really working for Luther Schoolfield) were William Preston and Otho Scott, both of whom had been on McCreary's defense team, and William Schley, one of Baltimore's most prominent lawyers. Rachel's legal representation, after the huffy departure of Davis Hoopes, consisted of William H. Norris and two special appointees sent by the Governor of Pennsylvania: James Campbell, who was the state's attorney general at the time and would go on to become the postmaster general of the United States, and Thomas S. Bell, a retired justice of the Pennsylvania Supreme Court living in West Chester. Both appointees would prove to be, from the perspective of Chester County, at best ill-chosen and at worst an embarrassment.

The proceedings began with an opening statement by William Norris. He summarized the facts of the case, veering briefly to acknowledge something of which everyone in the room was already fully and nervously aware—the political tightrope they were all walking in pursuing a verdict. Norris took the occasion to respond obliquely to the claims made earlier by the unhappy Davis Hoopes in withdrawing from the case. Hoopes had charged that what he had assumed would be a quiet inquiry into the *identity* of Rachel/Eliza had become politicized by others who had their own agendas. In his statement, Norris answered Hoopes, without using his name, by declaring that the state of Pennsylvania did not intend to use the trial as a platform for a quarrel with Maryland but sought only to "quietly" defend one of its own citizens. Hoopes had been right that the only relevant question for a jury was one of identity. Was it Rachel Parker or Eliza Crocus that Thomas McCreary brought to Baltimore? Answering that question would consume nearly eight days.[14]

The spectators at this trial included a substantial number of African Americans, presumably local people, given Maryland's prohibitions against free blacks entering the state. Rachel, Elizabeth, and Rebecca Parker were present in the courtroom from the beginning—not to testify, of course, but to be identified by the white witnesses. Ned Parker and his son Jim were brought into the court on the sixth day of the trial so that they too could be identified. The Baltimore newspapers had no comment on the reunion of the Parker family in these awkward circumstances. The correspondent for the *Village Record*, however, the pseudonymous Toby, was more attuned to such local, personal-interest aspects of the case. What Toby found in the courtroom reunion of the Parker family was the same pathos and high drama he had been finding in the case all along. According to Toby, Beck's greeting to her daughter Elizabeth, whom she had not seen since her kidnapping a full year before, was a chilly one:

> Her first words were those of upbraiding, as if the abused, sorrowing child had not already born [*sic*] enough, and accused her of being the author of all this trouble. Her greeting with Rachel was more cordial, but Becky never gets enthusiastic. . . . Elizabeth appears to be "father's child," while Rachel was "mother's." When Edward Parker, the father, entered the Court, Elizabeth seeing him as she chanced to look up, uttered a stifled scream of joy, and flying to him, wound her arms around his neck and kissed him again and again, and he greeted her no less fondly—lavishing on her such loving epithets as "pappy's honey!" "Neddy's pet!" etc., making this little tableau of family reunion quite affecting. Neddy was Becky's first love, but some absence or wrong, or something else had played very foul with her virgin affections, and the seal of death seemed on them and also on his, for the once husband and wife, the once young and fondly loving couple, met without emotion, with a cold greeting of "well Neddy," "well Becky."

Just as the lawyers attempted to scrub the case clean of its very messy and bitter political history, so Toby in his rendering of this scene makes its history an entirely familial one. His description abstracts the family almost completely from the charged racial and political context that first separated them and then brought them together in a Maryland courtroom. What remains is a "little tableau of family reunion" that leaves Toby mildly surprised by its complexity and lack of sweetness—just as he had been surprised by the distanced strangeness he saw in Elizabeth when she returned from New Orleans.[15]

The testimony in support of Rachel's freedom was overwhelming. It continued for seven days, with forty-nine witnesses called, most of them from Chester County, and a reported thirty more still waiting to testify when the trial ended. Eight of the witnesses had already taken the stand at McCreary's trial, and six of these—Ephraim Blackburn, Lewis Melrath, William Morris, James Pollock, James Hutchinson, and Robert Hughes—had also been called to testify at the second inquest on Joseph Miller's body. These six were therefore making their third appearance before a Maryland jury. Among the new witnesses at this trial were fourteen women, including Joseph Miller's wife, sister, mother, and sister-in-law. Other women were neighbors of the Millers' or the Parkers'. Witness after witness specifically identified the young black woman in the courtroom as Rachel Parker. John McCreary, one of Thomas's nephews, swore that he "could tell [Rachel] if I met her a thousand miles from here and amongst ten thousand niggers." Other testimonies were equally confident, if less colorful. Edward Chambers had "not the least doubt that [Rachel] is the girl whom I have known from infancy." Rebecca Miller, Joseph's widow, said she "would have no more difficulty in identifying the girl than she would have in identifying one of her own children." Mary Wilkinson had "no doubt of her identity." William Morris spoke "with a perfect certainty" in identifying Rachel. Rachel was brought to stand before the jury twice to show two scars: one from the vaccination James Hutchinson gave her and one on her foot from an axe wound that was wrapped in a rag when she first came to live with the Miller family.[16]

And so it went for seven days. The defense lawyers were generally quiet, as person after person swore that the young woman in the courtroom was Rachel Parker and not Eliza Crocus and as the defense case therefore looked weaker and weaker. The one effort by Dickehut's lawyers to come up with an account of how Juno Crocus and her daughters might have ended up in Chester County turned out to be a feeble one. The account involved the story of the "engine," a piece of heavy machinery used by the Tyson Mining Company of Baltimore, which operated a chrome mine within a mile of the Miller farm. When the mine closed in 1847, Tyson hired three teams from a local merchant farmer, Amor Carter, to haul the "engine" back to Baltimore. The defense tried to argue that when Carter's teams returned to West Nottingham, having deposited the apparatus in Baltimore, one of the wagons concealed the escaping Juno Crocus, her husband, and their two daughters. The argument had to be abandoned when more than one witness testified to having seen Rachel at the Millers' place at least a year before the "engine" was hauled away.[17]

The eighth day of the trial, January 12, began oddly. When it was time for court to begin, there were no lawyers in the courtroom—only jurors, witnesses, spectators, reporters, and the Parker family. The defense had called no witnesses, although there were at least twelve who were apparently prepared to testify, including Thomas McCreary, Matthew Donnelly, and John Merritt. Everyone waited. Some must have wondered if the defense had found another surprise witness, like John Merritt, who was about to be sprung on them. There was, in fact, a surprise coming, but of a kind very different from Merritt's damning (and perjured) testimony. Rumors began to make the rounds in the room that the defense was going to abandon the case. Finally, Otho Scott, one of Dickehut's lawyers, confirmed the rumors by announcing that Luther Schoolfield was withdrawing his claim. There would be no more witnesses, no more argument, and no verdict. This time, there was no pandemonium as there had been in the wake of Merritt's story. What followed instead was an astonishingly controlled performance by both legal teams as well as the judge—a well-orchestrated exercise in obfuscation and manipulation that, as it turned out, almost no one would take seriously.

None of those who spoke at the conclusion of the trial had very much to say about Rachel or Elizabeth Parker, their kidnapping, or their time in jail. What they did talk about was the unfinished business of Christiana; it was no secret that there were those, on both sides, who were looking to the trial as either vindication for the treason charges at Christiana or payback for the death of Gorsuch. By ending it without a verdict, the lawyers made it clear that they thought they and everyone else involved had dodged a very dangerous bullet. As Otho Scott put it, this was "one of those cases which, from its connection with questions arising with a sister state, was likely to cause some agitation and excitement."

Scott reported that both he and Luther Schoolfield were stunned by the testimonies they had heard in support of a black girl: "No white girl in either of the States could be found who could prove her identity so conclusively as Rachel Parker had done." Given the competing testimonies and the depth of feeling on both sides, it seemed to Scott that the verdict was not going to be good, and it was therefore best to conclude without one. Schoolfield concurred with that decision, he reported; he "was anxious to relieve the jury of any further trouble or difficulty—he did not want a Maryland jury to find a verdict in his favor if the evidence was not of the clearest character." Scott did want to make it clear, however, that he and Schoolfield had good reasons for pursuing the case in the first place: McCreary, Merritt, and Donnelly had all sworn that Rachel and Elizabeth had admitted they were runaways. McCreary believed them, Scott reported. "Otherwise he would not have gone in open day in Chester county, where he was well known, and taken Rachel away."

William Preston spoke next to express his satisfaction with the proceedings. The way the trial ended was consistent, he pointed out, with the way national politics had been conducted recently, especially the politics of slavery: "It was gratifying to him that the cause had thus terminated—a termination that has been induced in a spirit of compromise—that spirit which has already been so beneficially exerted by our most distinguished men in another contest in reference to the right of negro property in this country." Preston's blithe comparison of this case to the Compromise of 1850 would fall on very attentive ears in Pennsylvania, partly because of its reference to the strengthened Fugitive Slave Act that was part of that compromise, but mainly because of its intimation of a deal, a quid pro quo, worked out by the lawyers. Why was Preston talking about compromise? If a deal was made, who was getting what? Who was giving up what? These questions Preston did not address.

William Norris, Rachel's lawyer, began his remarks by comparing himself to Napoleon; both of them had considered it their duty to defend the weak as well as the powerful. He then went on to offer a back-handed compliment to Maryland by praising the state's magnanimity in the face of defeat: "He felt animated with delight that when Maryland claimants were convinced that they were wrong, that they had the magnanimity to avow their mistake. . . . He hoped that this little mustard seed of a case would spring up and grow till its effects were felt in the happiest results."

Judge Constable echoed Norris's characterization of the defense's decision as "magnanimous" and offered his hope that the case might help to allay "asperities" on both sides of the Mason-Dixon Line. It would be a cause for great regret, he noted, if the disposition of this case should result in an increase of prejudice on either side. He was therefore fully appreciative of "the adjustment of the case just made," another tantalizing reference to some kind of deal made behind closed doors.

The remarks that turned out to be most disturbing to Pennsylvanians came from James Campbell. Campbell wanted, he said, to explain why Governor Bigler of Pennsylvania had sent him and Judge Bell as special appointees to the trial. No one should think that they were sent in "a foul spirit of abolitionism" or because the governor did not trust the Maryland lawyers to do their job properly. In fact, Pennsylvania was eager to "bind still stronger the ties which should ever hold Maryland and Pennsylvania together." To this end, he said, the Pennsylvania authorities "are ready and willing to surrender to you your slaves and to teach every one of our citizens that it is their duty to aid and encourage you in the pursuit of them." Not surprisingly, the citizens of Pennsylvania would not be at all pleased to hear from Campbell that they would have to assume the *duty* of helping to catch fugitives in order to placate the slaveholders of Maryland.

When all the speeches were made, Rachel Parker was declared free. The jury was dismissed and then immediately reconstituted so that it could declare Elizabeth Parker free as well. And it was all over—or seemed to be. The sisters were congratulated by their supporters, and arrangements were made for James Campbell to escort them back to Chester County. They were taken the long way around, through York and Lancaster Counties, perhaps in a kind of victory lap. The *Village Record* reported that "the girls were in the best of spirits, and were received with general rejoicing by their friends." For the Parkers, a simple, surprise announcement had put an end to what the Philadelphia Female Anti-Slavery Society called "that long year of anguish, suspense, and terror." As it turned out, however, the many issues and questions that had been raised over the course of the "Parker affair" were far from settled. Campbell's comments were galling, as was the question of the closed-door compromise. The "little mustard seed" that William Norris hoped to see growing did in fact sprout, but clearly not in the way Norris intended.[18]

For a while, efforts to smooth over sectional antagonisms continued. Judge Bell, seemingly oblivious to the hostility he and Campbell had aroused, sent a letter to all the Chester County newspapers, thanking the witnesses from the county, especially the ladies, who "exchanged the comforts of home for the inconveniences and supposed dangers of sojourn in a strange city." Bell went on to declare the verdict to be both an instance of "the triumph of truth over prejudice and falsehood" and a "gratifying proof that our Southern brethren are disposed to accord to the negroes, their ascertained rights." Another extremely polite and conciliatory letter appeared in the Chester County newspapers over the signature of John Miller Dickey, who signed himself as chairman of a meeting of witnesses and others who had attended Rachel's trial. The letter implied that the matter of the kidnapping of the Parker sisters was settled and all that remained to do was to arrest the people who killed Joseph Miller. Most of the letter was taken up with courtesies: thanking the "friends of humanity" in Maryland who had offered help and hospitality to the visitors from Pennsylvania, expressing appreciation to the "distinguished counsel" on both sides, and acknowledging the consideration shown by the Court of Baltimore County. Finally, after all the cordiality, the letter asked Governor Bigler of Pennsylvania to offer a reward for the "discovery and apprehension" of the "murderers" of Miller. No names were mentioned, but there was little doubt in Chester County that the person who needed to be apprehended was Thomas McCreary.[19]

That letter, however, appeared in the same edition of the *Village Record* as a much less complacent one from Toby, dated January 15, three days after the trial ended. The tone and content of the two letters make it difficult to believe that Toby and John Miller Dickey were responding to the same trial or living in the same county. Dickey's letter was largely about gratitude and relief; Toby's was about anger and frustration, much of it directed at James Campbell's mention of the "duty" of Pennsylvanians to help Marylanders catch their runaway slaves: "The whole current of feeling runs strong and violent against the settlement as made, and Campbell and his speech, and his course in the matter are denounced on all hands in most bitter and unmeasured terms. His speech is regarded as most contemptibly worded to catch southern favor for political effect, and degrading to every Pennsylvanian, and most unspeakably obnoxious to every Nottinghamite." Toby did not explain the "settlement as made" that was so offensive to the people whose testimony had brought the trial to such a sudden end. Clearly, the lawyers for the two sides had reached some sort of agreement. But what was it? Toby himself probably did not know for certain what was in the deal, only that there was a deal. But he implied that the source of the deal was Campbell, who had been sent to Baltimore by the governor of Pennsylvania with the terms of the deal in his pocket.[20]

Dickey's letter, with its polite request to the governor to fund a reward for the arrest of Joseph Miller's killers, obviously did not satisfy the people whom it purported to represent—the witnesses and others closely involved in the two trials. On January 18, the West Chester newspapers carried the announcement of a $1,000 reward offered for the arrest and conviction of the murderer or murderers. The money was being put up by Joseph Miller's "friends and neighbors, for ourselves and in behalf of the family of said deceased." The notice was signed by Abner Richardson and Lewis Melrath, both of whom had been part of the group that originally accompanied Miller to Baltimore, and by Joseph Stubbs, the Quaker owner of a paper mill in Nottingham. This group clearly did not trust either John Miller Dickey and his committees or Governor Bigler and his lawyers to see that justice was done. They were the "friends and neighbors" of Joseph Miller; Dickey and the governor were not. They had been with Miller on the day he died; Dickey and the governor had not.[21]

The press, south and north, soon began venturing predictably polarized explanations for the surprise ending to the trial. Virginia's *Alexandria Gazette* read it as an example of the disinterested virtue of Maryland slaveholders, who had refused, in the interest of the Union, to retaliate against Pennsylvania for the brutal assassination of one of her citizens (Gorsuch) killed in the pursuit of his legal rights. *Frederick Douglass's Paper* was convinced that the whole trial had been staged by Gorsuch's friends as a payback for Christiana. The *Massachusetts Spy* editorialized that it was not a sense of justice that made the defense give up its case but a need to keep any more witnesses from taking the stand. The evidence was getting dangerously close to the death of Joseph Miller, said the *Spy*; to prevent that particular can of worms from being opened, Schoolfield's lawyers were willing to close down the case and send both the Parkers home. The writer of an anonymous letter to West Chester's *Village Record* strongly implied that the trial was abandoned because two of the lawyers for the defense, William Schley and Otho Scott, found the evidence in favor of Rachel's freedom so compelling that they had determined to withdraw from the case. The *Pennsylvania Freeman* was especially outraged by the performances of the lawyers on both sides, theorizing that the defense folded simply because they knew they were beaten; the whole posture of generosity and mutual respect on the part of the lawyers was meant to cover that plain fact. The *Freeman* closed its article by asserting what many were obviously thinking—that "there is more than meets the eye in the closing scenes of this remarkable trial." The *Freeman* was right.[22]

The specific nature of the vague "compromise" or "settlement" that closed Rachel's trial was revealed only slowly. The revelations began in February with the decision to try Thomas McCreary and John Merritt in Pennsylvania on the charges they had dodged in Maryland. Accordingly, they were indicted for the crime of kidnapping by a West Chester grand jury. Both Rachel Parker and Rebecca Miller, Joseph Miller's widow, were brought in to testify. With the jury's return of a true bill, Governor Bigler of Pennsylvania had no choice but to prepare a requisition, asking that Governor Enoch Louis Lowe of Maryland send McCreary to Pennsylvania for trial. The Chester County sheriff dutifully took the requisition to Annapolis. And then nothing happened. Rumors and speculations, some closer to the truth than others, began to appear in the press. One rumor making the rounds was that Lowe had refused to accept the requisition because of the infamous compromise that had been reached at Rachel Parker's trial: Maryland would allow Rachel to go free, and Pennsylvania would not press kidnapping charges against McCreary. Word that such a deal had been struck brought other

Maryland and Pennsylvania newspapers to furious life. The *Pennsylvania Freeman* was incredulous. If a "compromise" was reached, according to the newspaper (which consistently used quotation marks around the word), then it should be made public immediately. But the paper found it hard to believe that the Pennsylvania lawyers would risk their reputations by making such an outrageous agreement, which amounted to "compromising with crime." At the same time, the newspaper was troubled by the odd conduct of the counsel from Pennsylvania, which "leads us to fear that they did or said *something* which will afford [Lowe] a plausible excuse for refusing to surrender the kidnappers."[23]

The *Elkton Democrat* was also picking up and sifting through the rumors and unconfirmed stories that came its way. When the Pennsylvania grand jury indicted McCreary, the paper fumed that "the bloodhounds of abolition," not satisfied with the Baltimore compromise, were still after McCreary and "pant[ing] for his blood." A month later, the newspaper cited a "highly respectable source" who had learned that certain persons in Chester County, having given up on the requisition process, were planning to take matters into their own hands, seize McCreary by force, and throw him in the West Chester jail. That, bristled the *Democrat*, was a very bad idea. The Pennsylvanians would do well to remember what happened the last time they tried to ambush McCreary: "Our citizens will defend McCreary to the last extremity against all such incursions, and there are those here who would rejoice at the opportunity such a mad attempt would afford. . . . If some eight or ten men could not capture McCreary in a barroom in Lancaster county, there would be little chance for ten times that number to capture him here where relief would be swift and sure." No one tried.[24]

It was not until the middle of June that the newspapers could move past the rumors and say with assurance that a requisition had been made by Pennsylvania's Bigler and refused by Maryland's Lowe, and not until the end of the month that they were able to make public the correspondence between the two governors that finally confirmed the rumors. In his letter to Bigler, Lowe defended his refusal to hand over Thomas McCreary on several grounds: (1) that McCreary thought he was arresting a runaway and so was morally innocent, (2) that it was appropriate for a governor to make his own decisions about the validity of requisitions from one state to another, (3) that he did not think that McCreary could get a fair trial in Pennsylvania, "where so strong prejudices exist against him," and (4) that there was the all-important deal. The verdict, Lowe wrote, "was given in favor of the freedom of the Parker girls, in virtue of an arrangement between the counsel in Baltimore, that their acquittal was to be followed by a cessation of effort to convict McCreary of kidnapping." By agreeing to the "arrangement," the lawyers for Rachel Parker had essentially admitted the moral innocence of McCreary and Merritt, and Governor Lowe declared himself content to abide by their decision.[25]

Governor Bigler replied at great length, salting his letter with assurances of his wish to preserve the "very amicable relations which have existed between Maryland and Pennsylvania" but giving no ground to Lowe. The strength of his arguments for a new trial in Pennsylvania and the occasional intensity of his language suggest that the "deal" that freed McCreary probably did not come from Bigler himself and must, as many suspected, have been put on the table by Judge Bell. Most of the letter was devoted to demolishing Lowe's claim that it was appropriate, and even standard practice, for a governor to decide, on the merits of the case, whether to honor a requisition or not. The very idea, Bigler wrote, was "truly startling." On the question of whether McCreary could get a fair trial in Pennsylvania, Bigler acknowledged that "excitement and misdirected feeling may, on special occasions, prevail without," but Pennsylvania courtrooms were more civil and well-ordered places than those in Maryland: "The sacred portals of justice in this orderly Commonwealth, are seldom if ever invaded by popular clamor." As for the "understanding" that would keep Pennsylvania from prosecuting McCreary and Merritt, Bigler declared that all the lawyers had overstepped their bounds. There was no connection that he could see between the freedom trial of Rachel Parker and an indictment for kidnapping against McCreary and Merritt. If there was a reason for the kidnapping trial not to go forward, that was for the grand jury in Pennsylvania to determine, not the governor of Maryland.[26]

Bigler's letter was dated May 26, 1853. After its contents were published, the newspapers generally fell silent on the matter, as if everyone were waiting to see how Lowe would respond. The African American *National Era* did go on record as finding that Governor Lowe's "imputations are as insolent as his logic is bad." But the same newspaper, in the same issue, also expressed its disgust with Pennsylvania's deference to its bullying neighbor, attacking Bigler for toadying to Maryland and declaring, both illogically and unhelpfully, "The little respect we have on hand goes to McCreary and Lowe. There is that much of Adam in us yet, that we like the metal in the heel of the tyrant's boot better than the dough in the sycophant's heart." The Philadelphia Female Anti-Slavery Society found the same terminology appropriate to describe its disgust with the public face Pennsylvania had put on for this trial. The Parker sisters had been restored to freedom, but at the cost of a "disgraceful sycophancy to the slave power."[27]

Governor Lowe put an end to the controversy and the waiting by simply not responding. He never answered Bigler's letter, at least not publicly, and after that spring, little more was heard about the matter from the newspapers, the governors, or the people of Chester County. Thomas McCreary never again went to trial, then or later, in Pennsylvania or anywhere else. The Parkers' long story never reached a conclusion, but it did end. It was finally over.

9

AFTERWARD

THE VIOLENT HISTORY of conflicts along the North/South border ended with emancipation and the last battles of the Civil War. In the aftermath, some who had been intimately involved in the conflicts were able to transmute the violence and terror into exciting and even profitable memories of a time that was gone for good. By 1880, when a West Chester newspaper ran this notice, even the once-hated abolitionism had become only an interesting and harmless relic of the old days: "Edwin H. Coates, of Philadelphia, one of the old-line Abolitionists, and for 30 years an active worker on the 'Underground Railroad,' will give his celebrated lecture entitled 'Reminiscences of the Slaves' Escape from Bondage to Freedom' in Odd Fellows Hall." Others, not surprisingly, could not see the end of the conflict so completely in terms of what was past and now largely irrelevant except as entertainment. For them, the war left much unfinished business and many battles still to fight, especially for African Americans. Thomas Garrett and William Still, who had been two of the most prominent and effective contributors to the work of the Underground Railroad in the border states, both worried about what lay ahead, cautioning that the end of slavery was by no means a guarantee of freedom for African Americans. Garrett wrote in 1870: "I now rejoice most heartily that African Slavery is forever ended in this country. But there is much yet for philanthropists to do for this people before they can fully enjoy the great boon granted them by the Fifteenth Amendment." In the 1878 edition of his history of the Underground Railroad, Still acknowledged how distant the goal of true freedom and equality remained for African Americans, fifteen years after the "wonderful changes" brought by emancipation: "I believe no more strongly at this moment than I have believed ever since the Proclamation of Emancipation was made by Abraham Lincoln, that as a class, in this country, no small exertion will have to be put forth before the blessings of freedom and knowledge can be enjoyed by these people."[1]

For the free blacks of Pennsylvania and other border areas, people like Rachel and Elizabeth Parker, the end of the Civil War brought emancipation in the form of freedom from the threat of kidnapping. As both Garrett and Still had recognized, however, the political changes following the war did not make many other significant differences in the patterns of their experience. When Thomas McCreary kidnapped the Parkers, their lives had been altered in dramatic and unimagined ways—for the space of one year. When that year closed with the end of Rachel's trial, the lives of Rachel and Elizabeth returned to what was largely a pre-war normalcy and predictability. They remained poor, illiterate black women in a place that had clear ideas about the entitlements and the limitations of poor black women. The lives of both women, even though they were relatively long ones, ended pretty much as they had begun.

Rachel, who had been the tractable, likeable teenager, the good worker, spent most of her adult life working as a domestic for white families as her mother had done, earning praise as a good "Mammy." She married, had children and grandchildren, and died among her family. We can follow at least the major changes in her life. Tracking her sister, on the other hand, is more difficult. Elizabeth, the restless and difficult child, the determinedly independent one, moved more quickly and more fully out of the range of history and memory (and the census taker) than her sister did, and no one seemed to make much of an effort to find her. When she did reappear in public and was asked about her experiences, she may have lied, but nobody bothered to check. No one paid much attention to either sister once the whites of Chester County had secured the Parkers' freedom, as if freedom—from slavery or jail—should have been enough for them, as if that were all they could need or want. No one acknowledged how constrained and limited their freedom was and always had been, nor did anyone acknowledge the courage and resilience they had shown throughout their ordeal.

Rachel returned from Baltimore to the Miller farm in West Nottingham, the place that had been home to her for seven years before her kidnapping. She remained with Rebecca Miller, Joseph's widow, for a few weeks after her release from jail and then moved to the farm home of Hart G. Coates; his wife, Eliza; and their six children, in Lancaster County. (Rebecca Miller remained in West Nottingham for the rest of her life. She died there in 1893 and was buried beside her husband in the hilltop cemetery at Union ME Church, the old House's Meeting House.) The *Village Record* reported in 1856 that Rachel was doing well, by the county's lights and in its terms: she was said to be an "estimable and well behaved girl." In 1865, after twelve years of living in the Coateses' home, Rachel married George Wesley, a Civil War veteran who served with the 13th U.S. Colored Infantry.[2] Rachel was thirty-one when they married; George, who was from Maryland and may have been an escaped slave, was twenty-two. They lived on the Coates farm for the eight years of their marriage while Rachel continued to work for the family. George's younger sister Mary also worked for the Coates family as a live-in domestic while Rachel and George were there. Rachel gave birth to four children during those years: Lucinda, or Lucy, born in 1865; Joseph, born in 1868; Elizabeth, born in 1869; and Judith, born in 1872. For the space of at least eight years, then, Rachel gave herself to the simultaneous running of two households and the care of a growing number of children—the six Coates children and, eventually, her own four.[3]

When Rachel and George separated in 1873, Rachel moved back into the Coateses' home, bringing her two youngest children—Elizabeth and Judith, ages four and one—with her. (It is unclear why Lucy and Joseph, ages eight and five, did not come with Rachel, although it is possible they were already working for other white families at that point. We know that by the time Joseph was twelve, he was working for a farm family in the nearby township of Little Britain.) Rachel remained with the Coates family for another twenty-five years, working for Eliza Coates's sons after Eliza died. By 1900, Rachel, who was then sixty-five, had left the Coateses' and was living with her oldest child, Lucy, and Lucy's husband, James R. Jones, in Lower Oxford. When Rachel died in 1918 at the age of eighty-three, her obituary named three surviving children, all married: Lucy Jones, Joseph Wesley, and Elizabeth White. The fourth child, Judith, seems not to have survived into adulthood. Joseph married in 1888; he and his wife had three sons and a daughter named Charlotte. By 1910, eight-year-old Charlotte was living with her grandmother Rachel and her aunt Lucy in Lower Oxford. Also in the household were two-year-old John Jones, who was a nephew of Lucy's husband, James, and two other children who were apparently being cared for by the Joneses or by Rachel.[4]

Rachel was still living with Lucy in Lower Oxford at the time of her death. Her obituary gave the cause as "infirmities of age." Howard Coates commented ten years later that her death was not much noticed at the time. But Coates did offer a brief, belated tribute to her. Rachel was, he wrote, a "trusted, faithful servant, after the manner of the colored Mammy of the South. And to attest her appreciation, my mother directed that a small annuity be paid to her yearly during her life. She helped care for me as a boy of seven and lived in the family to play 'Mammy' to all my children, for over forty-five years." It seems that Rachel was, in the eyes of the white people who knew her, still considered estimable, still remembered as well behaved and reliable.[5]

When the *Village Record* reported in 1856 that Rachel was settled and behaving well, all it could say of her sister Elizabeth was that she was somewhere in the northern part of Chester County. The rebellious child who wandered the roads of the county apparently became a wandering adult. After her return from Baltimore in 1853, she does not appear in the records again until 1880, when she gave her age as thirty-eight. By that time she had become Elizabeth Miller, a widow, living in West Chester and working as a housekeeper. There is no evidence of whom she married or when. Living in the same household on East Marshall Street were a widower and his two children. Also in the household was eight-year-old Lottie J. Miller, who was probably Elizabeth's daughter. After that one mention in 1880, Lottie disappears from the records. She might have married and changed her name; she might have left the state; she might have died.

In the early 1890s, Elizabeth still lived in West Chester but at a different address. She was found there by a reporter for the *Daily Local News*, who asked if she would tell again the story of her kidnapping. She did tell it, and the paper published it. The same paper then printed the story again in 1941, long after Elizabeth's death. Neither of these appearances of Elizabeth's story acknowledged the version that had originally been collected by Toby back in 1853. The 1941 story appeared under the headline "Girl Slave's Vivid Story of Cruel Days," with a brief explanation: "Mrs. Elizabeth Miller, a colored woman who fifty years ago lived at 427 East Barnard Street, West Chester, is quoted as telling at that time a thrilling story of her kidnapping when she was a girl of ten years. She was a daughter of Edward Parker, who died here about the year 1892." In her retelling, Elizabeth's story was both more dramatic and less convincing than it had been when she first told it to Toby. It is hardly surprising that her story changed over the course of forty years or that, when someone solicited her story again after all those years, she might have decided to make it more "thrilling" and to make the wrongs done to her even greater than they had seemed at the time. When someone thought to ask for her story, that is, she told a good one.

In the 1941 version, she described her treatment by McCreary and by unspecified "slave traders" in New Orleans as more severe than she had in the original: McCreary kept her in a box for a day and a half with her legs bent and her feet tied to her hands, and she was beaten and tortured in New Orleans in an attempt to get her to identify herself as Henrietta Crocus. The number of people in the ship that took her to New Orleans was much greater in the second version than in the original (260 as opposed to 50), and the amount of money she brought when she was sold was also greater (a whopping $2,000 as opposed to the more realistic $900 she originally reported). In the first account she was sold from a slave pen, and in the second one she was sold at auction and became the object of a bidding war. Elizabeth ended her revised account by declaring some moral victory for herself and Rachel, some small justice: "The man McCreary, who kidnapped myself and my sister, died in poverty, a miserable sot."[6]

Elizabeth herself may or may not have died in poverty. She was still in West Chester in 1900. The census listed her as having two children, although it did not name them. Lottie J. Miller was not mentioned. The last record of Elizabeth is from 1920, when she was seventy-nine, living in York, Pennsylvania, in a home that she owned on Salem Avenue. There is no record of her death.

Beck, the mother of Rachel and Elizabeth, was still living with her husband in Lancaster County in 1860, according to the census for that year. She was fifty-eight. She must have been living in at least some comfort and security by that point; her fifty-seven-year-old husband was listed as owning real estate valued at over $18,000. (In his interview with Elizabeth, Toby had described Samuel Miller as "a well-to-do widower, of some fifty years of age, possessing a comfortable two-story log house, twenty acres of land, and a well earned and deserved reputation for honesty, industry, and sobriety.") Beck disappears from the records after 1860.[7]

Others who were involved in this dramatic story of viciousness and compassion, greed and generosity, enslavement and rescue also lived out the rest of their lives in relative quiet, also in largely predictable ways. Francis Corkran remained committed to Quakerism, the antislavery cause, Abraham Lincoln, and Republican politics through the Civil War. He wrote to a friend in September 1864: "All I can say is may the great God who rules the world and who holds in his hands the destinies of nations, strengthen the mind and control the heart of Abraham Lincoln in such a manner that will ensure the suppression of the present unholy Rebellion—the triumph of right over wrong and though last not the least—a thorough and complete vindication of that great American idea that man is capable of self government." Corkran retired as Collector of the Port of Baltimore and from most of his political activities after the war. He concentrated on his successful lumber and coal business, moving it from Baltimore to nearby Lutherville, Maryland, where he had built a home. He and his wife had two daughters and four sons; one of the sons joined him in the business, and they opened a second coal yard in Towsontown, Maryland. Corkran apparently could not abandon politics entirely, however: he was appointed postmaster at Lutherville in 1873. He died there in 1886, at the age of seventy-two.[8]

Levi K. Brown, another of the Baltimore Quakers who aided the Chester County friends of Joseph Miller and the Parkers on their trips to the city, would take on an important role in the Quaker outreach to Native Americans. Late in his life he would travel to the West with another Quaker, Joseph Janney; together they would publish *A Report of a Visit to the Santee and Ponca Indians, in Nebraska and Dakota* (1886).

John Miller Dickey retained his zeal for colonization after his involvement in the Parker affair, with ample support from others in the county. In 1853, the *Jeffersonian* of West Chester praised the efforts of the local colonization society in language that, if it was not supplied by Dickey, would at least have met with his approval. The society helped to "civilize and Christianize" African natives and used "its hallowed influence" to bring "our Southern brethren to regard emancipation with favor, through the light of a most successful experiment, without wounding their feelings or impinging upon their reserved rights." The influence of the genteel, cautious Dickey may have had a lot to do with the society's reputation for keeping their politics polite. Dickey also remained active in the administration of the Oxford Female Seminary, of which he was a cofounder. (In 1859 the school was offering a semester of study in the ordinary curriculum for $60, with an additional charge of $10 for piano, French, and drawing lessons.) After Dickey's death in 1878, his son helped to foster his father's reputation for heroism in the Parker affair, claiming that he made many trips to Baltimore in spite of threats from ruffians there and that "once he was very near death at their hands."[9]

The "notorious" slave catcher and kidnapper George Alberti died in 1869 at the age of seventy-nine. The *New York Times* noted but did not mourn his passing, remarking that he was for much of his life "beyond all question, the most unpopular man in Philadelphia." The *Times* pulled out all the stops in damning Alberti and his work, calling him "the oppressor of the poor—the professional bail-goer—the gallows-man—the heartless vindicator of the merciless Fugitive Slave law—the man at sight of whom children ran affrighted." The newspaper expressed surprise that Alberti did not die considerably earlier and less peacefully than he did, given the nature of his career.[10]

Matthew Donnelly and his family, including his brother-in-law and probable co-conspirator John Merritt, disappear from the records for a while after Donnelly's bankruptcy in 1849 and the kidnappings of the Parkers in 1851. They reappear in Covington, Kentucky, in 1860. This move out of state could well have been a retreat from a new set of creditors. It might also have been a flight from those county neighbors who suspected that Donnelly had been deeply involved in the kidnappings of Elizabeth Parker and others. If the people of Chester County succeeded in getting Thomas McCreary indicted for kidnapping by a Pennsylvania grand jury, Matthew Donnelly could be next. In 1869 the Donnellys and Merritt evidently thought it safe to return to Chester County, back to their old neighborhood, where Matthew bought 230 acres at Pleasant Garden on Big Elk Creek. He was fifty-one years old; he listed his occupation as farmer. By this point, the Donnellys' household included their son FitzHenry, his wife, and their two small children, both born in Kentucky. The Donnellys' return to Pleasant Garden brought a return of their financial woes. In 1873, Matthew was sued for debt by the woman who had sold him the farm four years earlier; the property was seized by the sheriff and sold back to the original owner for $100. She clearly did well in the transaction, while he lost everything. The next record of Donnelly is the notice of his death three years later, in 1876, in Washington, DC. After the Pleasant Garden farm was sold, John Merritt moved to Cecil County, Maryland, Thomas McCreary's home, and died there in 1905 at the age of seventy-three.

Luther Schoolfield remained in Baltimore until his death in 1884, when he was seventy-seven. His last known occupation was as a real estate broker. He and his wife, Elizabeth, had twelve children, the last one born in 1858. Luther outlived his wife and three of his children.

Thomas McCreary died in 1870 in his hometown of Elkton, Maryland. Elizabeth Parker may or may not have been right about the misery of McCreary's life at its end, but it was unquestionably a less sensational life than it had been. McCreary settled into at least the appearance of respectable citizenship in Elkton, living with his wife and two daughters and apparently keeping his slave-catching efforts within the law. He was appointed one of two constables for Cecil County in 1852. In 1856 the governor of Maryland gave him an additional appointment, that of inspector of lumber for the county. McCreary evidently managed his two positions simultaneously, since in late 1856 the *Elkton Democrat* reported that "officer" McCreary had succeeded in locating and arresting a fugitive slave and her two accomplices a few miles outside of town. In 1860 he listed his occupation for the census as tanner and currier. By 1870, the last year of his life, he was serving as sexton of the local Trinity Episcopal Church.[11]

Back in 1852, the correspondent for the West Chester *Village Record*, the pseudonymous Toby, had offered something like a prophetic obituary for the victorious McCreary, after his kidnapping trial had ended without a conviction. McCreary, Toby wrote, "is unquestionably as old in sin as in years, and as hard of heart as his head is hoary. He has long escaped justice, and may do it now again, but in the natural course of life he cannot escape it long, and will then meet it where bail is never taken, and escape hopeless—and that is not in this world."[12] When McCreary died, at about the age of seventy, his real obituary appeared in several area newspapers, including the *Baltimore Sun*. The obituary, an astonishing document, made an effort to cast McCreary as a folk hero, a kind of Robin Hood who stole from the (still reviled) abolitionists rather than the rich, "a man of iron nerve and lion heart" who was hell on lawbreakers and their friends, especially their Pennsylvania antislavery friends, but would never break the law himself—except when the law was just plain wrong. The obituary acknowledged that McCreary had been charged with kidnapping the Parker girls, but reported that the charge proved to be groundless.

> McCreary, though charged with the offense, was above anything of the kind. He was bold and adventurous, even to rashness, in arresting runaway slaves, but would disturb no one known to be free. He had a number of broad-brimmed Quakers in Chester

and Lancaster counties in his pay, who used to come stealthily to his domicile in Elkton in the small hours of the night, and furnish him with information as to the hiding places of those of whom he was in quest.[13]

The information in the obituary, the writer explained cheerfully, had come straight from the horse's mouth: "We had this explanation . . . from McCreary's own lips, and have no reason to doubt its truth." There were, of course, plenty of people who would have reason to doubt the truth of McCreary's claim to having Quaker informants and plenty who knew that he was far from being "above" the kidnapping of free people. But the obituary did not make room for them. McCreary had managed to provide the script for his own obituary. He had the last word. And he never went to jail.

ACKNOWLEDGMENTS

Y FIRST THANKS go to the many librarians and archivists, professional and volunteer, who welcomed me, guided me to the right sources, made suggestions, shared their considerable knowledge, and in general provided the invaluable research assistance I could not have done without. I am indebted especially to Pamela Powell and Diane Rofini at the Chester County Historical Society, who were immensely helpful; to the staff at the Kent County (Maryland) Public Library, who provided lifesaving technical aid; and to the librarians at the Miller Library of Washington College, who were unfailingly welcoming. Thanks also go to the staffs at the Chester County Archives, the Maryland State Archives, the Maryland Historical Society, the Cecil County (Maryland) Historical Society, the Oxford (Pennsylvania) Public Library, the Lincoln College Library, and the Friends Library at Swarthmore College.

The project has benefited enormously from the attention of three careful, generous, and very smart readers: Jim Maddox, Jonathan Strong, and Jane Scott. Their advice, gently but firmly delivered, helped to turn a wobbly and meandering manuscript into a book. Every writer should have such readers.

I am very grateful for the intellectual home provided by the Kent County Historical Society and especially by its librarian, Joan Anderson, and her Wednesday morning research group. The Society's community history group, a remarkable gathering of scholars, has also offered both encouragement and direction. All of these people not only have shared and fostered my passion for local history; they have also showed me a lot about how it is done.

APPENDIX

⸺ ⬦ ⬦ ⸺

T*he newspaper account that follows is the interview with Elizabeth Parker that "Toby" conducted on January 22, 1853, and published in the West Chester* Village Record *on January 25 and February 1, 1853.*

ELIZABETH PARKER

The Kidnapped Girl of Nottingham

Written by Toby for the *Village Record*
Nottingham, January 22, 1853

A NIGHT OR TWO SINCE, in company with two esteemed friends, I visited the home of the returned and famous Parker girls—Elizabeth and Rachel.

We found them—or rather Elizabeth only, Rachel being temporarily absent at home—restored after many a weary day of sorrow and confinement, of suffering and adventure, to that blessed refuge and rest for all abused and stricken ones—the cottage of their mother. What a long, long, aching, terrible year of absence from both those loved objects, the past one has been to them.

Rachel's history is familiar to us all, there is outrage and murder in it, and sadly and willingly I am silent about her.

Elizabeth's story is as yet untold, and it was hers we went to hear. She has had adventures—she was kidnapped, sent off to a southern city and sold—has served in slavery, and was returned and tried and declared free, and all in a little more than a year!

Becky, renowned Becky—"little Beck"—the mother, has recently married again. Becky has, during all her life, manifested a decided love for matrimonial connection, with equally decided partiality for *variety* in such alliances—the changes she has made being more than one or two, either, and that too, without waiting until slow death should sever her from the old before she joined herself to the new, and it is said, too, if the whole truth be told, that these changes were made without a very rigid scrutiny on her part into the entire legality of her "writing of divorcement." But be that as it may, she is at present—which is all that I have to do with—joined in holy wedlock with a Mr. Miller, a well-to-do widower, of some fifty years of age, possessing a comfortable two-story log house, twenty acres of land, and a well-earned and deserved reputation for honesty, industry and sobriety. He, himself, met us at the door, which was opened as soon as we knocked, although it was after night—and after recent occurrences it behoves all people of color to have a care and repel all night stragglers.

Mr. Miller's greeting was very gentlemanly—Mrs. M.'s was more noisy. "Well Becky," I said familiarly on entering, extending my hand to her, for I was anxious to establish a friendly and [illegible] feeling at once. She took my hand first, and looked hard at me next—"Why la sakes!" she exclaimed, fussing round among the chairs, "if this isn't Mr. Toby! Why how in the land do you do?" I told her I did very well just then by her hot stove, and added a wonder that she got back from Baltimore with a whole skin. "La sakes!" she said, "they wouldn't have nuthin at all to do with me down thar—nuthin at all, they wouldn't hardly look at me, I was too old for them. They thought I warn't worth anything, I reckon."

"You got your back up about it, I suppose," said I, "and felt rather slighted."

"La sakes! no *sir*, I didn't want 'em claimin' me, indeed, for I knew I didn't b'long to none of 'em, and didn't 'low to, nuther."

"You wouldn't like to be called Juno, then?" I asked.

"All but the Juno."

"Did Rachel know me when she saw me in court the other day?" I asked, for Rachel and I had seldom met, and I did not recognise her.

"Yes, *sir*, indeed she did; as soon as ever she seed you, she said to me, 'La, mammy, look—if there isn't Mr. Toby!'"

Sitting on the hearth by the chimney jam, quiet, old, slightly bent, and wearing a bonnet, sat another colored woman, whom after a moment or two I recognized as "*Old* Haney." She is well known over Nottingham, though few, I presume, know her now, or ever did, by any other name than "Old Haney." She had dandled me in her lap when a child, she was "*Old* Haney" then, and that is more years ago than I care to mention. I passed my hand to her with quite a feeling of joy at seeing her old familiar face. "Why Haney," I said, "is that you? I am very glad to see you, but indeed I thought you had gone to Heaven many long years ago." She smiled sadly—she used to smile and laugh very prettily—and said in low tones "that by the goodness of God she was still in the land of the living. She didn't know how long she would remain yet, but it could not be long."

On the opposite side of the stove from me sat Mr. Miller, and a fine, honest looking negro he is, and a stalwart son—and also two young girls whom I took for Rachel and Elizabeth, not seeing them distinctly.

"Well Rachel," I said, "you had a hard battle down in Baltimore." Instead of answering the individual who passed in my mind for Rachel disappeared suddenly from her chair out of sight behind the stove, in a manner very much resembling a Chinese salaam, and an audible "ti-he, ti-he, ti-he" was heard issuing from somewhere about where her head would be. "La sakes!" sung out Becky, "that isn't Rachel—that's another gal of mine, [she was Miller's daughter] her name is Hiekiah."

I then addressed the other girl—"Well, Elizabeth, I guess there is no mistake about you. You have seen a good deal of the world while you were away?" "Yes sir-r, [she has a way of getting out 'sir,' that I cannot find a letter to represent the sound exactly,] I've passed through a good deal since I was in Pennsylvania afore."

Elizabeth's voice is rather pleasant, she speaks rapidly, and gets her words out with an air, and tries to be a little stilted. The advertisement posted up for the runaways, Eliza and Henrietta Crocus, said that Henrietta—who stands for Elizabeth—was two or three shades lighter than Eliza—or Rachel. Elizabeth, when perfectly well, is about as deep a black as you can imagine, but at present she is a little lighter, owing to confinement and other causes, and looks, as our neighbor Anderson very pithily stated to the court in Baltimore, "very much like as if she had been drawn through a sick cow!"

She is smart and intelligent, and seems to have improved very much by her travels. Her airs are very much like those our country girls assume after being a year in town. She is often slightly sullen, and not disposed to be communicative, but spoke freely to us. Her history was obtained, however, by piecemeal, in answer to our questions. My readers would of course like to have her own language. I will write her history so, and connectedly.

"I do not know what month it was, sir, but I had been at Mr. Donnelly's about a month, when one night Mr. Donnelly told me he wanted me to bring in the slop bucket, and said it was out by the barrel. Mr. Merritt, he was in the room, and he said he would go and get it, and then Mr. Donnelly got up and said he would get it hisself. He went out, Mr. Donnelly did, and after about quarter of an hour he come back and said to me that I could go out for the bucket and that it was by the barrel, but did not say why he had not brought it hisself. I went out and had got about half way across the yard, when a man that I had not seen before caught me by the neck, and put a stick in my mouth."

"Put what in?" one of us asked.

"A stick, sir-r, a gag, sir-r. It was a stick of wood, pretty thick, with a string at each end.—They put the stick in my mouth and tied it by the strings. I couldn't holler at all. One man then took me by the head and another one by the feet, and they carried me to the road and put me into a two horse wagon there. One of the men then got in and drove me off. The other man went away—I didn't know him, he had a dark coat and long whiskers—it was not Merritt. It was Thomas McCreary that drove the wagon. The cars had passed for Baltimore when we got to Elkton so he took me to his own house and kept me until the next night."

Written by Toby for the *Village Record* (Concluded)
February 1, 1853

I LEFT POOR ELIZABETH with a "stick" in her mouth, at McCreary's home in Elkton. This kind of gag, like the tender mercies of the wicked, was really cruel, and she said to me that it hurt very much, cutting her mouth so that it was not well for weeks, and injuring her teeth. The curse of God rests on kidnapping and the kidnapper, and the little loving kindness, ever, that wells up in action in every human heart, is frozen up and lost in the great icy chambers of his cold and deadened soul. Were I asked what the three great blessed boons of life were, I would answer: "Home, Love, and Liberty." The man who wantonly invades my sacred home, and tears me from it and from love and those that love me, and sells my Liberty and me to a stranger, and an oppressor, and glories in his gain, and does to other ones the same, is a wretch that man cannot adequately punish. I war not with the laws of the land. In the cause before us if McCreary, wearing due authority in law, honestly in his own mind, made the capture he did—I say no more. I believe he believed them to be free, but he didn't care. Let us go on with Elizabeth's story.

"It was Sunday [*sic*] night I was taken; no cars run on the railroad on Sunday, so he kept me on at his house all day and kept the gag in my mouth all the time; once he come and asked if I didn't want something to eat, I told him no, by shaking my head, and he never offered to take the stick away. Some time in the day he brought a Mr. McCullough, of Elkton, to see me, and he asked him if I was not his slave—he said no and they both went off. Sunday night at twelve o'clock, he put me in the cars and took me to Baltimore, and took me then to Messrs. Campbell's trading house [she carefully avoided ever saying 'slave pen' or 'jail,' it was always 'traders house,'] after he got me there, he took me into a room by myself, and took the stick out of my mouth and then he described to me a Mr. Schoolfield and his children, and told me the names of each one, and then he pulled out a six barreled rifle and pointed it at me, and told me he was going to take me into a room where Mr. Schoolfield and his family were, and if I did not call them all by name as he had told me and say that I was Schoolfield's slave, he would shoot me down on the floor of the room. I then went along with him and did as he had told me; I could tell each one by the description he gave; I had to tell everybody who asked, that I belonged to Schoolfield, for I was afraid of McCreary; was at Campbell's about two weeks; there were about thirty there; they had sent a vessel off to New Orleans a week or two before I came; we were pretty well accommodated there; we got corn cake and rice, and potatoes, generally, to eat and had pretty good beds for sleeping on; most of us had to seek our own food; staid there about two weeks; was then put on board of a ship to go to New Orleans; didn't like the idea much; [as near as we could tell she did not have much (illegible) in the matter, the novelty and adventure I imagine pleased her a little;] it was very cold [so] a steam ship had to go ahead and break the ice for our ship to get out; there were about twenty others on board, one half of them belonging to the Messrs. Campbells the rest to Mr. [illegible]; we were very well accommodated on board the ship; could go out of the cabin up on the hurricane deck whenever we wanted, and had plenty to eat and had first rate beds; some of the beds were on the floor and some were hung up, swinging beds; we were about one month making the passage; we didn't have [illegible] and I liked the voyage right well; the Messrs. Campbells have a brother who has a trader's house in New Orleans; when we arrived all who were from Messrs. Campbell's house, in Baltimore, went there and the rest were sent to Mr. [illegible]; there were forty or fifty colored people at Campbell's traders house; we were all kept together in one room [illegible] the men on one side and the women on the other; we were allowed to sit on the [illegible] or walk about if there were no purchasers in, but if any came in, we had all to stand up on a [illegible] him, the buyer would walk along, and when he found some person he liked the looks of, he would get them out in the middle of the floor, and make 'em jump backwards and forwards, and run and swing themselves about, and then he would look at their teeth and examine their backs."

"What for? What did he examine their backs for?" we asked; "To see if they were scawered, sir, to see if they had any scaws on 'em, sir, and if they had, they wouldn't have 'em, that were not a good sign. After I had been there a few days, I was allowed to go out in the street along with some of the rest; there was always somebody, an overseer or somebody with us though; at night, we all slept in the room where we were kept during the day, we had little hard beds, we laid down in a row, our head out to the middle of the room, the men on one side, the women on the other."

"I had been there about two weeks when a man from the country, picked me out and examined me; he was a farmer, he made me run about, examined my back, and then my teeth."

"That was to see if she was a good feeder," interrupted Becky, "that was the reason they would not have anything to do with me in Baltimore, I hadn't teeth enough."

We laughed and Elizabeth went on: "Mr. Campbell would not sell me to that man though, he said he wouldn't sell me to go into the country at all. A day or two after that a colored man came, who wanted to buy a girl for his master, he picked me out, examined me, asked me a good many questions, and then went out into another room with Mr. Campbell, and I suppose bought me, for a little while after he came back and told me to go with him. I don't know exactly what he paid for me, I think it was $900, he took me home with him; he lived with Mrs. Churo."

"Was she a foreigner," we asked.

"No sir, she was a Creowl, sir, a creowl, she kept a flower garden and kept some sows and made molasses candy. The man who bought me took me in to her, she told me she liked my looks, and all she wanted of me was to sell milk and candy and flowers, and that if I was honest and done the best I could, she would treat me well, so I set into work in the morning. I took out milk to the market and sold it out by the pint and quart, at 10 o'clock I came home and took out molasses candy—this Mrs. Churo made herself, it was done up in long platted sticks, and was fust-rate, I sold it at a levy a stick, and I sold a heap of it, at 4 o'clock I went home again and got flowers and took them out. I would go to the theatres and stand with them, I stood inside and could get to see the performances, I like to see 'em play fust-rate. I would sometimes leave early and go to dance parties [balls] and would sell a good many flowers there. On Saturday nights the colored people had their dance parties—the white people never had none that night. I always sold a heap of flowers there, I never danced any myself, I never got acquainted with any of the bucks down there. I was always allowed to be home by ten o'clock at night. One night I had been at a dance party and was kept late, it was about twelve o'clock when I was going home, when a watchman met me and stopped me, he asked where I was going? I told him I was agoing home—he asked me who I belonged to? I said I belonged to Madam Churo—he said I didn't. I told him I did—he said then that he knew all Mrs. Churo's slaves and that I wasn't one of them. I told him I was one she had lately bought.

"'Have you a pass?' he asked.

"'Yes sir,' I said. I had, and I showed it to him and then I just thought I would just tell the truth so I told him, I don't belong to Madam Churo nuther for I belonged to myself, and that I was a free girl, I was stolen out of Pennsylvania and sent from Baltimore down here and sold.

"'Who sold you?' he asked.

"I told him it was Mr. Campbell, and then he took me off to the watch house and kept me all night. The next morning he sent for Mr. Campbell—when he came he asked him if he had sold me; he said he had, he then asked him, for his bill of sale of me to him, and he couldn't show any; Mr. Campbell then sent out for a lawyer, and when he came they talked awhile, and then Mr. Campbell gave the watchman some money and then they sent me home. Not long after that two men came to me one day and asked me all about myself; [the men I suppose who were telegraphed to by the Baltimoreans] and they told me at last that I was to be sent back and stand a trial for my freedom. I was very glad to hear that, not long after that Mr. Campbell paid back to Mrs. Churo what she had paid him for me and took me away back to the traders house.

"Mrs. Churo was a very nice woman and I got along with her fust-rate, she had several other slaves besides me men and women, the men attended to the garden, some of the other girls went out with milk and candy and flowers too.

"When we were at Mrs. Churo's we generally got rice and bread and meat, but we girls, who stood in the street often bought our meals there. Mrs. Churo had two daughters, I don't know how old they were older than I was though, I don't know if they had any beaux or not; they generally got up about 10 o'clock. Mrs. Churo was up early. I sometimes dressed her, we had fust-rate feather beds there and we all slept in her house where she was herself. I wasn't never whipped, saw a man whipped one day in the street, he was whipped with the cat of nine tails. It looks very dreadful, none of Mrs. Churo's people were ever whipped that I knew of. I did not see any body have very hard times of it.

"I staid in Campbell's Traders House two weeks before I was put on board of the ship for Baltimore. We were two weeks this time making the voyage.

"I was put at Campbell's traders house again when I arrived in Baltimore. I was standing one day at an upper window looking out into the yard and fronting the gate, when the gate opened and looking who came in, I saw James Hutchinson, James Mullen, and Robert Hughes; I knew them as soon as I saw them; I was pleased first-rate to see them; there were about 30 or 40 of us there, some of us in the other room were ordered down; I did not go, I was not told to; the next time I was sent on along with the rest; I spoke or smiled to 'em as I went along.

"Most of the time that I staid at Mr. Campbell's traders house after I came back, until my trial, I had to help cook. The table was set out in the yard, and there we had to eat; I had not shoes, and working over a hot stove in the house, and then out on the cold ground in my bare feet gave me a bad cold."

Here Elizabeth's story ended. She had a very bad cold, and had several bad fits of coughing while we were there.

"Will people live and learn," said Becky, when Elizabeth was done, "this 'ere trip of her'n will do her good. She'll be settled now."

Elizabeth was never a favorite of her mother's. Mr. Anderson, it may be recollected, testified in Court that the last time Elizabeth came to see her mother while she lived at his house, she "whaled" her, and drove her off, and told her to never come back again, and she never did, and he believed that it was that "whaling" that done all the mischief. She got down there to Donnelly's and among them she was carried off. So mothers, it will seem, must be careful, and use the rod discreetly, and not "whale" their daughters too obstreperously.

The first time after the "whaling" that Becky and her castigated offspring met was in the Court room in Baltimore. There was no very cordial demonstration of effusion exhibited on either side on that occasion. Becky *might* have fallen on her daughter's neck and exclaimed joyfully amidst fast flowing tears, "my daughter who was dead is alive again. She that was lost is found," for it was certainly a very unheard of thing, that a child of Africa, on whom the manacles of slavery were once fastened, should get them stricken off again, and the child restored to its mother. I say, Becky, the mother *might* have done all that, but she didn't. Her first words were those of upbraiding, as if the abused, sorrowing child had not already borne enough; and accused her of being the author of all this trouble. Her greeting with Rachel was more cordial, but Becky never gets enthusiastic. She shook hands with her at arms length, saying, "Why, Rachel child, how does thee do?" (Becky is about one sixth a Quaker, on occasion,) and they stuck to each other's sides afterward; Elizabeth appears to be "father's child," while Rachel was "mother's." When Edward Parker, the father, entered the Court, Elizabeth seeing him as she chanced to look up, uttered a stifled scream of joy, and flying to him, wound her arms around his neck and kissed him again and again, and he greeted her no less fondly—lavishing on her such loving epithets as "pappy's honey!" "Neddy's pet!" etc., making this little tableau of family reunion quite affecting. Neddy was Becky's first love, but some absence or wrong, or something else had played very foul with her virgin affections, and the seal of death seemed on them and also on his, for the once husband and wife, the once young and fondly loving couple, met without emotion, with cold greeting of "well Neddy," "well Becky."

Elizabeth, by her story, appears to have been pretty well treated during her absence, and had rather a pleasant, easy life of it, and I do not suppose, as far as the matter of usage and labor was concerned, that she cared very much whether she returned or remained. Indeed, I heard that she stated in Baltimore that she did not want to come back, but she said to us that she was very glad to get back, and I believe that to be the truth, for to all of us, high and low, rich and poor, black or white, *Liberty* is very, very sweet.

NOTES

CHAPTER 1

1. Most accounts and records give Rachel's birth date as 1834, which would make her seventeen when she was kidnapped. Elizabeth's age is less clear, perhaps because she seemed older than her years. A Chester County resident who knew Elizabeth put her age at twelve to fourteen at the time of her kidnapping, although the only census record of her birth date gives it as 1841, which would make her between ten and eleven years old when she was taken.

2. Philadelphia Female Anti-Slavery Society, Annual Report (Philadelphia, 1853), 12; *Village Record*, January 18, 1853; Harriet Beecher Stowe, *The Key to Uncle Tom's Cabin* (Boston: John P. Jewett, 1853), 173.

3. William C. Kashatus, *Just Over the Line: Chester County and the Underground Railroad* (West Chester, PA: Chester County Historical Society, 2002), 91; W. U. Hensel, *The Christiana Riot and the Treason Trials of 1851: An Historical Sketch* (Lancaster, PA: New Era Printing, 1911), 7; James M. Wright, *The Free Negro in Maryland, 1634–1860* (New York: Octagon Books, 1971), 25–26. Pennsylvania's 1780 law also removed distinctions between the treatment of black criminals and the treatment of white criminals.

4. Fergus M. Bordewich, *Bound for Canaan: The Underground Railroad and the War for the Soul of America* (New York: Harper Collins, 2005), 133; Edward Turner, *The Negro in Pennsylvania: Slavery, Servitude, Freedom* (Washington, DC: American Historical Association, 1911), 231–233; *Maryland Ga-*

zette, March 6, 1823; Max Grivno, *Gleanings of Freedom: Free and Slave Labor along the Mason-Dixon Line, 1790–1860* (Urbana: University of Illinois Press, 2011), 46, 127.

5. Stanley Campbell, *The Slave-Catchers: Enforcement of the Fugitive Slave Law, 1850–1860* (Chapel Hill: University of North Carolina Press, 1970), 112; speech of Governor Benjamin F. Perry quoted in Steven Deyle, *Carry Me Back: The Domestic Slave Trade in American Life* (New York: Oxford University Press, 2005), 86; *Pennsylvania Freeman*, May 7, 1846.

6. R. C. Smedley, *History of the Underground Railroad in Chester and the Neighboring Counties of Pennsylvania* (Mechanicsburg, PA: Stackpole Books, 2005), 340–342; W. W. Thomson, *Chester County and Its People* (Chicago: Union History, 1898), 395.

7. *Chestertown Telegraph*, December 23, 1825; *Emancipator*, March 11, 1846; Stanley Harrold, *Border War: Fighting over Slavery before the Civil War* (Chapel Hill: University of North Carolina Press, 2010), 127.

8. *Anti-Slavery Bugle*, September 22, 1849; *Blue Hen's Chicken* quoted in the *Anti-Slavery Bugle*, December 22, 1849; *Village Record*, January 15, 1850; *Elkton Democrat*, June 30, 1849.

9. Isaac Mason, "Life of Isaac Mason as a Slave," in *From Bondage to Belonging: The Worcester Slave Narratives*, ed. B. Eugene McCarthy and Thomas L. Doughton (Amherst: University of Massachusetts Press, 2007), 267. Hugh Wallis, the man from whom Isaac Mason fled, did sell a group of nine slaves to a relative in Terrebone Parish, Louisiana, two years after Mason ran away. They brought a total price of $3,750.

10. Mason, "Life of Isaac Mason as a Slave," 271. Both Mason and Mitchell changed their names before they reached Pennsylvania. Mason's original name was William Thompson, and Mitchell's was Albert Ambrose.

11. Emerson W. Wilson, ed., *Mount Harmon Diaries of Sidney George Fisher, 1837–1850* (Wilmington: Historical Society of Delaware, 1976), 172–173.

12. John Smith Futhey and Gilbert Cope, *History of Chester County, Pennsylvania: With Genealogical and Biographical Sketches* (Louis H. Everts, 1881), 1:427; *Pennsylvania Freeman*, January 28, 1847; August 18, 1837; February 20, 1851. Burleigh was known for his skill as a debater, his eloquence as an orator, and the shabbiness of his dress, all of which led to some poetic advice from an anonymous fellow Quaker: "Thy logic is good / And may not be withstood; / Thy eloquence simple and true. / Could the outer man catch / Enough neatness to match / With the inner—'twere wise so to do, Charley

C.! / With the inner—'twere wise so to do" (*Abolitionrieties: or, Remarks on Some of the Members of the Pennsylvania State Anti-Slavery Society*, unpublished pamphlet, 1840).

13. *Pennsylvania Freeman*, January 9, 1846.

14. *Pennsylvania Freeman*, March 25, 1847; February 20, 1857.

15. Pauli Murray, *Proud Shoes: The Story of an American Family* (New York: Harper and Row, 1978), 95; Marianne H. Russo and Paul A. Russo, *Hinsonville, a Community at the Crossorads: The Story of a Nineteenth-Century African-American Village* (Selinsgrove, PA: Susquehanna University Press), 15; "Hosanna Meeting House," unpublished typescript, Chester County Historical Society.

16. *Jeffersonian*, November 11, 1851.

17. Gary Nash and Jean Soderlund, *Freedom by Degrees: Emancipation in Pennsylvania and Its Aftermath* (New York: Oxford University Press, 1991), 174.

18. U.S. Census, 1850.

19. Kashatus, *Just Over the Line*, 94–96.

20. Ryan Jordan, *Slavery and the Meetinghouse: The Quakers and the Abolitionist Dilemma, 1820–1865* (Bloomington: Indiana University Press, 2007), 92; Jean R. Soderlund, *Quakers and Slavery: A Divided Spirit* (Princeton, NJ: Princeton University Press, 1985), 177; Baltimore Yearly Meeting of Friends, Report of the Committee of the Yearly Meeting of Friends, Baltimore, 1842; Futhey and Cope, *History of Chester County, Pennsylvania*, 1:427; *Pennsylvania Freeman*, July 27, 1848.

21. Kashatus, *Just Over the Line*, 59; Pennsylvania Anti-Slavery Society, Fourteenth Annual Report Presented to the Pennsylvania Anti-Slavery Society, by Its Executive Committee, October 7, 1851.

22. Smedley, *History of the Underground Railroad*, xiv; Philadelphia Yearly Meeting of Friends (Orthodox), Report, Third Month 16, 1860, 1–2; Richard S. Newman, "'Lucky to Be Born in Pennsylvania': Free Soil, Fugitive Slaves, and the Making of Pennsylvania's Anti-Slavery Borderland," *Slavery and Abolition* 32, no. 3 (September 2011): 415. Back in 1837, the Anti-Slavery Society had taken a position very close to the one that would be taken by the Philadelphia Yearly Meeting in 1851. Rejecting both colonization and the use of force as solutions, the president of the Society, F. J. Le Moyne, urged free blacks to be docile, submissive, and patient: "LET EVERY ONE OF THE COLOURED PEOPLE, MALE OR FEMALE, *as far as in their power lies*, FULFILL ALL THEIR MORAL, SOCIAL, AND RELIGIOUS DUTIES. . . . We lament, before God, the

prejudices that exist, and we exhort you to be patient and faithful in the discharge of every duty. Remember that your good conduct will greatly aid the efforts that are making for the abolition of slavery, and the enjoyment of your rights" (Philadelphia Anti-Slavery Society, *Address to the Coloured People of the State of Pennsylvania* [Philadelphia, 1837], 4, 7).

23. Ralph Clayton, *Cash for Blood: The Baltimore to New Orleans Domestic Slave Trade* (Bowie, MD: Heritage Books, 2002), passim; *Delaware Republican*, February 17, 1853.

24. Eric Ledell Smith et al., "Rescuing African American Kidnapping Victims in Philadelphia as Documented in the Joseph Watson Papers at the Historical Society of Pennsylvania," *Pennsylvania Magazine of History and Biography* 129, no. 3 (July 2005): 320; Smedley, *History of the Underground Railroad*, 26; Julie Winch, "Pennsylvania and the Other Underground Railroad," *Pennsylvania Magazine of History and Biography* 111, no. 1 (January 1987): 7.

25. *Cincinnati Gazette* story quoted in the *Baltimore Sun*, May 6, 1843; *Baltimore Sun*, May 18, 1844; April 21, 1846; August 11, 1847; *Pennsylvania Freeman*, August 13, 1849; *Washington Reporter*, August 22, 1849.

26. *Baltimore Sun*, May 10, 1847.

27. Harriet Beecher Stowe, *Uncle Tom's Cabin*, in *Three Novels by Harriet Beecher Stowe* (New York: Library of America, 1982), 513; Eber M. Pettit, *Sketches in the History of the Underground Railroad* (Fredonia, NY: W. McKinstry and Son, 1879), n.p.; James H. W. Howard, *Bond and Free: A True Tale of Slave Times* (Harrisburg, PA, 1886), 83.

28. William Still, *The Underground Railroad: A Record of Facts, Authentic Narratives, Letters, &c* (Medford, NJ: Plexus Publishing, 2005), 398; *Massachusetts Spy*, July 28, 1852.

CHAPTER 2

1. William Still, *The Underground Railroad: A Record of Facts, Authentic Narratives, Letters, &c* (Medford NJ: Plexus Publishing, 2005), 251; Theodore Parker, *The Trial of Theodore Parker* (Boston, 1855), 130; Samuel May, *The Fugitive Slave Law and Its Victims* (New York: American Anti-Slavery Society, 1856), 161; William P. Newman to Frederick Douglass, October 10, 1850, in *The Black Abolitionist Papers*, ed. C. Peter Ripley (Chapel Hill: University of North Carolina Press, 1991), 4:61, 63–64.

2. *Philadelphia Inquirer*, November 11, 1860; Joseph Nogee, "The Prigg

Case and Fugitive Slaves, 1842–1850," *Journal of Negro History* 39 (July 1954): 201–202. The section of the 1847 law prohibiting the use of jails to house fugitives was repealed in March 1851. The *Baltimore Sun* applauded the repeal and used it to give Pennsylvania an admonishment disguised as a compliment. According to the *Sun*, the repeal demonstrated Pennsylvania's desire to right itself and be a better neighbor and citizen: "Pennsylvania demonstrates her genuine feeling of brotherhood with the confederated States of the South, by refusing longer to throw obstacles in the way of carrying out the compromises of the constitution" (April 16, 1851).

3. J. R. Dorsey, *Documentary History of Slavery in the United States, by a Native of Maryland* (Washington, DC: 1851), 52; Stanley Harrold, *Border War: Fighting over Slavery before the Civil War* (Chapel Hill: University of North Carolina Press, 2010), 139.

4. *Pennsylvania Freeman*, March 13, 1851.

5. Quoted in Steven Lubet, *Fugitive Justice: Runaways, Rescuers, and Slavery on Trial* (Cambridge, MA: Harvard University Press, 2010), 41.

6. *Pennsylvania Freeman*, January 28, 1847; *New York Evening Post* quoted in May, *The Fugitive Slave Law and Its Victims*, 1; Stanley Campbell, *The Slave-Catchers: Enforcement of the Fugitive Slave Law, 1850–1860* (Chapel Hill: University of North Carolina Press, 1970), vii–viii.

7. Still, *The Underground Railroad*, 251, 418, 409; *Washington Reporter*, January 15, 1851; "Resolutions by a Committee of Philadelphia Blacks," in *The Black Abolitionist Papers*, 4:69.

8. Edward Raymond Turner, *The Negro in Pennsylvania: Slavery, Servitude, Freedom* (Washington, DC: American Historical Association, 1911), 243; Pennsylvania Anti-Slavery Society, Fifteenth Annual Report, October 25, 1852, 3–4; *Kent News*, October 12, 1852.

9. Pauli Murray, *Proud Shoes: The Story of an American Family* (New York: Harper and Row, 1978), 96; R. C. Smedley, *History of the Underground Railroad in Chester and the Neighboring Counties of Pennsylvania* (Mechanicsburg, PA: Stackpole Books, 2005), 318.

10. William Parker, "The Freedmen's Story," *Atlantic Monthly* 17 (February 1866): 159; Ella Forbes, *But We Have No Country: The 1851 Christiana, Pennsylvania Resistance* (Cherry Hill, NJ: Africana Homestead Legacy Publishers, 1998), 34.

11. Smedley, *History of the Underground Railroad*, 95–96; William Parker quoted in Margaret Hope Bacon, *Rebellion at Christiana* (New York: Crown

Publishers, 1975), 56; Henry Harris's story is given in Murray, *Proud Shoes*, 96–97.

12. James H. W. Howard, *Bond and Free: A True Tale of Slave Times* (Harrisburg, PA, 1886), 268. Some research suggests that the violent resistance to the Fugitive Slave Act in parts of Pennsylvania may have helped to turn citizens against the Act and make them even more reluctant to support it than they might have been before. In his study of voters in Harrisburg, Pennsylvania, between 1850 and 1852, Gerald G. Eggert found that citizens reacted negatively to several factors in addition to the violence that made them reluctant to support the return of fugitives. These included the difficulty of determining whether blacks were free or runaways, the separation of families, kidnappings, the absence of a statute of limitations on runaways, and the opportunities for corruption opened up by the law. "The Impact of the Fugitive Slave Law on Harrisburg: A Case Study," *Pennsylvania Magazine of History and Biography* 109, no. 4 (October 1985): 533.

13. Pennsylvania Society for Promoting the Abolition of Slavery, "Five Year Abstract of the Transactions of the Pennsylvania Society for Promoting the Abolition of Slavery, the Relief of Free Negroes Unlawfully Held in Bondage, and for Improving the Condition of the African Race" (Philadelphia, 1853), n.p.; *Frederick Douglass's Paper*, October 12, 1849.

14. *Cecil Whig*, January 10, 1852; *Village Record*, July 22, 1851.

15. *Lancaster Examiner and Herald*, February 18, 1852; *American Republican*, July 22, 1851.

16. *Pennsylvania Freeman*, August 13, 1849.

17. Pennsylvania Society for Promoting the Abolition of Slavery, "Five Year Abstract."

18. The newspaper accounts of the Mitchell kidnapping differ on several points. Tom Mitchell was variously called in the press Thomas Mitchell, Robert Michener, or simply Albert. In fact, his original name was Alfred Ambrose; he took the name "Tom Mitchell" when he ran away. Some newspaper accounts say he had been a fugitive for four years; others say eight, nine, or twelve years. McCreary claimed that Mitchell ran away from Cecil County, while Isaac Mason, who came from Kent County and knew Mitchell personally, said that Mitchell was from Kent County.

19. *Albany Evening Journal*, August 27, 1849; *Cecil Democrat*, September 1, 1849; *Cecil Whig*, September 1, 1849.

20. Isaac Mason, "Life of Isaac Mason as a Slave," in *From Bondage to Be-*

longing: The Worcester Slave Narratives, ed. B. Eugene McCarthy and Thomas L. Doughton (Amherst: University of Massachusetts Press, 2007), 271; *Daily Local News*, May 3, 1889.

21. *Daily Local News*, October 6, 1893.

22. *American Republican*, September 11, 1849.

23. *Albany Evening Journal*, August 27, 1849; *Cecil Whig*, September 1, 1849.

24. *Frederick Douglass's Paper*, October 12, 1849.

25. *Pennsylvania Freeman*, March 13, 1851. Cecil County was still imposing extraordinary punishments on free blacks as late as 1863. In that year, one free black man was given twenty-five lashes for stealing horses, and another was sentenced to be sold for one year for stealing beef (*Cecil Whig*, February 2, 1863).

26. *Cecil Whig*, January 10, 1852; Lois E. Horton, "Kidnapping and Resistance: Antislavery Direct Action in the 1850s," in *Passages to Freedom: The Underground Railroad in History and Memory*, ed. David Blight (Washington, DC: Smithsonian Books, 2004), 153–154; Ellwood Griest, *John and Mary; or, The Fugitive Slaves: A Tale of South-Eastern Pennsylvania* (Lancaster, PA: Inquirer Printing and Publishing, c. 1873), 52. Carol Wilson has pointed out that for the most militant critics of slavery, the term *kidnapped* could be used to designate any enslaved African Americans and not just those who had been abducted (*Freedom at Risk: The Kidnapping of Free Blacks in America, 1780–1865* [Lexington: University Press of Kentucky, 1994], 5).

27. *Pennsylvania Freeman*, July 24, 1851.

28. *Village Record*, July 3, 1851.

29. *Pennsylvania Freeman*, July 24, 1851. In a later fugitive slave case, heard in Philadelphia in 1857, the judge again convened the hearing so early in the morning that the defense counsel arrived after the alleged fugitive had been remanded to the claimant. When the defense counsel protested the early hour, the judge (Kane) is reported to have replied that "there is no rule of Court which fixes a time for the hearing of cases. In the fugitive slave cases, there is often an attempt made to interfere with the execution of the law, and for that reason, they should be peremptorily heard" (May, *The Fugitive Slave Law and Its Victims*, 92).

30. *Pennsylvania Freeman*, July 24, 1851. The Naudains were a prominent Delaware family with connections to Cecil County, Maryland. Arnold S. Naudain (1790–1872) was a physician who served in the U.S. Senate for two

terms. The identity of the Arnold S. Naudain who was involved in the kidnapping is not clear, but it is possible that he was either the son or the nephew of the senator. In his account in the *Freeman*, Thomas Garrett said of Naudain that "he has the character of a religious and respectable man, and I presume will hardly lose caste with his neighbors for this high handed act."

31. *Cecil Whig*, reprinted in the *Kent News*, January 3, 1852.

32. *Baltimore Sun*, August 9, 1870.

33. Quoted in *Kent News*, January 3, 1852; *Cecil Whig*, January 10, 1852; January 17, 1852. Daniel Robinson Hundley, the great apologist for all things southern, certainly including slavery, laid the entire problem of runaway slaves at the feet of the abolitionists (*Social Relations in Our Southern States* [New York: Henry B. Price, 1860], 346–347):

> As a general thing no honest, industrious slave ever desires to run away at all, even though solicited to do so by the secret emissaries of the abolitionists; and where such an one is seduced to leave the protecting care of his master, and all the blessings and comforts of the "old plantation" for the freedom to enjoy a precarious and hard-earned livelihood in the Free States or Canada, he is almost sure to embrace the first opportunity to return back again, a "sadder but a wiser man."

CHAPTER 3

1. *American Republican*, January 11, 1853; Gary Nash and Jean Soderlund, *Freedom by Degrees: Emancipation in Pennsylvania and Its Aftermath* (New York: Oxford University Press, 1991), 182; *Village Record*, January 18, 1853.

2. On Rachel Parker's death certificate, her mother's name is given as Rebecca Chandler.

3. *Baltimore Sun*, January 8, 1852; *Oxford News*, November 22, 1951; *Baltimore Sun*, January 10, 1852. Monique Bourque notes that in Pennsylvania's rural counties, including Lancaster and Chester, the most frequently cited conditions associated with admission to almshouses for African Americans between 1800 and 1850 were insanity and poverty, followed by pregnancy. "Populating the Poorhouse: A Reassessment of Poor Relief in the Antebellum Delaware Valley," *Pennsylvania History* 70, no. 3 (Summer 2003): 247.

4. Nash and Soderlund, *Freedom by Degrees*, 190.

5. Chester County, Pennsylvania, Records of the Poorhouse, 1801–1825;

Nash and Soderlund, *Freedom by Degrees*, 190; *Pennsylvania Freeman*, November 28, 1850; *Kent News*, November 21, 1857. A House of Refuge school for black children was opened in Philadelphia in 1849. W.E.B. Du Bois reported that in 1856 the school had three teachers and nineteen students, the Orphans Shelter School in the city had two teachers and seventy-three students, and the Temporary Home for Colored Children had one teacher and nineteen students. *The Philadelphia Negro: A Social Study* (Philadelphia: University of Pennsylvania Press, 2011), 86.

6. Bourque, "Populating the Poorhouse," 246; *American Republican*, January 11, 1853.

7. *Oxford News*, November 22, 1951.

8. *Village Record*, January 13, 1852.

9. Chester County, Pennsylvania, Prison Docket, 1840–1857. A black family named Glasgow lived in Hinsonville, the African American community in Chester County that was the site of Hosanna Meeting House. Samuel Glasgow of that family was said to be an Underground Railroad agent. See William C. Kashatus, *Just Over the Line: Chester County and the Underground Railroad* (West Chester, PA: Chester County Historical Society, 2002), 56.

10. Nash and Soderlund, *Freedom by Degrees*, 173.

11. *Village Record*, January 22, 1853.

12. *Baltimore Sun*, January 12, 1853; *Village Record*, February 17, 1852; *American Republican*, January 11, 1853.

13. *Village Record*, January 8, 1853. Donnelly's name also appears as Donelly, Donnally, and Donley in the newspapers and the census records.

14. Nash and Soderlund, *Freedom by Degrees*, 183; Joan M. Jensen, *Loosening the Bonds: Mid-Atlantic Farm Women, 1750–1850* (New Haven, CT: Yale University Press, 1986), 89.

15. *American Republican*, January 11, 1853; *Village Record*, January 18, 1853.

16. Among the other occupations practiced by more than one person were mason (nine), teacher (nine), cooper (eight), tailor (six), forgeman (six), and auger maker (five).

17. *Baltimore Sun*, January 9, 1852.

18. *Maryland Gazette*, January 7, 1836; John L. Carey, *Slavery in Maryland Briefly Considered* (Baltimore: John Murphy, 1843), 82–83.

19. John Dixon Long, *Pictures of Slavery in Church and State* (Philadelphia, 1857), 73–74; Henry J. Cadbury, "Negro Membership in the Society of

Friends," *Journal of Negro History* 21 (April 1936): 178; Herbert Aptheker, "The Quakers and Negro Slavery," *Journal of Negro History* 25 (July 1940): 360–361.

20. *Village Record*, January 13, 1852.

21. Ellwood Griest, *John and Mary; or, The Fugitive Slaves: A Tale of South-Eastern Pennsylvania* (Lancaster, PA: Inquirer Printing and Publishing, c. 1873), 32–33.

22. W. U. Hensel, *The Christiana Riot and the Treason Trials of 1851: An Historical Sketch* (Lancaster, PA: New Era Printing, 1911), 18.

23. Chester County, Pennsylvania, Sheriff's Deeds, 1830–1857; Chester County Insolvent Debtors' Records, 1849; Chester County Prison Docket, 1840–1857. Among the creditors on Donnelly's list was John Miller Dickey, minister of the Presbyterian Church in nearby Oxford, a founder of Lincoln University, and one of the leaders of the successful effort to secure the release of Rachel and Elizabeth Parker from jail. Donnelly owed Miller $38.

24. *Oxford News*, November 22, 1951; November 29, 1951; Pauli Murray, *Proud Shoes: The Story of an American Family* (New York: Harper and Row, 1978), 98.

25. *Baltimore Sun*, January 5, 1853; *Oxford News*, November 22, 1951.

26. *Pennsylvania Freeman*, February 12, 1852.

27. *American Republican*, January 11, 1853; church records, Chester County Historical Society; *Village Record*, April 5, 1853. The Millers' church erected a new building in 1861 and changed its name to Goar's Methodist Meeting House. It was later renamed Union ME Church.

28. *Village Record*, January 18, 1853.

29. *American Republican*, January 11, 1853.

30. *Pennsylvania Freeman*, February 12, 1852.

31. Lancaster County Historical Society, *Historical Papers and Addresses of the Lancaster Historical Society* (Lancaster, PA, 1911), 117; Murray, *Proud Shoes*, 98.

32. These details of Elizabeth's kidnapping come from her account as reported in the West Chester *Village Record*, January 25, 1853.

33. These details of Rachel's kidnapping come from her account as reported in the *Village Record*, January 25, 1853. A later account of the kidnapping, published in the *Oxford Press* (February 21, 1918) on the occasion of Rachel's death, identified a third man involved in the kidnapping as George Alexander; according to the newspaper, Alexander was the driver of the buggy.

CHAPTER 4

1. *Liberator,* October 25, 1850.

2. *Baltimore Sun*, December 21, 1850. Denning, one of the major Baltimore traders, turned in at least one kidnapper and is on record as having returned several fugitives who were sold to him as slaves, some of them from Pennsylvania.

3. *Kent News*, December 21, 1850; *Baltimore Sun*, December 16, 1850; November 14, 1851; May 18, 1852.

4. *Kent News*, May 22, 1852; *Easton Star*, January 7, 1851; *Baltimore Sun*, December 20, 1850; *Pennsylvania Freeman*, January 23, 1851; *Baltimore Sun*, June 27, 1852. There were other, inexplicable (or at least unexplained) complications in the Jim Brown case. Zenos Dawson, one of the men accused of abducting the boy, was implicated in another kidnapping of a child in Church Hill less than a month after his reported arrest. This time, however, he was an arresting constable himself. Dawson took into custody in Church Hill a man named John Downes, accused of attempting to sell an eight-year-old boy who had been stolen from Delaware. Downes was free again within a few months. Zenos Dawson was still acting as constable in Church Hill in 1855.

5. Kent County Criminal Court Records, First Session, 1851; *Kent News*, February 1, 1851; February 8, 1851. Walter Campbell would later receive both Elizabeth and Rachel Parker from their kidnapper.

6. The *Kent News* reported on December 19, 1857, that a slave from Kent county named Amelia, who was assumed to be a runaway, had in fact been abducted and taken to New Orleans; the paper reported that Amelia had been "recovered," but it mentioned no arrests.

7. *Philadelphia Inquirer*, December 16, 1840, December 3, 1860; R. C. Smedley, *History of the Underground Railroad in Chester and the Neighboring Counties of Pennsylvania* (Mechanicsburg, PA: Stackpole Books, 2005), 107–108.

8. Smedley, *History of the Underground Railroad*, 99; *Pennsylvania Freeman*, January 23, 1851. James Houston, the proprietor of the Gap Tavern, wrote immediately to the *Freeman* vigorously contesting the reports of his establishment's involvement in the kidnapping and calling the author of the article "a base and infamous slanderer" (*Pennsylvania Freeman*, January 24, 1851).

9. Samuel May, *The Fugitive Slave Law and Its Victims* (New York: American Anti-Slavery Society, 1856), 181–182; *Philadelphia Inquirer*, December 3, 1860.

10. *Philadelphia Inquirer*, December 3, 1860.

11. Roderick Nash, "William Parker and the Christiana Riot," *Journal of Negro History* 46 (January 1961): 24; W. U. Hensel, *The Christiana Riot and the Treason Trials of 1851: An Historical Sketch* (Lancaster, PA: New Era Printing, 1911), 16; Frances Williams Browin, "But We Have No Country," *Quaker History* 57, no. 2 (Autumn 1968): 84.

12. There are many published accounts of the Christiana episode; I have used a number of them, but I have relied primarily on Thomas P. Slaughter's very full and detailed version in *Bloody Dawn: The Christiana Riot and Racial Violence in the Antebellum North* (New York: Oxford University Press, 1991).

13. Daniel Forbes, *A True Story of the Christiana Riot* (Quarryville, PA: Sun Printing House, 1898), 20–21; Margaret Hope Bacon, *Rebellion at Christiana* (New York: Crown Publishers, 1975), 7.

14. Bacon, *Rebellion at Christiana*, 121.

15. *Baltimore County Jacksonian*, reprinted in the *Easton Star*, September 16, 1851; Browin, "But We Have No Country," 90; *Kent News*, September 20, 1851; Slaughter, *Bloody Dawn*, 88; *Pennsylvania Freeman*, October 23, 1851.

16. *Pennsylvania Freeman*, October 10, 1851; January 2, 1851; December 25, 1851.

17. *Kent News*, November 23, 1850.

18. P. A. Browne, "A Review of the Trial, Conviction and Sentence of George F. Alberti, for Kidnapping," in *Fugitive Slaves and American Courts: The Pamphlet Literature*, ed. Paul Finkelman, series 2 (Clark, NJ: Lawbook Exchange, 2007), 2:23; Theodore Parker, *The Trial of Theodore Parker* (Boston, 1855), 140–141. The indicted men were held for another month in the Lancaster County jail on possible charges of riot and murder. They were eventually released for lack of evidence.

19. Pauli Murray, *Proud Shoes: The Story of an American Family* (New York: Harper and Row, 1978), 93; Ella Forbes, "'By My Own Right Arm': Redemptive Violence and the 1851 Christiana, Pennsylvania Resistance," *Journal of Negro History* 83, no. 3 (Summer 1998): 159; *Jeffersonian*, September 23, 1851.

20. Maryland House of Delegates, "Report of the Select Committee Appointed to Consider So Much of the Governor's Message as Relates to the Murder of Edward Gorsuch and the Trial of the Treason Case in Philadelphia, May 19th, 1852" (Maryland, 1852), 1579; *Report of Attorney General Brent, to His Excellency Governor Lowe, in Relation to the Christiana Treason Trials* (Annapolis, MD: Thomas E. Martin, 1852), 17.

21. *Kent News*, September 29, 1851; *Pennsylvania Freeman*, September 9, 1851; Frederick Douglass, *Life and Writings of Frederick Douglass*, ed. Eric Foner (New York: International Publishers, 1950), 3:437–438.

22. Browin, "But We Have No Country," 95.

23. William Still, *The Underground Railroad: A Record of Facts, Authentic Narratives, Letters, &c* (Medford, NJ: Plexus Publishing, 2005), 252; *Pennsylvania Freeman*, March 13, 1851; *Kent News*, September 20, 1851; *Herald and Torch Light*, October 13, 1887. Kline was arrested again in 1857 for counterfeiting in New York.

24. *Pennsylvania Freeman*, January 16, 1851; Pennsylvania Anti-Slavery Society, Fourteenth Annual Report Presented to the Pennsylvania Anti-Slavery Society, by Its Executive Committee, October 7, 1851, 11; *Massachusetts Spy*, July 28, 1852.

25. *North American*, April 7, 1848; February 15, 1855; November 11, 1873; *Philadelphia Inquirer*, March 20, 1855.

26. *Albany Evening Journal*, July 26, 1853.

27. *Boston Post*, reprinted in the *Massachusetts Spy*, April 5, 1854; *Liberator*, August 5, 1853.

28. *Pennsylvania Freeman*, January 9, 1851; *Boston Evening Transcript*, August 11, 1851. The arrest and conviction of Alberti had incensed some southern newspapers, such as the *Macon* [GA] *Telegraph*, which contended: "Nothing has transpired to exhibit more truly the settled hate of the North towards the South than this case. Never was the judicial ermine so utterly disgraced as by the Judge who presided on this occasion. If a perusal of this report does not convince every fair minded man of the utter worthlessness of the Fugitive Slave Law, and of the settled determination of the Northern people to render it practically void, they would not believe though one rose from the dead" (August 5, 1851).

29. *Times-Picayune*, February 14, 1852; *Baltimore Argus*, reprinted in the *Pennsylvania Freeman*, April 1, 1852.

30. Browne, "A Review of the Trial, Conviction and Sentence of George F. Alberti," 24; Pennsylvania State Anti-Slavery Society, Fifteenth Annual Report, October 25, 1852, 16.

31. *Massachusetts Spy*, August 3, 1853. William Still recounts an episode that took place in Philadelphia after Alberti's pardon. A slaveholder from Kent County, Maryland, had hired Alberti to find and arrest a runaway who had been spotted in Philadelphia. The Pennsylvania Anti-Slavery Society got wind

of the arrangement and sent someone pretending to be Alberti's representative to the slaveholder. That person solicited the relevant information—the runaway's name, age, description, and so on—and posted it around town on placards three feet square, with a warning that the man should flee. He did, and the slaveholder went home empty-handed. The Society was enormously pleased to have foiled the famous Alberti (Still, *The Underground Railroad*, 387–388).

32. *Daily Register*, reprinted in the *Pennsylvania Freeman*, August 18, 1853.

33. Hensel, *The Christiana Riot and the Treason Trials of 1851*, 19.

34. Slaughter, *Bloody Dawn*, 134.

35. Steven Lubet, *Fugitive Justice: Runaways, Rescuers, and Slavery on Trial* (Cambridge, MA: Harvard University Press, 2010), 136.

36. Pennsylvania State Anti-Slavery Society, Fifteenth Annual Report, 11; *Village Record*, January 27, 1852; Pennsylvania Yearly Meeting of Progressive Friends, Report, 1853.

37. *Easton Star*, December 19, 1854.

CHAPTER 5

1. *Village Record*, January 22, 1853. All other quotations in my account of Elizabeth's interview with Toby are from this source, unless otherwise noted.

2. Harriet Beecher Stowe, *Uncle Tom's Cabin*, in *Three Novels by Harriet Beecher Stowe* (New York: Library of America, 1982), 452.

3. Henry Stockbridge Sr., "Baltimore in 1846," *Maryland Historical Magazine* 6 (1911): 26; *Easton Star*, August 15, 1848.

4. Ralph Clayton, *Cash for Blood: The Baltimore to New Orleans Domestic Slave Trade* (Bowie, MD: Heritage Books, 2002), 57, 125; Frederic Bancroft, *Slave Trading in the Old South* (Baltimore: J. H. Furst, 1931), 121, 317; *New York Daily Tribune*, July 30, 1863.

5. The circular was reproduced in the *Village Record*, January 18, 1853.

6. *Baltimore Sun*, January 12, 1852.

7. *Times-Picayune*, January 20, 1852; Stockbridge, "Baltimore in 1846," 25; *Baltimore Sun*, May 27, 1844.

8. Clayton, *Cash for Blood*, 125; Walter Johnson, *Soul by Soul: Inside the Antebellum Slave Market* (Cambridge, MA: Harvard University Press, 1999), 129.

9. Johnson, *Soul by Soul*, 195–197.

10. Bancroft, *Slave Trading in the Old South*, 13–14.

11. Steven Deyle, *Carry Me Back: The Domestic Slave Trade in American Life* (New York: Oxford University Press, 2005), 153; *New Orleans as It Is* (New Orleans, 1850), 70.

12. Maurie D. McInnis, *Slaves Waiting for Sale: Abolitionist Art and the American Slave Trade* (Chicago: University of Chicago Press, 2011), 160.

13. *Times-Picayune*, January 2, 1851; October 26, 1852.

14. Ebenezer Davies, *American Scenes, and Christian Slavery: A Recent Tour of Four Thousand Miles in the United States* (London: J. Snow, 1849), 17.

15. Fredrika Bremer describes a similar episode she witnessed in a New Orleans slave pen in December 1851: "A gentleman took one of the prettiest of [the women] by the chin, and opened her mouth to see the state of her gums and teeth, and with no more ceremony than if she had been a horse." *The Homes of the New World: Impressions of America*, trans. Mary Botham Howitt (Ulan Press, 2011), 5.

16. Michael Tadman, *Speculators and Slaves: Masters, Traders, and Slaves in the Old South* (Madison: University of Wisconsin Press, 1989), 289.

17. *Times-Picayune*, November 23, 1851; January 2, 1851.

18. The name "Chero" or "Churo" that Elizabeth used for her purchaser is probably spelled phonetically. Neither of those names appears in the New Orleans directories, but the name Ciuro does appear a few times. José Ciuro immigrated to New Orleans from Spain in 1837 and was operating a coffee house in the city in 1842; Ramon Ciuro and his wife were listed in 1877 and 1878 as umbrella makers and repairers. Since I do not know which spelling of the name, if any, is correct, I have chosen to spell the name as it appears in Elizabeth's narrative.

19. Johnson, *Soul by Soul*, 46; McInnis, *Slaves Waiting for Sale*, 65.

20. William Jay, *Miscellaneous Writings on Slavery* (John J. Jewett, 1853), 382; Robert William Fogel and Stanley L. Engerman, *Time on the Cross: The Economics of American Negro Slavery* (New York: Little, Brown, 1974), 76; Tadman, *Speculators and Slaves*, 289; Johnson, *Soul by Soul*, 45–46; Bancroft, *Slave Trading in the Old South*, 330. The *Kent News* reported (January 20, 1855) on a sale of seven slaves in Easton, Maryland, that brought in a total of $5,215, including over $1,000 each for two men in their thirties and $780 for a twenty-five-year-old woman with a one-year-old child.

21. *New Orleans as It Is*, 71.

22. *Village Record*, April 13, 1842.

23. *Baltimore Sun*, January 12, 1853.

24. Philadelphia Female Anti-Slavery Society, Annual Report, 1853, 12.

CHAPTER 6

1. My account of the events of December 31, 1851, and January 1, 1852, is drawn from trial testimonies that appeared in a variety of newspaper reports, especially in the *Baltimore Sun* and the [West Chester] *Village Record*.

2. Eli Haines was a member of a prominent Quaker abolitionist family from Lancaster County that was known to have forwarded many fugitives who were sent there.

3. R. C. Smedley, *History of the Underground Railroad in Chester and the Neighboring Counties of Pennsylvania* (Mechanicsburg, PA: Stackpole Books, 2005), 233. The newspapers usually spelled the name Furness as Furnace; it also appears sometimes as Furniss.

4. Arthur E. James, *The Potters and Potteries of Chester County, Pennsylvania* (Exton, PA: Schiffer Publishing, 1978), 37; Frances Cloud Taylor, *The Trackless Trail: The Story of the Underground Railroad in Kennett Square, Chester County, Pennsylvania, and the Surrounding Community* (Kennett Square, PA, 1976), 27–28. Members of the Vickers family were among the most productive of the Quaker potters in the county.

5. William T. Kelley, "The Underground Railroad in the Eastern Shore of Maryland and Delaware," *Friends Intelligencer* 55 (1898): 379; James A. McGowan and William C. Kashatus, *Harriet Tubman: A Biography* (Santa Barbara, CA: Greenwood Press, 2011), 155. The *Easton Gazette* reported in 1858 (January 23) on the flight of another Quaker from Caroline County, Arthur Leverton, seventeen years after Corkran had left the county: "The fact of his precipitated flight appears to be conclusive evidence of his guilt. . . . It is said he has long been suspicioned of tampering with slaves; and it is supposed that the apparent prompt and determined action of the slaveholders, and the conviction of his own guilt, brought to his mind a certain suit, the component parts of which are generally of tar and feathers, and constructed more with a view of dispatch than comfort or neatness, which led him to 'make tracks for parts unknown.'" Leverton moved to Indiana.

6. Rebecca Townsend Turner papers, Friends Historical Library, Swarthmore, PA.

7. *Baltimore Sun*, January 10, 1852; *Oxford Press*, February 21, 1918.

8. *Baltimore Sun*, March 26, 1861; November 18, 1886.

9. *Baltimore Sun*, November 15, 1886; February 26, 1861.

10. Francis S. Cochran to Montgomery Blair, May 20, 1862, Abraham Lincoln Papers, Manuscript Division, Library of Congress. The spelling of Corkran's name varies, but in most references in the press it appears as Corkran.

11. *Baltimore Sun*, January 10, 1852; *Daily National Intelligencer*, October 13, 1863; *Baltimore Sun*, November 11, 1886; Lucretia Coffin Mott, *Selected Letters of Lucretia Coffin Mott*, ed. Beverly Wilson Palmer (Urbana: University of Illinois Press, 2002), 278.

12. *Cecil Democrat*, September 1, 1849.

13. *Baltimore Sun*, January 10, 1852.

14. *Baltimore Sun*, January 4, 1855; June 28, 1865.

15. *Village Record*, January 13, 1852. Corkran described his movements on that day in his testimony at Thomas McCreary's trial, reported in the *Baltimore Sun* for January 10 and January 14, 1852, and at Joseph Miller's second inquest, reported in the *Baltimore Sun* for January 12, 1852. My account is taken primarily from these sources.

16. *Baltimore Sun*, January 12, 1852.

17. "Memorial of Baltimore Monthly Meeting concerning John Needles," Baltimore Monthly Meeting Records, Friends Historical Library, Swarthmore College. John Needles's brother-in-law, a Quaker named James Bowers, was tarred and feathered in Kent County, Maryland, by a group of slaveholders who suspected him (probably correctly) of aiding and encouraging runaways.

18. Henry Stockbridge Sr., "Baltimore in 1846," *Maryland Historical Magazine* 6 (1911): 26; Robert H. Gudmestad, *A Troublesome Commerce: The Transformation of the Interstate Slave Trade* (Baton Rouge: Louisiana State University Press, 2003), 164.

19. *Baltimore Sun*, January 12, 1852; *Village Record*, January 13, 1852.

20. Barbara Jeanne Fields, *Slavery and Freedom on the Middle Ground: Maryland during the Nineteenth Century* (New Haven, CT: Yale University Press, 1985), 91.

21. *Baltimore Sun*, January 12, 1852.

22. *Village Record*, January 13, 1852.

23. *Village Record*, October 12, 1870.

24. *Baltimore Sun*, January 3, 1852.

25. *Oxford Press*, February 28, 1918; *Village Record*, October 12, 1870.

26. *Baltimore Sun*, January 12, 1852.

27. *Village Record*, January 13, 1852.

28. Pennsylvania State Anti-Slavery Society, Fifteenth Annual Report, October 25, 1852, 13; *Pennsylvania Freeman*, January 8, 1852; *Baltimore Argus*, January 13, 1852; *Baltimore Sun*, January 10, 1852; *Cecil Whig*, January 10, 1852.

29. *Village Record*, October 12, 1870; *Pennsylvania Freeman*, April 29, 1852; *Village Record*, October 12, 1870; *Baltimore Sun*, January 12, 1852. My account of the inquest comes primarily from the *Baltimore Sun* story of January 12.

30. *Baltimore Sun*, January 12, 1852.

CHAPTER 7

1. Baltimore City Jail, Monthly Reports, 1846–1855, Maryland State Archives. The number of white people admitted during the year included 1,351 men, 83 women, and 106 boys (no girls). The number of black people included 319 men, 148 women, 19 boys, and 4 girls. The most common charges were assault and battery, felony, rioting, and violating ordinances.

2. My reconstruction of Schoolfield's activities and of the progress of McCreary's trial is based primarily on reports in the *Baltimore Sun* from January 8 through January 14, 1852.

3. *Baltimore Sun*, January 12, 1852.

4. *Baltimore Sun*, January 14, 1852.

5. *Baltimore Sun*, April 4, 1843.

6. *North American*, March 11, 1847; *Philadelphia Inquirer*, September 19, 1861; *Easton Gazette*, December 8, 1860. In 1847, Preston, Maulsby, and Scott served as prosecutors in a highly publicized case against the divorced wife of Francis Thomas, a former governor of Maryland. Thomas's wife had sued him for divorce, charging him with various kinds of erratic and unstable behavior. Thomas then turned around and sued her for defamation of character. The trial brought out such irrefutable evidence of craziness on the part of Thomas that the case had to be dropped. The three prosecutors were all forced to apologize to the former wife for taking her husband's side against her, explaining that they, like many others, had become susceptible to Thomas's delusions. In spite of this public gaffe, all three remained active in political and civic life in Maryland.

7. *Baltimore Sun*, January 8, 1852; January 10, 1852.

8. *Baltimore Sun*, January 12, 1852; *American Republican*, February 17, 1852.

9. *New York Herald*, January 12, 1852.

10. *Cecil Whig*, January 17, 1852; *American Republican*, January 13, 1852; *Baltimore Sun*, January 14, 1852.

11. *Baltimore Sun*, January 14, 1852.

12. Ibid.

13. *Baltimore Sun*, January 15, 1852.

14. *Cecil Whig*, January 17, 1852.

15. Ibid.

16. *National Era*, March 4, 1852; *Pennsylvania Freeman*, January 15, 1852; February 12, 1852.

17. The West Chester *Village Record* (January 13, 1852) stated its own opinion about Miller's death in typically dramatic form. Miller had reasons to be distressed, the newspaper acknowledged; he might have feared suffering the fate of Caster Hanway or, worse,

> these terrors might have become intolerable, and in an unhappy moment of mental darkness he may have been impelled to seek death's awful oblivion. But this, his friends, who knew best his state of mind, utterly refuse to believe, and there are many other reasons to doubt it. There are shadows of evidence showing a different fate—faint gleams, reflected from suspicious circumstances, which may grow bright and clear, and grow—to proof of murder!

18. Quoted in the *Baltimore Sun*, January 30, 1852.

19. *Pennsylvania Freeman*, January 29, 1852.

20. *Baltimore Sun*, January 30, 1852.

21. *Germantown Telegraph* quoted in *Lancaster Examiner and Herald*, January 28, 1852.

22. *American Republican*, January 20, 1852.

23. James McCauley, Diary, Cecil County [Maryland] Historical Society.

CHAPTER 8

1. *History of the Nottingham Presbyterian Church, 1811–2011* (Nottingham, PA, 2012), 3. The Dickey properties for sale were listed in the *Village Record*, October 21, 1862.

2. Gilbert Cope and Henry Graham Ashmead, *Historic Homes and Institutions and Genealogical and Personal Memoirs of Chester and Delaware Counties, Pennsylvania*, (New York: Lewis Publishing, 1904), 1:154.

3. W. W. Thomson, ed., *Chester County and Its People* (Chicago: Union History, 1898), 395; John Smith Futhey and Gilbert Cope, *History of Chester County, Pennsylvania: With Genealogical and Biographical Sketches* (Philadelphia: Louis H. Everts, 1881), 1:521; *Pennsylvania Freeman*, February 20, 1857; Special Report of the [Pennsylvania] Commissioner of Education, June 30, 1870, 382. In 1852, the Pennsylvania Colonization Society had declared colonization the only way of "saving ourselves and our posterity from those dangers which are apprehended from the presence of two separate and distinct races in our land—a danger affecting the peace and safety of the one race, and possibly the very existence of the other." African Americans, according to the Society, belonged to "a race which must always be a distinct and incongruous people—to whom our climate is not congenial, who seem not to be of us, and who appear under a necessity to give place to the influx and increase of the whites" (William V. Pettit and Rev. John P. Durbin, D.D., Addresses Delivered in the Hall of the House of Representatives, Harrisburg, Pa., on Tuesday Evening, April 6, 1852 [Philadelphia, 1852], 4, 17). By 1897, Lincoln University, the former Ashmun Institute, had produced 554 graduates; of these, 235 were serving as ministers in the United States, and only 13 had gone to Africa as missionaries.

4. Futhey and Cope, *History of Chester County, Pennsylvania*, 1:521; Cope and Ashmead, *Historic Homes and Institutions*, 1:152.

5. *Lancaster Examiner and Herald*, February 4, 1852; *American Republican*, February 17, 1852.

6. One person who attended the meeting put the number present at fifty, another at fifty to seventy-five, another at sixty to eighty; the reporter for the *American Republican* in West Chester (February 17, 1852) noted only that the crowd was "numerous and respectable."

7. *American Republican*, February 17, 1852.

8. *Village Record*, February 17, 1852; *American Republican*, February 17, 1852.

9. *National Era*, April 29, 1852.

10. *Baltimore Sun*, April 29, 1852.

11. *Pennsylvania Freeman*, April 29, 1852.

12. *Village Record*, July 13, 1852.

13. *Baltimore Sun*, January 5, 1853. "Next friend" is a legal term for some-

one who acts on behalf of another person who is not able, for legal reasons, to act on his or her own behalf.

14. *Baltimore Sun*, January 5, 1853. Unless otherwise noted, my summary of the trial of Rachel Parker is taken from reports in the *Baltimore Sun* between January 4 and January 13, 1853.

15. *Village Record*, January 25, 1853.

16. *Village Record*, January 18, 1853.

17. *Oxford News*, December 27, 1951.

18. *Village Record*, January 18, 1853; Philadelphia Female Anti-Slavery Society, Annual Report, Philadelphia, 1853.

19. *Village Record*, January 15, 1853; *Pennsylvania Freeman*, June 30, 1853.

20. *Village Record*, January 11, 1853; January 25, 1853.

21. *American Republican*, January 18, 1853.

22. *Alexandria Gazette*, January 17, 1853; *Frederick Douglass's Paper*, February 19, 1852; *Massachusetts Spy*, January 26, 1853; *Village Record*, January 18, 1853; *Pennsylvania Freeman* quoted in *Liberator*, February 4, 1853.

23. *Pennsylvania Freeman*, March 10, 1853; March 17, 1853.

24. *Elkton Democrat*, February 26, 1853; March 26, 1853.

25. Lowe's letter is summarized in the Philadelphia *Public Ledger*, June 17, 1853.

26. *Pennsylvania Freeman*, June 30, 1853.

27. *National Era*, June 30, 1853; Philadelphia Female Anti-Slavery Society, Annual Report, 1853.

CHAPTER 9

1. *Daily Local News*, March 5, 1880; James A. McGowan, *Station Master on the Underground Railroad: The Life and Letters of Thomas Garrett* (Moylan, PA: Whimsie Press, 1977), 157; William Still, *The Underground Railroad: A Record of Facts, Authentic Narratives, Letters, &c* (Medford, NJ: Plexus Publishing, 2005), xvii.

2. More than five hundred African American men from Chester County served in the Civil War.

3. *Village Record*, August 19, 1856.

4. The 1910 census gives the notation "aid" by the names of two children living in the household with Rachel and her family, a six-year-old boy and a sixteen-year-old girl.

5. *Oxford Press*, February 21, 1918; *Daily Local News*, August 18, 1928.

6. *Daily Local News*, February 8, 1941.

7. *Village Record*, January 25, 1853.

8. Francis S. Corkran to John G. Nicolay, September 8, 1864, Abraham Lincoln Papers, Manuscript Division, Library of Congress.

9. *Jeffersonian*, August 13, 1853; *National American* [Bel Air, Maryland], April 22, 1859; Fred Fowler, "Some Undistinguished Negroes," *Journal of Negro History* 5, no. 4 (October 1920): 483; *Lincoln University Herald* 22 (January 1918): 4.

10. *New York Times*, July 27, 1869.

11. *Baltimore Sun*, November 11, 1856; *Elkton Democrat* quoted in the *Baltimore Sun*, November 10, 1856.

12. *Village Record*, January 1, 1852.

13. *Baltimore Sun*, August 9, 1870.

BIBLIOGRAPHY

PENNSYLVANIA NEWSPAPERS

American Republican (West Chester)
Daily Local News (West Chester)
Harrisburg Patriot
Jeffersonian (West Chester)
Lancaster Examiner and Herald
Oxford News
Oxford Press

Pennsylvania Freeman
Philadelphia Inquirer
Public Ledger
Village Record (West Chester)
Washington Reporter
West Chester Register

MARYLAND NEWSPAPERS

Baltimore Argus
Baltimore Sun
Cecil [County] *Democrat*
Cecil [County] *Whig*
Chestertown Telegraph
Easton Gazette

Easton Star
Elkton Democrat
Kent [County] *News*
Maryland Gazette
National American (Bel Air)

OTHER NEWSPAPERS

Albany Evening Journal
Alexandria [Virginia] *Gazette*
Anti-Slavery Bugle

Boston Evening Transcript
Daily National Intelligencer
Delaware Republican

Emancipator

Frederick Douglass's Paper

Herald and Torch Light

Liberator

Massachusetts Spy

National Era

New York Daily Tribune

New York Evening Post

New York Herald

New York Times

North American

Times-Picayune (New Orleans)

———

Abolitionrieties; or, Remarks on Some of the Members of the Pennsylvania Anti-Slavery Society. Unpublished pamphlet, 1840.

Abraham Lincoln Papers. Manuscript Division, Library of Congress. Available at http://memory.loc.gov/ammem/alhtml/alhome.html. Accessed April 16, 2013.

Aptheker, Herbert. "The Quakers and Negro Slavery." *Journal of Negro History* 25 (July 1940): 331–362.

Bacon, Margaret Hope. *Rebellion at Christiana.* New York: Crown Publishers, 1975.

Baltimore City Jail. Monthly Reports, 1846–1855. Maryland State Archives.

Baltimore Yearly Meeting of Friends. Monthly Meeting Records. Friends Historical Library, Swarthmore College.

Bancroft, Frederic. *Slave-Trading in the Old South.* Baltimore: J. H. Furst, 1931.

Blight, David, ed. *Passages to Freedom: The Underground Railroad in History and Memory.* Washington, DC: Smithsonian Books, 2004.

Bordewich, Fergus M. *Bound for Canaan: The Underground Railroad and the War for the Soul of America.* New York: Harper Collins, 2005.

Bourque, Monique. "Populating the Poorhouse: A Reassessment of Poor Relief in the Antebellum Delaware Valley." *Pennsylvania History* 70, no. 3 (Summer 2003): 235–268.

Bremer, Fredrika. *The Homes of the New World: Impressions of America.* Translated by Mary Botham Howitt. Ulan Press, 2011.

Browin, Frances Williams. "But We Have No Country." *Quaker History* 57, no. 2 (Autumn 1968): 84–95.

Browne, P. A. "A Review of the Trial, Conviction and Sentence of George F. Alberti, for Kidnapping." In *Fugitive Slaves and American Courts: The Pamphlet Literature*, edited by Paul Finkelman, Series 2, 27–50. Clark, NJ: Lawbook Exchange, 2007.

Cadbury, Henry J. "Negro Membership in the Society of Friends." *Journal of Negro History* 21 (April 1936): 151–213.

Campbell, Stanley. *The Slave-Catchers: Enforcement of the Fugitive Slave Law, 1850–1860*. Chapel Hill: University of North Carolina Press, 1970.

Carey, John L. *Slavery in Maryland Briefly Considered*. Baltimore: John Murphy, 1843.

Chester County, Pennsylvania. Insolvent Debtors' Records, 1849.

———. Prison Docket, 1840–1857.

———. Records of the Poorhouse, 1801–1825.

———. Sheriff's Deeds, 1830–1857.

Clayton, Ralph. *Cash for Blood: The Baltimore to New Orleans Domestic Slave Trade*. Bowie, MD: Heritage Books, 2002.

Cope, Gilbert, and Henry Graham Ashmead. *Historic Homes and Institutions and Genealogical and Personal Memoirs of Chester and Delaware Counties, Pennsylvania*. 2 vols. New York: Lewis Publishing, 1904.

Davies, Ebenezer. *American Scenes, and Christian Slavery: A Recent Tour of Four Thousand Miles in the United States*. London: J. Snow, 1849.

Deyle, Steven. *Carry Me Back: The Domestic Slave Trade in American Life*. New York: Oxford University Press, 2005.

Dorsey, J. R. *Documentary History of Slavery in the United States, by a Native of Maryland*. Washington, DC, 1851.

Douglass, Frederick. *Life and Writings of Frederick Douglass*. Edited by Eric Foner. 5 vols. New York: International Publishers, 1950.

Du Bois, W.E.B. *The Philadelphia Negro: A Social Study*. Philadelphia: University of Pennsylvania Press, 2011.

Eggert, Gerald G. "The Impact of the Fugitive Slave Law on Harrisburg: A Case Study." *Pennsylvania Magazine of History and Biography* 109, no. 4 (October 1985): 537–569.

Fields, Barbara Jeanne. *Slavery and Freedom on the Middle Ground: Maryland during the Nineteenth Century*. New Haven, CT: Yale University Press, 1985.

Fogel, Robert William, and Stanley L. Engerman. *Time on the Cross: The Economics of American Negro Slavery*. New York: Little, Brown, 1974.

Forbes, Daniel. *A True Story of the Christiana Riot*. Quarryville, PA: Sun Printing House, 1898.

Forbes, Ella. *But We Have No Country: The 1851 Christiana, Pennsylvania Resistance*. Cherry Hill, NJ: Africana Homestead Legacy Publishers, 1998.

————. "'By My Own Right Arm': Redemptive Violence and the 1851 Christiana, Pennsylvania Resistance." *Journal of Negro History* 83, no. 3 (Summer 1998): 159–167.

Fowler, Fred. "Some Undistinguished Negroes." *Journal of Negro History* 5, no. 4 (October 1920): 476–485.

Futhey, John Smith, and Gilbert Cope. *History of Chester County, Pennsylvania: With Genealogical and Biographical Sketches.* 2 vols. Philadelphia: Louis. H. Everts, 1881.

Griest, Ellwood. *John and Mary; or, The Fugitive Slaves: A Tale of South-Eastern Pennsylvania.* Lancaster, PA: Inquirer Printing and Publishing, c. 1873.

Grivno, Max. *Gleanings of Freedom: Free and Slave Labor along the Mason-Dixon Line, 1790–1860.* Urbana: University of Illinois Press, 2011.

Gudmestad, Robert H. *A Troublesome Commerce: The Transformation of the Interstate Slave Trade.* Baton Rouge: Louisiana State University Press, 2003.

Harrold, Stanley. *Border War: Fighting over Slavery before the Civil War.* Chapel Hill: University of North Carolina Press, 2010.

Hensel, W. U. *The Christiana Riot and the Treason Trials of 1851: An Historical Sketch.* Lancaster, PA: New Era Printing, 1911.

History of the Nottingham Presbyterian Church, 1811–2011. Nottingham, PA, 2012.

Howard, James H. W. *Bond and Free: A True Tale of Slave Times.* Harrisburg, PA, 1886.

Hundley, Daniel Robinson. *Social Relations in Our Southern States.* New York: Henry B. Price, 1860.

James, Arthur E. *The Potters and Potteries of Chester County, Pennsylvania.* Exton, PA: Schiffer Publishing, 1978.

Jay, William. *Miscellaneous Writings on Slavery.* Boston: John J. Jewett, 1853.

Jensen, Joan M. *Loosening the Bonds: Mid-Atlantic Farm Women, 1750–1850.* New Haven, CT: Yale University Press, 1986.

Johnson, Walter. *Soul by Soul: Inside the Antebellum Slave Market.* Cambridge, MA: Harvard University Press, 1999.

Jordan, Ryan. *Slavery and the Meetinghouse: The Quakers and the Abolitionist Dilemma, 1820–1865.* Bloomington: Indiana University Press, 2007.

Kashatus, William C. *Just Over the Line: Chester County and the Underground Railroad.* West Chester, PA: Chester County Historical Society, 2002.

Kelley, William T. "The Underground Railroad in the Eastern Shore of Maryland and Delaware." *Friends Intelligencer* 55 (1898): 238, 264–265, 379.

Kent County, Maryland. Criminal Court Records, First Session, 1851.

Lancaster County Historical Society. Papers and Addresses of the Lancaster Historical Society. Lancaster, PA, 1911.

Leslie, William R. "The Pennsylvania Fugitive Slave Act of 1826." *Journal of Southern History* 18 (1952): 429–425.

Lincoln University Herald 22 (January 1918).

Long, John Dixon. *Pictures of Slavery in Church and State*. Philadelphia, 1857.

Lubet, Steven. *Fugitive Justice: Runaways, Rescuers, and Slavery on Trial*. Cambridge, MA: Harvard University Press, 2010.

Maryland House of Delegates. "Report of the Select Committee Appointed to Consider So Much of the Governor's Message as Relates to the Murder of Edward Gorsuch and the Trial of the Treason Case in Philadelphia, May 19th, 1852." Maryland, 1852.

Mason, Isaac. "Life of Isaac Mason as a Slave." In *From Bondage to Belonging: The Worcester Slave Narratives*, edited by B. Eugene McCarthy and Thomas L. Doughton, 238–285. Amherst: University of Massachusetts Press, 2007.

May, Samuel. *The Fugitive Slave Law and Its Victims*. New York: American Anti-Slavery Society, 1856.

McCauley, James. Diary, 1852. Cecil County Historical Society, Elkton, Maryland.

McGowan, James A. *Station Master on the Underground Railroad: The Life and Letters of Thomas Garrett*. Moylan, PA: Whimsie Press, 1977.

McGowan, James A., and William C. Kashatus. *Harriet Tubman: A Biography*. Santa Barbara, CA: Greenwood Press, 2011.

McInnis, Maurie D. *Slaves Waiting for Sale: Abolitionist Art and the American Slave Trade*. Chicago: University of Chicago Press, 2011.

Mott, Lucretia Coffin. *Selected Letters of Lucretia Coffin Mott*. Edited by Beverly Wilson Palmer. Urbana: University of Illinois Press, 2002.

Murray, Pauli. *Proud Shoes: The Story of an American Family*. New York: Harper and Row, 1978.

Nash, Gary, and Jean Soderlund. *Freedom by Degrees: Emancipation in Pennsylvania and Its Aftermath*. New York: Oxford University Press, 1991.

Nash, Roderick. "William Parker and the Christiana Riot." *Journal of Negro History* 46 (January 1961): 24–31.

Newman, Richard S. "'Lucky to Be Born in Pennsylvania': Free Soil, Fugitive Slaves, and the Making of Pennsylvania's Anti-Slavery Borderland." *Slavery and Abolition* 32, no. 3 (September 2011): 413–430.

New Orleans as It Is. New Orleans, 1850.

Nogee, Joseph. "The Prigg Case and Fugitive Slaves, 1842–1850." *Journal of Negro History* 39 (July 1954): 185–205.

Parker, Theodore. *The Trial of Theodore Parker.* Boston, 1855.

Parker, William. "The Freedmen's Story." *Atlantic Monthly* 17 (February 1866): 152–166.

Pennsylvania Anti-Slavery Society. "Address to the Coloured People of the State of Pennsylvania." Philadelphia, 1837.

——. Fifteenth Annual Report. October 25, 1852.

——. Fourteenth Annual Report Presented to the Pennsylvania Anti-Slavery Society, by Its Executive Committee. October 7, 1851.

Pennsylvania Society for Promoting the Abolition of Slavery. "Five Year Abstract of the Transactions of the Pennsylvania Society for Promoting the Abolition of Slavery, the Relief of Free Negroes Unlawfully Held in Bondage, and for Improving the Condition of the African Race." Philadelphia, 1853.

Pennsylvania Yearly Meeting of Progressive Friends. Report, 1853.

Pettit, Eber M. *Sketches in the History of the Underground Railroad.* Fredonia, NY: W. McKinstry and Son, 1879.

Pettit, William V., and Rev. John P. Durbin, D.D. Addresses Delivered in the Hall of the House of Representatives, Harrisburg, Pa., on Tuesday Evening, April 6, 1852. Philadelphia, 1852.

Philadelphia Female Anti-Slavery Society. Annual Report, 1853.

Philadelphia Yearly Meeting of Friends (Orthodox). Report, Third Month 16, 1860.

Report of Attorney General Brent, to His Excellency Governor Lowe, in Relation to the Christiana Treason Trials. Annapolis, MD: Thomas E. Martin, 1852.

Ripley, C. Peter, ed. *The Black Abolitionist Papers.* 5 vols. Chapel Hill: University of North Carolina Press, 1991.

Russo, Marianne H., and Paul A. Russo. *Hinsonville, a Community at the Crossroads: The Story of a Nineteenth-Century African-American Village.* Selinsgrove, PA: Susquehanna University Press, 2005.

Slaughter, Thomas P. *Bloody Dawn: The Christiana Riot and Racial Violence in the Antebellum North.* New York: Oxford University Press, 1991.

Smedley, R. C. *History of the Underground Railroad in Chester and the Neighboring Counties of Pennsylvania.* 1883. Mechanicsburg, PA: Stackpole Books, 2005.

Smith, Eric Ledell, et al. "Rescuing African American Kidnapping Victims in Philadelphia as Documented in the Joseph Watson Papers at the Historical Society of Pennsylvania." *Pennsylvania Magazine of History and Biography* 129, no. 3 (July 2005): 317–345.

Soderlund, Jean R. *Quakers and Slavery: A Divided Spirit*. Princeton, NJ: Princeton University Press, 1985.

Special Report of the [Pennsylvania] Commissioner of Education. June 30, 1870.

Still, William. *The Underground Railroad: A Record of Facts, Authentic Narratives, Letters, &c.* Medford, NJ: Plexus Publishing, 2005.

Stockbridge, Henry Sr. "Baltimore in 1846." *Maryland Historical Magazine* 6 (1911): 20–34.

Stowe, Harriet Beecher. *The Key to Uncle Tom's Cabin*. Boston: John P. Jewett, 1853.

———. *Three Novels by Harriet Beecher Stowe*. New York: Library of America, 1982.

Switala, William J. *The Underground Railroad in Pennsylvania*. Mechanicsburg, PA: Stackpole Books, 2001.

Tadman, Michael. *Speculators and Slaves: Masters, Traders, and Slaves in the Old South*. Madison: University of Wisconsin Press, 1989.

Taylor, Frances Cloud. *The Trackless Trail: The Story of the Underground Railroad in Kennett Square, Chester County, Pennsylvania, and the Surrounding Community*. Kennett Square, PA, 1976.

Thomson, W. W., ed. *Chester County and Its People*. Chicago: Union History, 1898.

Turner, Edward Raymond. *The Negro in Pennsylvania: Slavery, Servitude, Freedom*. Washington, DC: American Historical Association, 1911.

Wilson, Carol. *Freedom at Risk: The Kidnapping of Free Blacks in America, 1780–1865*. Lexington: University Press of Kentucky, 1994.

Wilson, Emerson W., ed. *Mount Harmon Diaries of Sidney George Fisher, 1837–1850*. Wilmington: Historical Society of Delaware, 1976.

Winch, Julie. "Pennsylvania and the Other Underground Railroad." *The Pennsylvania Magazine of History and Biography* 111, no. 1 (January 1987): 3–25.

Wright, James M. *The Free Negro in Maryland, 1634–1860*. New York: Octagon Books, 1971.

INDEX

Abolitionism, 55–57; and Christiana upris-
ing, 88–89; and emancipation, 124; and
Quakers, 56, 124–125; and trial of Rachel
Parker, 163
Alberti, George: death of, 195–196; and Ed-
ward Ingraham, 84–85, 87; and Pennsylva-
nia Anti-Slavery Society, 223n1; reputation
of, 85, 87, 223n28; and Joel Thompson
case, 85–87, 223n28
Alexander, George, 220n33
Almshouses, 48–49, 218n3
Anderson, John, 51–52
Association in Aid of Freedmen of Maryland,
121–122

Baer, William, and Gap gang, 73
Baltimore, Maryland: city jail in, 147–148;
Quakers in, 114, 121–123, 135–136, 146,
160; slave trade in, 16–17
Bancroft, Frederic, 106, 111
Bell, Judge Thomas S., 176, 182, 186
Bigler, Governor William, 74, 160; and
George Alberti, 85–86; and trial of Rachel
Parker, 182, 183, 184–187
Birney, Colonel William, 99–100
Blandel, William, 149, 150–151
Bond and Free: A True Tale of Slave Times
(James H. W. Howard), 31–32

Borderers, 4, 32, 43
Bourque, Monique, 48–49, 218n3
Bremer, Fredrika, 225n15
Brosius family, 120
Brown, Ann, 37–38
Brown, Henry Lee, 33–34
Brown, Jim, 70–71
Brown, John, 73
Brown, Levi K., 195; and Baltimore Quakers,
135–136, 137
Browne, P. A., 87
Burleigh, Charles, 9–11, 62, 64, 212n12; and
John Miller Dickey, 10, 167

Cahill, William, 70
Campbell, Bernard, 99, 113
Campbell, James, and trial of Rachel Parker,
176, 181–183
Campbell, Stanley, 28
Campbell, Walter: and abduction of Henry
Lee Brown, 33; and abduction of Elizabeth
Parker, 114, 160, 174; and abduction of
Rachel Parker, 118, 126–128
Campbell brothers: and abduction of
Elizabeth Parker, 16, 65, 98; and Baltimore
premises, 99–100, 104; and New Orleans
premises, 106–109; and slave trade,
98–100, 109, 129

Carey, John L., 55–56
Chalfant, William, 50
Chester County Anti-Slavery Society, 15
Children as workers, 47–49
Christiana uprising, 11–12, 74–82; after-
    math of, 88–91
Churo, Mrs., 110–113
Clay, Henry, 26
Coates, Edwin H., 189
Coates, Hart G., 118–119, 131, 191
Cooper, Henry, 36
Cope, Gilbert: and Ebenezer Dickey, 167;
    and John Miller Dickey, 167–168
Corkran, Francis S.: and abduction of Rachel
    Parker, 117, 119–122, 125–136 *passim*,
    141; and abolitionism, 121, 124–125; and
    anti-slavery activity, 120–122; later life of,
    194; and Abraham Lincoln, support for,
    123–124, 194; and Tom Mitchell, 126;
    political appointments of, 123–124; and
    trial of Thomas McCreary, 155
Crocus, Allen, 146
Crocus, Eliza, 100, 145–146, 148, 149, 152;
    and identity of Rachel Parker, 145, 150,
    153, 154, 158
Crocus, Henrietta, 65, 145–146; and identity
    of Elizabeth Parker, 100, 101, 104
Crocus, Juno, 100, 145–146, 153

Davies, Ebenezer, 108
Dawson, Zenos, 221n4
Denning, John, 70, 221n2
Dickehut, Hannah, 100, 145, 149, 153–154
Dickey, Ebenezer, 166–167
Dickey, John Miller: and Charles Burleigh,
    10, 167; and colonization, 10, 167–168,
    195; and Matthew Donnelly, 220n23;
    and Lincoln University, 168; and Oxford
    Female Seminary, 168, 195; and Parker
    sisters, 114, 166–169, 182, 183
Dickey family, 166–167
Donnelly, Matthew: and abduction of Eliza-
    beth Parker, 1, 52, 60–61, 65, 113–114;
    financial problems of, 58–60; later life of,
    196
Donovan, Joseph S., 16
Dorsey, J. R., 25

Douglass, Frederick, 11, 30
Doyle, G. A., 6

Elkton, Maryland, 33, 38, 40–41, 85
Engerman, Stanley, 111
Evans, Henry S., 160, 166
Evans, Nathan, 6

Farming population in Chester County,
    Pennsylvania, 53
Ficcio, L. J., 60
Finnegan, Thomas, 18
Fisher, Sidney George, 9
Flint, Isaac S., 9
Fogel, Robert W., 111
Free blacks: kidnapping of, 2, 16, 17–18,
    24, 26; and the law, 38, 40, 146, 217n25;
    live-in workers, 52; in Maryland, 70–72;
    population in Pennsylvania, 13; post–
    Civil War, 190
Freeman, Benjamin, 14
Fugitive Slave Act of 1850, 2, 5, 11, 19, 45;
    and Christiana uprising, 75, 77; history
    of, 23–27; provisions of, 27; responses to,
    27–30, 216n12
Furness, Benjamin, 118–120, 132
Furness, Oliver, 119

Gap gang, and kidnapping, 72–74, 76; and
    John Merritt, 64
Garrett, Thomas, 37, 39–41, 189–190, 218n30
Gibson, Adam, 83, 87
Gittings, William H., 137, 141
Glasco, George, 47, 50, 58
Goodwin, Lyle, 154
Gorsuch, Dickinson, and Christiana upris-
    ing, 76
Gorsuch, Edward, 11, 12; and Christiana
    uprising, 75–77, 82; death of, 79–80
Gradual abolition in Pennsylvania, 3, 211n3
Grier, Robert C., 77–79
Griest, Ellwood (*John and Mary, or, The
    Fugitive Slaves*), 39, 57–58

Haines, Eli, 67, 117
Hanway, Castner: and Christiana uprising,
    76, 77, 78, 79; and Quakerism, 89

Hazle, Jonathan, 71–72
Henry A. Barling, 104, 105–106
Hensel, W. U., 74
Hiss, George M., 140–141, 143
Hoopes, Davis H.: trial of Thomas Mc-
  Creary, 151; and trial of Rachel Parker,
  172–176
Hopewell meeting, 169–170
Hopkins, William, 149–150, 154
Horton, Lois, 39
Hosanna Meeting House, 11, 15
Howard, James H. W. (*Bond and Free: A
  True Tale of Slave Times*), 31–32
Hutchinson, James, 160–161, 174

Informants, 31, 82
Ingraham, Edward: and George Alberti,
  84–85, 87; and Christiana uprising, 76,
  81; personal life of, 83–84; reputation of,
  82–83

Jackson, John, 38
Jackson, William, 12
Jay, William, 110
Jensen, Joan, 52–53
John and Mary, or, The Fugitive Slaves (Ell-
  wood Griest), 39, 57–58
Johnson, Rebecca Jane, 71–72
Johnson, Sarah, 149, 150, 152
Johnson, Walter, 104–105, 110, 111

Kane, John K., 77–78
Kelley, William T., 121, 124
The Key to Uncle Tom's Cabin (Harriet
  Beecher Stowe), 2
Kidnapping, definition of, 38–39
Kidnapping victims: Ann Brown, 37–38;
  Henry Lee Brown, 33–34; Jim Brown,
  70–71; John Brown, 73; Adam Gibson,
  83, 87; Rebecca Jane Johnson, 71–72;
  John Kinnard, 39–41; Tom Mitchell,
  8–9, 16, 18, 34–37, 126, 212n10, 216n18;
  Mary Whiting, 18; Elizabeth Williams,
  39–41
Kimbel, Rachel, 53
Kinnard, John, 39–41
Kirk, Jesse, 118, 132–133

Kline, Henry: and Christiana uprising, 76,
  78; and William Padgett, 82; reputation
  of, 82

Lamb, Eli, 121
Leverton, Arthur, 226n5
Lewis, Elijah, 76–77
Lincoln University, 168
Long, John Dixon, 56,
Lowe, Governor Enoch Louis, 184–187
Lubet, Steven, 89
Lynch, Patrick, 149, 150–151, 154

Martin, George, 35
Martin, Susannah, 148–149, 152
Mason, Isaac, 8–9, 16, 34, 35, 212nn9–10
Maulsby, William P., 228n6; and trial of
  Thomas McCreary, 151
May, Samuel, 24
McCauley, James, 163
McCreary, Jesse, 33
McCreary, Thomas: and abduction of
  Tom Mitchell, 8, 18, 34–37, 126; and
  abduction of Elizabeth Parker, 1–2, 65,
  98–103; and abduction of Rachel Parker,
  1, 65–67, 117, 119, 126–135; accomplices
  of, 64–65; arrest of, 127–128, 130; career
  of, 32–43 *passim;* and Fugitive Slave Act,
  21; later life of, 196–197; obituary for, 42,
  197–198; and Pennsylvania kidnappings,
  33–41; reputation of, 32, 37, 102; and trial
  for kidnapping, 145–146, 151–163
McCreary, William, 46, 52
McCrone, George, 39–41
McKim, J. Miller, 15, 29
Melrath, Alexander, 63
Melrath, Hannah, 53
Melrath, Lewis, 54, 118, 130, 134, 183
Merritt, John, 58, 60; later life of, 196; Mc-
  Creary's accomplice, 64; trial testimony
  of, 155–159
Miller, Joseph, 1, 3, 21; and abduction of Ra-
  chel Parker, 62, 66–67, 118–119, 127–134;
  autopsies of, 137, 138–143, 160–161; and
  Christiana uprising, 90–91, 130; death of,
  134–136, 157–159, 160, 165, 173; disap-
  pearance of, 132–133

Milner, Nathan, 47
Mitchell, Tom, 8–9, 16, 18, 34–37, 126, 212n10, 216n18
Moffit, Thomas, 70–72
Morris, William, 54, 118–119, 138, 140
Mott, James, 15
Mott, Lucretia, 125
Murray, Pauli, 30, 60, 65
Mutual Protection Societies, 6–7

Nash, Gary, 46
Naudain, Arnold, 40–41, 217n30
Needles, Jane, 148–149, 152
Needles, John, 121, 125, 126, 128–129
Newcomer, Lewis, 117, 120, 126
Newman, William, 24
New Orleans, slave trade in, 16, 106–111
Norris, William Henry: trial of Thomas McCreary, 151; and trial of Rachel Parker, 172, 176, 182

Padgett, William: and Christiana uprising, 75–76; and Henry Kline, 82
Parker, Edward, 46, 49–50, 177
Parker, Elizabeth: abduction of, 1, 21–22, 60–61, 65, 98; age of, 211n1; in Baltimore slave pen, 104, 114–115; as child worker, 51–52; and Henrietta Crocus, 65, 104–105; later life of, 190, 192–194; response to enslavement, 45–46, 98, 105; slave life in New Orleans, 98, 111
Parker, Rachel, 1, 16, 21; abduction of, 65–67; age of, 61, 211n1; children of, 191–192; and Christiana uprising, 171, 173–174, 179, 183–184; and Eliza Crocus, 150, 153, 154, 158; employment by Joseph Miller, 61–63; freedom trial of, 170–187; later life of, 190–192
Parker, Rebecca, 94, 96; childhood of, 47–49, 50, 51; children of, 46–47; later life of, 194; marriage of, 49
Parker, Theodore, 23
Parker, William, 30–31; and Christiana uprsising, 76–77, 81–82
Pennington, Augustine, 127–128; and trial of Thomas McCreary, 152, 155–158
Pennock, Samuel, 35

Pennsylvania Abolition Society, 15, 17, 34
Pennsylvania Anti-Slavery Society, 15, 32, 83, 87, 90, 213n22, 223n31
Pennsylvania Colonization Society, 230n3
Personal liberty laws, 25, 26, 215n2
Pettit, Eber, 19
Philadelphia Female Anti-Slavery Society, 2, 115, 181, 187
Philadelphia House of Refuge, 48, 219n5
Pitts, Charles H., 151
Plummer, William S., 169
Pollock, James, 66, 118
Pollock, Samuel, 66, 118, 132
Preston, William P., 228n6; trial of Thomas McCreary, 151–152; and trial of Rachel Parker, 175
Price, James, 71–72
Price, John O., 127–128, 132
Prigg v. Pennsylvania, 24–25
Pusey, Joshua, 8

Quakers, 5; and abolitionism, 56; in Baltimore, 114, 121–123, 135–136, 146, 160; in Chester County, 13; Pennsylvania Yearly Meeting of Progressive Friends, 9, 15, 89; persecution of, 121, 226n5, 227n17; position on slavery, 14–16; and pottery making, 120; and Underground Railroad, 6, 14; and working children, 48; Yearly Meeting of Philadelphia Quakers, 14, 15

Schley, William, 172, 175, 184
Schoolfield, Elizabeth, 149, 150
Schoolfield, Luther, 100–103; and Francis Corkran, 126–127; and jailing of Rachel Parker, 114, 146–147; later life of, 196; lottery business of, 102–103; and Joseph Miller, 142; and trial of Thomas McCreary, 148–150 152, 154, 169; and trial of Rachel Parker, 179–180
Schoolfield, William Henry, 149, 150, 153
Scott, Otho, 223n6; and trial of Thomas McCreary, 74, 151; and trial of Rachel Parker, 175, 184
Slatter, Hope, 16, 99, 107
Slaughter, Thomas P., 77

Slave catchers, 3, 10, 16, 30, 65, 81–82, 165; George Alberti, 84; borderers, 4; definition of, 38–39, 162; Thomas McCreary, 32, 39, 43, 102; John O. Price, 127

Slaveholders, 99, 151, 181, 183, 226n5, 227n17; and abolitionists, 125; and Christiana uprising, 75, 81, 88; and Fugitive Slave Act, 24–27; and fugitive slaves, 4–7, 30–31; and Tom Mitchell, 375; and slave trading, 129

Slaves, fugitive, 4–9, 11–12, 218n33; and Fugitive Slave Act, 19, 24–25; prices for, 107, 110–111

Smedley, R. C., 17, 30, 119; and Gap gang, 72–73

Smith, James Y., 52, 56, 61

Society for the Protection of Free Negroes Held in Bondage, 5

Soderlund, Jean, 46

Starr's Tavern, 138–139

Stevens, Thaddeus, 79

Still, William, 21, 23, 28, 189–190, 223n31

Stowe, Harriet Beecher: *The Key to Uncle Tom's Cabin*, 2; *Uncle Tom's Cabin*, 2, 19, 95–96

Swayne, Enoch, 35–36

Swayne, John, 12–13

Tadman, Michael, 109, 111

Temporary Home for Colored Children, Philadelphia, 48, 219n5

Thawley, Henry, 71

Thomas, Philip, 151, 155

Townsend, Samuel, 121, 128, 171

Tubman, Harriett, 11, 121

Turner, Edward, 29

Turner, Elizabeth Townsend, 121

Turner, Rebecca Sinclair, 125

Uncle Tom's Cabin (Harriet Beecher Stowe), 2, 19, 95–96

Underground Railroad, 4, 121, 189; and kidnapping, 64; and Quakers, 6, 37, 120

Wesley, George, 191

Whiting, Mary, 18

Whitson, Moses, 31

Whittier, John Greenleaf, 83

Williams, Elizabeth, 39–41

Wilson, Jonathan, 34–35

Woods, Benjamin, 140–141

Woolfolk, Austin, 16

Wright, Samuel, 17

Lucy Maddox is Professor Emerita of English and American Studies at Georgetown University. She is the author of *Removals: Nineteenth-Century American Literature and the Politics of Indian Affairs* and *Citizen Indians: Native American Intellectuals, Race, and Reform.*

EAST 2/16